On Character

LANDMARKS OF
CONTEMPORARY POLITICAL THOUGHT

Christopher C. DeMuth, series editor

On Character

Essays by James Q. Wilson

THE AEI PRESS

Publisher for the American Enterprise Institute
WASHINGTON, D.C.

1995

This is an expanded version of the 1991 edition. The author is grateful to the publishers listed in the back of the book for allowing him to reprint versions of what first appeared in their pages.

Available in the United States from the AEI Press, c/o Publisher Resources Inc., 1224 Heil Quaker Blvd., P.O. Box 7001, La Vergne, TN 37086-7001. Distributed outside the United States by arrangement with Eurospan, 3 Henrietta Street, London WC2E 8LU England.

The Library of Congress has cataloged the hardcover edition of this title as follows:

Library of Congress Cataloging-in-Publication Data
Wilson, James Q.
   On character: essays by James Q. Wilson.
     p.   cm.
   Includes bibliographical references and index.
   ISBN 0-8447-3786-0 (cloth).—ISBN 0-8447-3787-9 (pbk.)
   1. Character—Social aspects. 2. Social ethics. 3. United States—Moral conditions. I. Title.
   BJ1531.W55 1991
   170—dc20   91-9911

                                           CIP

1 3 5 7 9 10 8 6 4 2

THE AEI PRESS
Publisher for the American Enterprise Institute
1150 17th Street, N.W., Washington, D.C. 20036

Printed in the United States of America

To Roberta, again and always

Contents

ix

1

Introduction: Thinking about Character

I am a slow study. Not until the early 1980s, after nearly two decades of writing about crime and criminal justice, did I realize that I was seriously interested in the problem of character. Not only was I late in coming to this view, I had earlier devoted a few pages to explaining why I ought to avoid it. In *Thinking About Crime,* published in 1975, I said that trying to reduce crime by attacking its root causes was futile for two very good reasons—we did not know what these root causes were, and the most likely candidates for such causes, human character and the intimate social settings in which it was formed, were beyond the reach of public policy in a free society.

The second reason is still largely true, but the first one is less so. Scholars have learned a great deal about the influence of biological, familial, and peer-group influences on criminality. And although there is much we still do not know, we already know enough to say this: that what the average citizen has long believed about crime—that it occurs when people of weak or malicious character find themselves in tempting or opportune situations—is generally true. Public policy may be able to reduce the temptations or alter the opportunities, but the resulting improvement in public safety is likely to be marginal if the internal constraints on misconduct—that is to say, human character—decay. Government policy may not be able to improve character at a reasonable cost in freedom and money (although schooling, properly organized, may make a significant difference), but that is not the same thing as saying that character is wholly a private matter. Character is shaped, albeit indirectly, by public forces: by general opinion, by neighborhood expectations, by artistic conventions, by elite understandings—in short, by the ethos of the times.

In 1982–1983 I set forth that argument in an essay in the *Public Interest* and tested its acceptability in lectures at various colleges and universities. The middle-aged people who read the essay seemed to find my position defensible, but not the young people who listened to me on the campuses.

1

At Rice University I remarked that schools may affect the crime rate to the extent that they instill principles of decent conduct. The first question from the audience was asked by a student: "But, Professor, won't a school have to choose which values to instill? Won't they be middle-class values?"

"Yes," I said. "Of course." My response was reflexive, without thought. The student's evident disagreement was equally reflexive, but being polite, he did not press the matter. I have forgotten what else was said that evening, but I recall what I was thinking as the audience and I shuffled through the painful minuet of bringing to a close an occasion none of us had especially enjoyed: "Does this young man think that 'values' are arbitrary and that inculcating 'middle-class' ones is suspect? Why does he think that? Why do I disagree?"

I still had not answered these questions to my own satisfaction when a few years later I spoke at Beloit College. I described, as best I could, how character was formed. The first question was from an intelligent young woman, who rose and asserted that "character" was a code word for compliance and subservience; teaching character, she argued, was to teach young people to sit still with their hands folded and not to ask questions. Character, she implied, was the enemy of self-expression and personal freedom. Before making her point, she waited until I had called on her; when speaking, she did not raise her voice or speak insultingly; on finishing, she listened politely to my response.

Whatever my response was, it was inadequate. What I should have said to her was this: "Character" is not a code word, it is a real word that describes how you behaved even though you felt strongly that I was wrong and perhaps wicked. While claiming your right to speak, you acknowledged my right to speak; while making your point, you addressed yourself to my argument and not to my personality. You attacked my views but not my self-esteem. Character is not the enemy of self-expression and personal freedom, it is their necessary precondition.

I am not surprised to find that young people are skeptical of lectures on character delivered by middle-aged professors. It is the natural inclination of the middle-aged to talk about rules and obligations; it is the natural inclination of the young to dream about freedom and self-realization. But I am surprised to learn that a concern for character is taken as the infallible sign of a conservative disposition. Anyone who explains high rates of drug abuse, criminality, or family dissolution by some defect in character (rather than as a consequence of social inequality, unemployment, or political oppression) is immediately taken to be a reactionary, probably in the grip of some extreme evangelical obsession.

Now I confess to being conservative, at least by the standards of contemporary academia. But there is no necessary connection between a conservatively inclined politics and a character-oriented psychology. It is hard to find regimes more dedicated to creating a new personality and to stamping out hooliganism than those inspired by Marxist doctrine. If a young man wanted to kick up his heels, it is hard to know whether he would be worse off in Beijing or in Riyadh. The great revolutions animated by egalitarian sentiments have never been content to leave people alone to act as they pleased within the context of new, presumably more just social arrangements; they have inevitably insisted on changing people into the new Soviet man or the French citizen or the disciples of the teachings of Mao. By the standards of these regimes, a modest American concern for good manners and personal decency seems the height of democratic sensibility.

Presuppositions of the Enlightenment

In truth, of course, the youthful (and not-so-youthful) skeptics of lectures on character are not judging these views against a Marxist alternative but against the presuppositions of the Enlightenment. The great liberating transformation of Western life began in the eighteenth century, was brought to the cutting edge of philosophical discourse in the nineteenth, and swept everything before it in the twentieth. The Enlightenment, by which I mean the elevation of skeptical reason, the celebration of individual freedom, and the anticipation of human progress, was an attack on convention, as then understood, especially the conventions defended by revealed religion and prescriptive politics. It sought to emancipate man from a privileged church, an anointed king, and common opinion.

Although the great founders of the Enlightenment were English (Bacon, Locke, Newton, Mill, Bentham) or French (Voltaire, Condorcet), America and the American regime were its fullest expression. Our domestic apostles were Jefferson, Paine, and Franklin; their failure to produce many great writings to defend their emancipating cause reflected as much the absence of resistance to be overcome as any defect in the rhetorical powers at their disposal. They had no privileged church to subdue, no resident monarch to overthrow, and, in the frontier conditions of a young republic, precious little conventional opinion to defy.

By European standards the emancipation of American thought was easy, and so it was not obvious to us how much we still took for granted in our new-found state of enlightened freedom. But the magnitude of this assumption becomes clear if one asks what the founders did *not* put into the Constitution. Not only was it amended to make clear that freedom of expression was guaranteed and no official church could be established (the French Constitution supplied these rights as well), there was no positive grant of power to the national government to supervise education, to manage public welfare, or to attend to the health, safety, and morals of the people. There was, in short, no national police power. We assumed that the citizenry would have, in Madison's words, "sufficient virtue" to make republican government possible.[1] Indeed, republican government presupposes the existence of these qualities. George Will disagrees: "Presupposes? Those qualities [that is, virtue] must be willed."[2] The absence of any constitutional provision and political inclination for a tutelary state has led Will (and earlier led others) to consider our nation to be "ill-founded."

Well-founded or not, the Enlightenment basis of our popular regime has spread, like grass roots in a well-tended lawn, to cover virtually our entire political and social landscape. We, especially the youngest of us, react with dismay and alarm at talk of character's being a public problem rather than a private concern. And yet, as with the student at Beloit, we typically express our dismay and even our alarm in well-modulated language that gives due regard to the feelings (and not just the rights) of others. I am reminded of what Tocqueville observed in another context about the difference between what Americans profess and how they behave:

> Americans . . . are fond of explaining almost all of the actions of their lives by the principle of self-interest rightly understood. . . . In this respect I think they frequently fail to do themselves justice; for in the United States as well as elsewhere people are sometimes seen to give way to those disinterested and spontaneous impulses that are natural to man; but Americans seldom admit that they yield to emotions of this kind; they are more anxious to do honor to their philosophy than to themselves.[3]

As with self-interest, so with individual rights: we assert large claims to freedom, spontaneity, and self-expression but act in ways that for the most part respect constraints, moderate excesses, and reveal our capacity for self-control.

For the most part. The failures of character preoccupy us, especially the older ones of us. Whether those failures are larger and more ominous today than in the distant past is a matter on which scholars have no settled verdict, but there can be little doubt that they are greater than when most of us (middle-aged) folk were growing up—in the 1930s, the 1940s, and the 1950s. (As I suggest in chapter 6, the belief that things are worse today than when the observer was growing up is as often held by eighteen-year-olds as by fifty-year-olds.) Whatever a long historical perspective may teach us, we do not live long ago; we live today, and today we worry about the apparent collapse of character as evidenced by fashionable drug users, ominous youth gangs, aggressively (and often obscenely) importuning beggars, rude disrupters of public addresses, and vulgar purveyors of prurience. And we worry especially about those institutions (including, alas, some experimental colleges) that seem determined to encourage the most self-indulgent and solipsistic behavior.

This book, however, is not about those worries—all real, though some exaggerated. It is not in short a jeremiad about how the world is going to perdition on the skids of its own slippery, situational ethics. It is an attempt to bring together some reflections covering almost twenty-five years of research and observation about bits and pieces of the character puzzle, research and observation that I did not quite realize was about character until the man at Rice and the woman at Beloit stood up and asked their questions.

The first puzzle is what anyone can reasonably mean by "character." It cannot stand for every trait we like in another person, for some traits are matters of taste and style or accidents of personality that have no fundamental moral significance. I have not answered this question to my complete satisfaction, but I offer the following as a starting place: to have a good character means at least two things: empathy and self-control. Empathy refers to a willingness to take importantly into account the rights, needs, and feelings of others. Self-control refers to a willingness to take importantly into account the more distant consequences of present actions; to be in short somewhat future oriented rather than wholly present oriented.[4]

The significance of these two dispositions can best be seen by considering what almost any of us would regard as a defect in character: a persistent and wanton proclivity to criminality. There can be criminals who have a lot of self-control (they tend to specialize in the more lucrative forms of white-collar crime) but almost none who have both self-control and a high regard for the rights and feelings of others.[5] Persistent and wanton criminality is higher among young people than older ones and among males than females because, for reasons to be discussed in later chapters, young males are more likely to score low in both empathy and self-control. (And when we find high-rate female offenders, it is usually because they score low in just the same way.)

Criminality is the extreme case. Some people who score low on these two character traits do not, for reasons of circumstance or social control, get involved in crime at all, but they do get involved in other behaviors that we find threatening or wrong. Persons scoring low in empathy and self-control are more likely to be reckless drivers, spouse assaulters, drug users, and unreliable employees. People living immoral or disorderly (but not necessarily criminal) lives tend to do so both because they are unable to act in their own long-term best interests (that is, they are impulsive) and because they are unwilling to act for the interests of others (that is, they are self-centered). Some people lead orderly but nonetheless immoral lives because, although they have a great deal of self-control, they lack any effective concern for others. (The highly organized child who insists on having for himself all the toys when young and all his father's bequest when he is older is a stock, and all too real, figure of novels.)

Character, thus defined, leaves a lot of room for individual self-expression; having a good character is not synonymous with being introverted, subservient, religious, patriotic, or even Republican. To investigate character and to seek ways of improving it are not tantamount to taking ideological sides.

Facets of Character

In chapter 2 I try to defend the proposition that even (or especially) in a free society, understanding character is vital to the understanding of several public policy questions. In chapter 3 I give an account of how the public ethos, if not public policy, has shaped American character, with crime and temperance as the leading examples. Following that I try to explain how biology contributes to individual differences in character. In chapter 4 I describe some of what we know about how family experiences operate on this biological raw material. These three chapters set forth the broad dimensions of the problem: how character changes over time and why it differs among individuals at a given point in time. These essays have gaping intellectual holes in them; in particular none shows by rigorous analysis the causal patterns that contribute to the formation or malformation of character. In chapter 12 I offer a research agenda for filling those holes, an agenda I hope to pursue (in the company of others) over the next few years.

Chapters 5 through 8 look at character, or character-forming processes, among two groups of young people—high school students, most of whom will never go on to college, and college students, many of whom will go on to prosperous and powerful positions. The chapters on students at my old high school in Southern California were written only two years apart, but they are about generations that were twenty years apart. What I find in reflecting on young people at Jordan High in the 1940s (when I was there) and the 1960s (when I returned for a visit) was a remarkable degree of continuity. Although my return was in the

1960s when my employer, Harvard University, was in the throes of a student rebellion and although the 1960s had affected the style of student life and dress, that much-described decade did not seem to affect the core beliefs, concerns, and commitments of these young people. That fact will strike sophisticated people as a damning indictment of the insularity of high school and Eastern sophisticates as additional evidence of the shallowness of Southern California, but I find it neither. Jordan High was and is a blue-collar high school, and I am willing to bet that almost any blue-collar school in whatever region revealed, in the 1960s, more of the continuity and less of the rebelliousness of American character. Indeed, serious scholars (as opposed to the popular commentators on culture) long ago showed that the heralded generation gap of the 1960s was largely a myth.

Since my sympathies are obviously with the high school students, the reader will not be surprised to learn that when I looked at college students, especially those at elite schools such as Harvard, I had my enthusiasms under careful control. Harvard in the 1960s and early 1970s was not a happy place to be, and much as I admire and respect its intellectual accomplishments, I did not think much of the way in which students and professors behaved. I recall an old friend of mine who was for a brief period dean of Harvard College. After he had been barricaded in his office, hounded down Massachusetts Avenue, and repudiated by the faculty to whom he turned for support, he told me that "at Harvard, unfortunately, the men of conscience outnumber the men of honor." When I was asked many years later to give the commencement address at my own alma mater, the University of Redlands, I had those days in mind when I reflected on the difference between the life of the mind with its many and sudden infusions of cause and "conscience," and the life of the heart with its latent, irregular, but always powerful tug toward honor, duty, and commitment.

In chapters 10 through 12 I take up three practical problems of character: How should we police our cities when they are in disarray? What is the fundamental source of the ethical problems in business? What is the case for keeping certain drugs illegal? Chapter 13 is not the conventional academic call for more research; it is rather an effort to state in concrete detail what we need to know about how character is formed in the big cities of a free society and how our public policies will differ depending on what we learn. Chapter 14 explains social order in the context of the moral sense.

Neoconservatism?

The essays in this book are fragmentary precursors of work in progress. I am not quite satisfied with them, but many readers will find them unsatisfactory for reasons having little to do with their preliminary and incomplete quality. A story will explain the concerns of those readers and perhaps predict their response. In April 1980 the editors of the *Partisan Review* convened a conference at Boston University to discuss the meaning (if any) of neoconservatism. I was asked, along with Nathan Glazer, to defend this doctrine, one for which the editors had little sympathy but displayed much tolerance. Glazer and I found the experience somewhat uncomfortable, inasmuch as neoconservatism is not an ideology or a program of action; it is (or was), if anything, a skeptical posture toward some of the more popular clichés of liberalism in the 1960s and 1970s. To me it was not much more than applied social science, albeit an application animated for many adherents (but not for me) by a desire to settle old scores in the literary and political wars of the West Side of Manhattan. Since I was not from New York, was not raised on the Left, took no part in its internecine war of words, and could not even give a passable definition of a Trotskyite, I had almost nothing to say of interest to the conferees.

All I could do was remark that I was a neoconservative (if that is what you wanted to call me) because I was raised in a Catholic family in a Southern California city populated mostly by Midwestern Protestants. At school we unhesitatingly saluted the flag every morning; our disputes—and they were often vicious—were rarely over politics but often over dates, cars, sports, and (above all) male reputation. Almost everybody went to church on Sunday and during the rest of the week connived at breaking school and family rules about drinking, dating, and homework. We sent our fair share of boys to juvenile court and reform school. We often lost a football game but rarely the riot afterward. We were, in short, representative of that vast number of young people trying to reconcile a youthful desire for autonomy and excitement with a system of adult authority that as a structure we entirely respected even as we sought to escape from its particular restrictions. As we grew to adulthood, we began to enforce the rules ourselves, modifying them somewhat in keeping with the general drift of society toward allowing more freedom for self-expression and more tolerance for ethnic and religious differences. Some of the rules represent mere convention—in matters of dress, etiquette, and social expectations—and a thoughtful adult will try to give less weight to these than to the fundamental and enduring rules governing obligation, fairness, and self-control.

Given this background, what of significance could I say to a sophisticated audience? Not much. I remarked that a neoconservative such as myself understood the public's worry over crime and disorder and respected its allegiance to family, neighborhood, church, and country. I also worried over whether understandable fears combined with deep loyalties might stimulate unfair actions but asked my listeners to note the growing tolerance among the public for people who were different. At the same time this tolerance for individual differences did not, would not, and probably should not extend to individuals flouting the values we are supposed to have in common. There is in our society and across almost all societies a shared and natural sense of what constitutes, with respect to fundamental matters, right character. That sense does not come from intellectual deliberation or chosen ideology but from ordinary men and women struggling to discover how best to live familial and communal lives in which politics is for the most part irrelevant.

When I finished my brief remarks along these lines, the first question from the audience was this: What was my position on the third world and the Equal Rights Amendment?

2

The Rediscovery of Character: Private Virtue and Public Policy

When Irving Kristol asked me in 1985 to write an essay for the twentieth anniversary of the Public Interest, *this was the result. My intent was to set forth my worries about the extent to which economics had come to dominate policy analysis; the essay was a set of reflections about how noneconomic matters—in particular, human character—shaped the policy issues and, by implication, the policy solutions with which we were concerned.*

The most important change in how one defines the public interest that I have witnessed—and experienced—from 1965 to 1985 has been a deepening concern for the development of character in the citizenry. An obvious indication of this shift has been the rise of such social issues as abortion and school prayer. A less obvious but I think more important change has been the growing awareness that a variety of public problems can only be understood—and perhaps addressed—if they are seen as arising out of a defect in character formation.

The *Public Interest* began publication at about the time that economics was becoming the preferred mode of policy analysis. Its very first issue contained an article by Daniel Patrick Moynihan hailing the triumph of macroeconomics: "Men are learning how to make an industrial economy work" as evidenced by the impressive ability of economists not only to predict economic events accurately but to control them by, for example, delivering on the promise of full employment. Six months later I published an essay suggesting that poverty be dealt with by direct income transfers in the form of a negative income tax or family allowances. In the next issue, James Tobin made a full-scale proposal for a negative income tax, and Virginia Held welcomed program planning and budgeting to Washington as a means for rationalizing the allocative

11

decisions of government, a topic enlarged upon the following year by a leading practitioner of applied economics, William Gorham. Meanwhile, Thomas C. Schelling had published a brilliant economic analysis of organized crime, and Christopher Jencks a call for a voucher system that would allow parents to choose among public and private purveyors of education. In a later issue, Gordon Tullock explained the rise in crime as a consequence of individuals responding rationally to an increase in the net benefit of criminality.

There were criticisms of some of these views. Alvin L. Schorr, James C. Vadakian, and Nathan Glazer published essays in 1966, 1968, and 1969 attacking aspects of the negative income tax, and Aaron Wildavsky expressed his skepticism about program budgeting. But the criticisms themselves often accepted the economic assumptions of those being criticized. Schorr, for example, argued that the negative income tax was unworkable because it did not resolve the conflict between having a strong work incentive (and thus too small a payment to many needy individuals) and providing an adequate payment to the needy (and thus weakening the work incentive and making the total cost politically unacceptable). Schorr proposed instead a system of children's allowances and improved social security coverage. But he did not dissent from the view that the only thing wrong with poor people was that they did not have enough money and the conviction that they had a "right" to enough. Tobin was quick to point out that he and Schorr were on the same side, differing only in minor details.

A central assumption of economics is that "tastes" (which include what noneconomists would call values and beliefs, as well as interests) can be taken as given and are not problematic. All that is interesting in human behavior is how it changes in response to changes in the costs and benefits of alternative courses of action. All that is necessary in public policy is to arrange the incentives confronting voters, citizens, firms, bureaucrats, and politicians so that they will behave in a socially optimal way. An optimal policy involves an efficient allocation—one that purchases the greatest amount of some good for a given cost, or minimizes the cost of a given amount of some good.

This view so accords with common sense in countless aspects of ordinary life that, for many purposes, its value is beyond dispute. Moreover, enough political decisions are manifestly so inefficient or rely so excessively on issuing commands (instead of arranging incentives) that very little harm and much good can be done by urging public officials to "think economically" about public policy. But over the past two decades, this nation has come face to face with problems that do not seem to respond, or respond enough, to changes in incentives. They do not respond, it seems, because the people whose behavior we wish to change do not have the right tastes or discount the future too heavily. To put it plainly, they lack character. Consider four areas of public policy: schooling, welfare, public finance, and crime.

Schooling

Nothing better illustrates the changes in how we think about policy than the problem of finding ways to improve educational attainment and student conduct in the schools. One of the first reports of the 1966 study on education by James Coleman and his associates appeared in the *Public Interest*. As every expert on schooling knows, that massive survey of public schools found that differences in the objective inputs to such schools—pupil-teacher ratios, the number of books in the library, per pupil expenditures, the age and quality of buildings—had no independent effect on student achievement as measured by standardized tests of verbal ability.

But as many scholars have forgotten, the Coleman report also found that educational achievement was profoundly affected by the family background and peer-group environment of the pupil. And those who did notice this finding understandably despaired of devising a program that would improve the child's family background or social environment. Soon, many specialists had concluded that schools could make no difference in a child's life prospects, and so the burden of enhancing those prospects would have to fall on other measures. (To Christopher Jencks, the inability of the schools to reduce social inequality was an argument for socialism.)

Parents, of course, acted as if the Coleman report had never been written. They sought, often at great expense, communities that had good schools and never doubted for a moment that they could tell the difference between good ones and bad ones or that this difference in school quality would make a difference in their child's education. The search for good schools in the face of evidence that there was no objective basis for that search seemed paradoxical, even irrational.

In 1979, however, Michael Rutter and his colleagues in England published a study that provided support for parental understanding by building on the neglected insights of the Coleman report. In *Fifteen Thousand Hours*, the Rutter group reported what they learned from following a large number of children from a working-class section of inner London as they moved through a dozen nonselective schools in their community. Like Coleman before him, Rutter found that the objective features of the schools made little difference; like almost every other scholar, he found that differences in verbal intelligence at age ten were the best single predictor of educational attainment in the high

13

school years. But unlike Coleman, he looked at differences in that attainment across schools, holding individual ability constant. Rutter found that the schools in inner London had very different effects on their pupils, not only in educational achievement but also in attendance, classroom behavior, and even delinquency. Some schools did a better job than others in teaching children and managing their behavior.

The more effective schools had two distinctive characteristics. First, they had a more balanced mix of children—that is, they contained a substantial number of children of at least average intellectual ability. By contrast, schools that were less effective had a disproportionate number of low-ability students. If you are a pupil of below average ability, you do better, both academically and behaviorally, if you attend a school with a large number of students who are somewhat abler than you. The intellectual abilities of the students, it turned out, were far more important than their ethnic or class characteristics in producing this desirable balance.

Second, the more effective schools had a distinctive ethos: an emphasis on academic achievement, the regular assignment of homework, the consistent and fair use of rewards (especially praise) to enforce generally agreed-upon standards of conduct, and energetic teacher involvement in directing classroom work. Subsequent research by others has generally confirmed the Rutter account, so much so that educational specialists are increasingly discussing what has come to be known as the effective schools model.

What is striking about the desirable school ethos is that it so obviously resembles what almost every developmental psychologist describes as the desirable family ethos. Parents who are warm and caring but who also use discipline in a fair and consistent manner are those parents who, other things being equal, are least likely to produce delinquent offspring. A decent family is one that instills a decent character in its children; a good school is one that takes up and continues in a constructive manner this development of character.

Teaching students with the right mix of abilities and in an atmosphere based on the appropriate classroom ethos may be easier in private than in public schools. This fact helps explain why Coleman (joined later by Thomas Hoffer and Sally Kilgore) was able to suggest in the 1982 book, *High School Achievement*, that private and parochial high schools may do better than public ones in improving the vocabulary and mathematical skills of students and that this private-school advantage may be largely the result of the better behavior of children in those classrooms. In the authors' words, "achievement and discipline are intimately intertwined." Public schools that combine academic demands and high disciplinary standards produce greater educational achievement than public schools that do not. As it turns out, private and parochial schools are better able to sustain these desirable habits of work behavior—this greater display of good character—than are public ones.

Welfare

Besides the Coleman report, another famous document appeared at about the time the *Public Interest* was launched—the Moynihan report on the problems of the black family (officially, the U.S. Department of Labor document entitled *The Negro Family: The Case for National Action*). The storm of controversy that report elicited is well known. Despite Moynihan's efforts to keep the issue alive by publishing in the *Public Interest* several essays on the welfare problem in America, the entire subject of single-parent families in particular and black families in general became an occasion for the exchange of mutual recriminations instead of a topic of scientific inquiry and policy entrepreneurship. Serious scholarly work, if it existed at all, was driven underground, and policy makers were at pains to avoid the matter except, occasionally, under the guise of welfare reform, which meant (if you were a liberal) raising the level of benefits or (if you were a conservative) cutting benefits. By the end of the 1960s, almost everybody in Washington had in this sense become a conservative; welfare reform, as Moynihan remarked, was dead.

Twenty years after the Moynihan report, Moynihan himself could deliver at Harvard a lecture in which he repeated the observations he had made in 1965, but this time to an enthusiastic audience and widespread praise in the liberal media. At the same time, Glenn C. Loury, a black economist, could publish in the *Public Interest* an essay in which he observed that almost everything Moynihan had said in 1965 had proved true except in one sense—in 1985, single-parent families were twice as common as they were when Moynihan first called the matter to public attention. The very title of Loury's essay suggested how times had changed: whereas leaders once spoke of welfare reform as if it were a problem of finding the most cost-effective way to distribute aid to needy families, Loury was now prepared to speak of it as "the moral quandary of the black community."

Two decades that could have been devoted to thought and experimentation had been frittered away. We were no closer in 1985 than we were in 1965 to understanding why black children are usually raised by one parent rather than by two or exactly what consequences, beyond the obvious fact that such families are very likely to be poor, follows from this pattern of family life. To the extent the matter was addressed at all, it was usually done by assuming that welfare payments provided an incentive for families to dissolve. To deal with this, some people

15

embraced the negative income tax (or as President Nixon rechristened it, the Family Assistance Plan) because it would provide benefits to all poor families, broken or not, and thus remove an incentive for dissolution.

There were good reasons to be somewhat skeptical of that view. If the system of payments under the program for aid to families with dependent children (AFDC) was to blame for the rise in single-parent families, why did the rise occur so dramatically among blacks but not to nearly the same extent among whites? If AFDC provided an incentive for men to beget children without assuming responsibility for supporting them, why was the illegitimacy rate rising even in states that did not require the father to be absent from the home for the family to obtain assistance? If AFDC created so perverse a set of incentives, why did these incentives have so large an effect in the 1960s and 1970s (when single-parent families were increasing by leaps and bounds) and so little, if any, such effect in the 1940s and 1950s (when such families scarcely increased at all)? And if AFDC were the culprit, how could poor, single-parent families rise in number during a decade (the 1970s) when the value of AFDC benefits in real dollars was declining?

Behavior does change with changes in incentives. The results of the negative income tax experiments certainly show that. In experiments in Seattle and Denver, the rate of family dissolution was much higher among families who received the guaranteed annual income than among similar families who did not—36 percent higher in the case of whites, 42 percent higher in the case of blacks. Men getting the cash benefits reduced their hours of work by 9 percent, women by 20 percent, and young males without families by 43 percent.

Charles Murray, whose 1984 book, *Losing Ground*, has done so much to focus attention on the problem of welfare, generally endorses the economic explanation for the decline of two-parent families. The evidence from the negative income tax experiments is certainly consistent with his view, and he makes a good case that the liberalization of welfare eligibility rules in the 1960s contributed to the sudden increase in the AFDC caseload. But as he is the first to admit, the data do not exist to offer a fully tested explanation of the rise of single-parent families; the best he can do is to offer a mental experiment showing how young, poor men and women might rationally respond to the alternative benefits of work for a two-parent family and welfare payments for a one-parent one. He rejects the notion that character, the *Zeitgeist*, or cultural differences are necessary to an explanation. But he cannot show that young, poor men and women in fact responded to AFDC as he assumes they did, nor can he explain the racial differences in rates or the rise in caseloads at a time of declining benefits. He notes an alternative explanation that cannot be ruled out: during the 1960s, many persons who once thought of being on welfare as a temporary and rather embarrassing expedient came to regard it as a right that they would not be deterred from exercising. The result of that change can be measured: whereas in 1967, 63 percent of the persons eligible for AFDC were on the rolls, by 1970, 91 percent were.

In short, the character of a significant number of persons changed. To the extent one thinks that change was fundamentally wrong, then, as Loury has put it, the change creates a moral problem. What does one do about such a moral problem? Lawrence Mead has suggested invigorating the work requirement associated with welfare, so that anyone exercising a "right" to welfare will come to understand that there is a corresponding obligation. Murray has proposed altering the incentives by increasing the difficulty of getting welfare or the shame of having it so as to provide positive rewards for not having children, at least out of wedlock. But nobody has yet come to grips with how one might test a way of using either obligations or incentives to alter character so that people who once thought it good to sire or bear illegitimate children will now think it wrong.

Public Finance

We have a vast and rising governmental deficit. Amid the debate about how one might best reduce that deficit (or more typically, reduce the rate of increase in it), scarcely anyone asks why we have not always had huge deficits.

If you believe that voters and politicians seek rationally to maximize their self-interest, then it would certainly be in the interest of most people to transfer wealth from future generations to present ones. If you want the federal government to provide you with some benefit and you cannot persuade other voters to pay for your benefit with higher taxes, then you should be willing to have the government borrow to pay for that benefit. Since every voter has something he would like from the government, each has an incentive to obtain that benefit with funds to be repaid by future generations. There are, of course, some constraints on unlimited debt financing. Accumulated debt charges from past generations must be financed by this generation, and if these charges are heavy, there may well develop some apprehension about adding to them. If some units of government default on their loans, there are immediate economic consequences. But these constraints are not strong enough to inhibit more than marginally the rational desire to let one's grandchildren pay (in inflation-devalued dollars) the cost of present indulgences.

That being so, why is it that large deficits, except in wartime, have been a feature of public finance only in the past few decades? What kept

17

voters and politicians from buying on credit heavily and continuously beginning with the first days of the republic?

James M. Buchanan, in his 1984 presidential address to the Western Economic Association, has offered one explanation for this paradox. He has suggested that public finance was once subject to a moral constraint—namely, that it was right to pay as you go and accumulate capital and wrong to borrow heavily and squander capital. Max Weber, of course, had earlier argued that essential to the rise of capitalism was a widely shared belief (he ascribed it to Protestantism) in the moral propriety of deferring present consumption for future benefits. Buchanan has recast this somewhat: he argues that a Victorian morality inhibited Anglo-American democracies from giving in to their selfish desire to beggar their children.

Viewed in this way, John Maynard Keynes was not simply an important economist, he was a moral revolutionary. He subjected to rational analysis the conventional restraints on deficit financing, not in order to show that debt was always good but to prove that it was not necessarily bad. Deficit financing should be judged, he argued, by its practical effect, not by its moral quality.

Buchanan is a free-market economist, and thus a member of a group not ordinarily given to explaining behavior in any terms other than the pursuit of self-interest narrowly defined. This fact makes the more significant his argument that economic analysts must understand "how morals impact on choice, and especially how an erosion of moral precepts can modify the established functioning of economic and political institutions."

A rejoinder can be made to the Buchanan explanation of deficit financing. Much of the accumulated debt is a legacy of having fought wars, a legacy that can be justified on both rational and moral grounds (who wishes to lose a war or to leave for one's children a Europe dominated by Hitler?). Another part of the debt exists because leaders miscalculated the true costs of desirable programs. According to projections made in 1965, Medicare was supposed to cost less than $9 billion a year in 1990; in 1985, the bill was already running in excess of $70 billion a year. Military pensions seemed the right thing to do when men were being called to service; only in retrospect is their total cost appreciated. The Reagan tax cuts were not designed to impose heavy debts on our children but to stimulate investment and economic growth; only later did it become apparent that they have contributed as much to the deficit as to economic growth. The various subsidies given to special interest groups for long seemed like a small price to pay for ensuring the support of a heterogeneous people for a distant government; no one could have foreseen their cumulative burden.

No doubt there is some truth in the proposition that our current level of debt is the result of miscalculation and good intentions gone awry. But what strengthens Buchanan's argument is the direction of these miscalculations (if that is what they were) and the nature of these good intentions. In almost every instance, leaders proposing a new policy erred in the direction of understating rather than overstating future costs; in almost every instance, evidence of a good intention was taken to be government action rather than inaction. Whether one wishes to call it a shift in moral values or not, one must he struck by the systematic and consistent bias in how we debated public programs beginning in the 1930s but especially in the 1960s. It is hard to remember it now, but there once was a time, lasting from 1789 to well into the 1950s, when the debate over almost any new proposal was about whether it was *legitimate* for the government to do this at all. These were certainly the terms in which social security, civil rights, Medicare, and government regulation of business were first addressed. By the 1960s, the debate was much different: how much should we spend (not, should we spend anything at all); how can a policy be made cost-effective (not, should we have such a policy in the first place). The character of public discourse changed and I suspect in ways that suggest a change in the nature of public character.

Crime

I have written more about crime than any other policy issue. My remarks on our changing understanding of this problem are to a large degree remarks about changes in my own way of thinking about it. On no subject have the methods of economics and policy analysis had greater or more salutary effect than on scholarly discussions of criminal justice. For purposes of designing public policies, it has proved useful to think of would-be offenders as mostly young males who compare the net benefits of crime with those of work and leisure. Such thinking, as well as the rather considerable body of evidence that supports it, leads us to expect that changes in the net benefits of crime affect the level of crime in society. To the extent that policy makers and criminologists have become less hostile to the idea of altering behavior by altering its consequences, progress has been made. Even if the amount by which crime is reduced by these measures is modest (as in a free society it will be), the pursuit of these policies conforms more fully than does the rehabilitative idea to our concept of justice—namely, that each person should receive his due.

But long-term changes in crime rates exceed anything that can be explained by either rational calculation or the varying proportion of young males in the population. Little in either contemporary economics or conventional criminology equips us to understand the decline in reported crime rates during the second half of the nineteenth century and the first part of the twentieth despite rapid industrialization and urbanization, a large influx of poor immigrants, the growing ethnic heterogeneity of society, and widening class cleavages. Little in the customary language of policy analysis helps us explain why Japan should have such abnormally low crime rates despite high population densities, a history that glorifies samurai violence, a rather permissive pattern of child-rearing, the absence of deep religious convictions, and the remarkably low ratio of police officers to citizens.

In an essay published in 1983 I attempted to explain the counter-intuitive decline in crime during the period after the Civil War in much the same terms that David H. Bayley had used in a 1976 article dealing with crime in Japan. In both cases, distinctive cultural forces helped restrain individual self-expression. In Japan, these forces subject an individual to the informal social controls of family and neighbors by making him extremely sensitive to the good opinion of others. The controls are of long standing and have so far remained largely intact despite the individualizing tendencies of modernization. In the United States, by contrast, these cultural forces have operated only in certain periods, and when they were effective, it was as a result of a herculean effort by scores of voluntary associations specially created for the purpose.

In this country as well as in England, a variety of enterprises— Sunday schools, public schools, temperance movements, religious revivals, YMCAs, the Children's Aid Society—that were launched in the first half of the nineteenth century had in common the goal of instilling a "self-activating, self-regulating, all-purpose inner control." The objects of these efforts were those young men who, freed from the restraints of family life on the farms, had moved to the boardinghouses of the cities in search of economic opportunities. We lack any reliable measure of the effect of these efforts, save one: the extraordinary reduction in the per capita consumption of alcoholic beverages that occurred between 1830 (when the temperance efforts began in earnest) and 1850 and that persisted (despite an upturn during and just after the Civil War) for the rest of the century.

We now refer to this period as one in which Victorian morality took hold; the term itself, at least as now employed, reflects the condescension in which that ethos has come to be regarded. Modernity, as I have argued elsewhere, involves, at least in elite opinion, replacing the ethic of self-control with that of self-expression. Some great benefits have flowed from this change, including the liberation of youthful energies to pursue new ideas in art, music, literature, politics, and economic enterprise. But the costs are just as real, at least for those young persons who have not already acquired a decent degree of self-restraint and other-regarding-ness.

The view that crime has social and cultural as well as economic causes is scarcely new. Hardly any lay person, and only a few scholars, would deny that family and neighborhood affect individual differences in criminality. But what of it? How, as I asked in 1974, might a government remake bad families into good ones, especially if it must be done on a large scale? How might the government of a free society reshape the core values of its people and still leave them free?

They were good questions then, and they remain good ones today. In 1974 there was virtually no reliable evidence that any program seeking to prevent crime by changing attitudes and values had succeeded for any large number of persons. In 1974 I could only urge policy makers to postpone the effort to eliminate the root causes of crime in favor of using those available policy instruments—target hardening, job training, police deployment, court sentences—that might have a marginal effect at a reasonable cost on the commission of crime. Given what we knew then and know now, acting as if crime is the result of individuals' freely choosing among competing alternatives may be the best we can do.

In retrospect, nothing I have written about crime so dismayed some criminologists as this preference for doing what is possible rather than attempting what one wishes were possible. My purpose was to substitute the experimental method for personal ideology; this effort has led some people to suspect I was trying to substitute my ideology for theirs. Although we all have beliefs that color our views, I would hope that everybody would try to keep that coloration under control by constant reference to the test of practical effect. What works?

With time and experience we have learned a bit more about what works. There are now some glimmers of hope that certain experimental projects aimed at preparing children for school and equipping parents to cope with unruly offspring may reduce the rate at which these youngsters later commit delinquent acts. Richard J. Herrnstein and I have written about these and related matters in *Crime and Human Nature*. Whether further tests and repeated experiments will confirm that these glimmers emanate from the mother lode of truth and not from fool's gold, no one can yet say. But we know how to find out. If we discover that these ideas can be made to work on a large scale (and not just in the hands of a few gifted practitioners), then we will be able to reduce crime by, in effect, improving character.

Character and Policy

The traditional understanding of politics was that its goal was to improve the character of its citizens. The American Republic was, as we know, founded on a different understanding—that of taking human nature

21

pretty much as it was and hoping that personal liberty could survive political action if ambition were made to counteract ambition. The distinctive nature of the American system has led many of its supporters (to say nothing of its critics) to argue that it should be indifferent to character formation. Friend and foe alike are fond of applying to government Samuel Goldwyn's response to the person who asked what message was to be found in his films: if you want to send a message, use Western Union.

Since I yield to no one in my admiration for what the founders created, I do not wish to argue the fundamental proposition. But the federal government today is very different from what it was in 1787, 1887, or even 1957. If we wish it to address the problems of family disruption, welfare dependency, crime in the streets, educational inadequacy, or even public finance properly understood, then government, by the mere fact that it defines these states of affairs as problems, acknowledges that human character is, in some degree, defective and that it intends to alter it. The local governments of village and township always understood this, of course, because they always had responsibility for shaping character. The public school movement, for example, was from the beginning chiefly aimed at moral instruction. The national government could afford to manage its affairs by letting ambition counteract ambition because what was originally at stake in national affairs—creating and maintaining a reasonably secure commercial regime—lent itself naturally to the minimal attentions of a limited government operated and restrained by the reciprocal force of mutual self-interest.

It is easier to acknowledge the necessary involvement of government in character formation than it is to prescribe how this responsibility should be carried out. The essential first step is to acknowledge that at root, in almost every area of important public concern, we are seeking to induce persons to act virtuously, whether as schoolchildren, applicants for public assistance, would-be lawbreakers, or voters and public officials. Not only is such conduct desirable in its own right, it appears now to be necessary if large improvements are to be made in those matters we consider problems: schooling, welfare, crime, and public finance.

By virtue, I mean habits of moderate action; more specifically, acting with due restraint on one's impulses, due regard for the rights of others, and reasonable concern for distant consequences. Scarcely anyone favors bad character or a lack of virtue, but it is all too easy to deride a policy of improving character by assuming that this implies a nation of moralizers delivering banal homilies to one another.

Virtue is not learned by precept, however; it is learned by the regular repetition of right actions. We are induced to do the right thing with respect to small matters, and in time we persist in doing the right thing because now we have come to take pleasure in it. By acting rightly with respect to small things, we are more likely to act rightly with respect to large ones. If this view sounds familiar, it should; it is Aristotle's. Let me now quote him directly: "We become just by the practice of just actions, self-controlled by exercising self-control."

Seen in this way, there is no conflict between economic thought and moral philosophy: the latter simply supplies a fuller statement of the uses to which the former can and should be put. We want our families and schools to induce habits of right conduct; most parents and teachers do this by arranging the incentives confronting youngsters in the ordinary aspects of their daily lives so that right action routinely occurs.

What economics neglects is the important subjective consequence of acting in accord with a proper array of incentives: people come to feel pleasure in right action and guilt in wrong action. These feelings of pleasure and pain are not mere tastes that policy analysts should take as given; they are the central constraints on human avarice and sloth, the core of a decent character. A course of action cannot be evaluated simply in terms of its cost-effectiveness because the consequence of following a given course—if it is followed often enough and regularly enough—is to teach those who follow it what society thinks is right and wrong.

Conscience and character, naturally, are not enough. Rules and rewards must still be employed; indeed, given the irresistible appeal of certain courses of action—such as impoverishing future generations for the benefit of the present one—only some rather draconian rules may suffice. But for most social problems that deeply trouble us, the need is to explore, carefully and experimentally, ways of strengthening the formation of character among the very young. In the long run, the public interest depends on private virtue.

3

Incivility and Crime

I spent the summer of 1983 reading American and British social history in an effort to find a solution to an intellectual puzzle: Why did crime rates appear to have declined during much of the Industrial Revolution? My answer was first given as a lecture at Wake Forest University and then written as an essay for the Public Interest. *After several revisions, a different version of it later appeared in* Crime and Human Nature *(written with Richard Herrnstein) and a still different one was given as a lecture in London in 1989. What follows is the 1989 version.*

Of late, modernization has been accompanied by criminality. Although there are some noteworthy exceptions (Japan being the most prominent), the economic advancement of a nation has been purchased at the price, among other things, of higher levels of property crime and to a lesser extent of violent crime. Yet the evidence is also quite clear that those individuals who are most likely to commit crimes are not the most obvious beneficiaries of modernization; the criminals today, like the criminals of yesteryear, tend to be the poor and the unschooled. How can we explain the failure of economic progress to produce higher levels of law-abidingness, especially since that progress has reduced the relative size of the population most likely to break the law?

This question is all the more puzzling when we realize that only economic progress in its *contemporary* form seems to be associated with increased criminality. In the early nineteenth century crime and disorder were quite common in the large cities of Europe and the United States but then became less so during the second half of that century, though the size and density of these cities were increasing dramatically. Ted Robert Gurr found that in London, Stockholm, and Sydney the number of murders, assaults, and thefts that came to the attention of the police declined irregularly, but consistently, for half a century or more.[1] Public safety continued to improve in these cities well into the twentieth century. In Boston, Philadelphia, Rochester, Muncie, and New York City, crime rates rose in the early nineteenth century and then began to decline beginning around the middle of that century.[2] Philadelphia is the best-studied city in this regard. There Roger Lane counted 3.3 murder indictments per hundred thousand persons in the middle of the nineteenth century but only 2.1 by century's end, a decline of 36 percent.[3]

The second half of the nineteenth century was a period of industrialization and urbanization and in the United States one in which millions of immigrants entered the nation. Despite rapid economic growth and convulsive social changes, crime rates appear to have declined or at worst to have traced an irregular pattern around a relatively stable trend line.

The contemporary period has also been one of economic growth and urbanization, but unlike a century ago these changes have been accompanied by higher rates of crime. In the United States between 1960 and 1978, the robbery rate more than tripled, the auto theft rate more than doubled, and the burglary rate nearly tripled.[4] Beginning around 1955, the rate of serious ("indictable") offenses in England began increasing at about 10 percent per year.[5] Murder rates during the 1960s rose in, among other cities, Amsterdam, Belfast, Colombo, Dublin, Glasgow, and Helsinki; the general crime rate rose in, among other countries, Denmark, Finland, Norway, and Sweden.[6]

Crime rates are less in underdeveloped nations than in developed ones, although the rate of crimes against persons is higher in the former than in the latter.[7] As a nation progresses economically, the total crime rate increases, but the fraction of those crimes that are violent ones decreases.[8]

One obvious, but partial, explanation for the difference between these two centuries is the age structure of the population. In the second half of the nineteenth century, in both the United States and much of Europe, the proportion of young persons in the population declined as life expectancy increased. During the 1960s and 1970s the proportion of youngsters in the population increased as the baby-boom generation came of age.

But age cannot be the whole story. In Roger Lane's study of Philadelphia, the increase in the median age of that city's residents was not enough to explain all of the decrease in homicide rates during the nineteenth century.[9] Scholars who have examined the upsurge in American crime during the 1960s and 1970s have concluded that the shift in age composition explained no more than half the increase, and probably less.[10]

We have quite clear evidence that much of the recent increase in crime is the result of the greater rate at which young people commit crimes. Marvin Wolfgang and his associates at the University of Pennsylvania followed the criminal careers of two groups of boys, those born in Philadelphia in 1945 (and who remained in that city until they were eighteen) and those born in Philadelphia in 1958 (and also remained in that city for at least eighteen years). Although roughly the same percentage (about one-third) of each cohort had at least one arrest, the number of arrests of those boys in the second cohort who had committed at least one crime was much higher than of the members of the first cohort. The boys who grew up during the 1960s and who had started on a life of crime committed twice as many burglaries, three times as many homicides, and five times as many robberies as the boys who grew up in the 1950s.[11] To put it in technical language, the age-specific arrest rate (and thus presumably the age-specific crime rate) of the newer cohort was much higher than that of the older cohort. The evidence we have from the nation as a whole confirms the Philadelphia data. The probability that a person aged fifteen to twenty-nine would commit a murder in the United States increased by nearly 50 percent between 1955 and 1972.[12]

Urbanization also tends to increase crime by increasing the frequency with which persons encounter criminal opportunities (goods to be stolen or persons to be assaulted) and criminal associates (gangs and criminal subcultures that one can join) and by increasing the chances of evading social sanctions by virtue of the anonymity that cities tend to confer. There is no doubt that violent crime is more common in big cities than in small ones. But Philadelphia was not a bigger city in the 1960s than it had been in the 1950s (in fact it was smaller). Yet, as we have seen, young boys growing up there were more criminal, and more violently criminal, in the 1960s than they had been in the 1950s. Moreover, in the 1890s more than a million Philadelphians went about their daily business in an environment so orderly that a present-day resident of that city who was transported back a century in time could be pardoned for thinking he had entered Arcadia.[13] While New York City, Istanbul, Manila, and Calcutta all experienced increases in the homicide rate as they grew in population during the first half of the twentieth century, Bombay, Helsinki, Tokyo, Madrid, Belfast, and Nairobi had murder rates that declined as their populations grew during this same period.[14] And in the second half of the nineteenth century, urbanization was associated with declining crime rates.

Perhaps the economic cycle has affected crime rates in a way that might explain the differences between this century and the last. There is some evidence that in the nineteenth century property crimes increased during periods of recession and decreased during times of affluence.[15] But that connection between economic conditions and criminality no longer seems to exist, or to exist to the same degree.[16] In the United States crime rates drifted down between 1933 and 1960, although the first part of this era included a severe depression (1933–1940) and the second part

27

was one of reasonable prosperity (1941–1960). And a more recent increase in crime (and in age-specific crime rates) occurred during a period of unparalleled prosperity (1960–1980). Even the scholars who find evidence that economic factors have some effect on contemporary crime rates concede that "the major movements in crime rates during the last half century cannot be attributed to the business cycle."[17]

One can perhaps put the matter even more strongly: whereas in the nineteenth century property crime was linked to the business cycle, today it is not. If true, that represents a profound change in the relationship between human behavior and historical forces. Criminality has been decoupled from the economy. If the prototypal novel of crime in the nineteenth century was written by Charles Dickens or Victor Hugo, today it would have to be written by whom? Someone, I conjecture, attuned to the effect, not of the economy, but of culture. Tom Wolfe comes to mind.

The "Civilizing Process"

Not having written or read the definitive novel, I offer instead an argument, one that I have advanced before.[18] In the mid-nineteenth century England and America reacted to the consequences of industrialization, urbanization, immigration, and affluence by asserting an ethos of self-control, whereas in the late twentieth century they reacted to many of the same forces by asserting an ethos of self-expression. In the former period big cities were regarded as threats to social well-being that had to be countered by social indoctrination; in the latter period cities were seen as places in which personal freedom could be made secure. The animating source of the ethos of self-control was religion and the voluntary associations inspired by religious life, but religion itself did not produce the resulting social control; rather the processes of habituation in the family, the schools, the neighborhood, and the workplace produced it. The ethos of self-expression was secular, but it was not secularism itself that led to the excesses of self-expression; rather it was the unwillingness of certain elites to support those processes of habituation that even in the absence of religious commitment lead to temperance, fidelity, moderation, and the acceptance of personal responsibility.

Gurr, following the lead of the German sociologist Norbert Elias, suggested that the nineteenth century witnessed the full flowering of the civilizing process, that is, the acceptance of an ethos that attached great importance to the control of self-indulgent impulses.[19] Eric Monkkonen said much the same thing when he observed that from about 1840 into the early decades of the twentieth century a set of Victorian values acquired a remarkable hegemony in England and America, concurrent with the advent of industrialization.[20] Martin J. Wiener has argued that this was more than mere coincidence. The British middle classes, who had invented industrialization and benefited enormously from it, viewed the resulting economic and urban growth with suspicion and disdain. Educated opinion placed industrialism into a kind of "mental quarantine," elevating in its place a conception of the "English way of life" that glorified the countryside—"ancient, slow-moving, stable, cozy, and 'spiritual.' " The English character was defined as inherently conservative, and its greatest task lay in "taming and 'civilizing' the dangerous engines of progress it had unwittingly unleashed."[21] Bertrand Russell would later sneer that "the concept of the gentleman was invented by the aristocracy to keep the middle classes in order," but in truth the concept of the gentleman enabled the middle classes to supplant the aristocracy.[22] The landed elite gave way to the industrialists on its own cultural terms: the former ceded power to the latter on condition the latter become as much like the former as possible.

In the United States there was no aristocracy that the members of the new bourgeois might ape; in its place was evangelical religion. The first few decades of the nineteenth century witnessed a series of religious revivals that later become known as the Second Great Awakening. Those revivals involved an intense debate over the meaning of the Bible and how man might enter into the right relationship with God. Whatever spiritual effect they may have had, their social effect was enormous. People caught up in them created or joined a host of voluntary associations designed to improve society by improving the character of its members.

Those associations included temperance societies, antislavery movements, Sunday schools, children's aid groups, and the Young Men's Christian Association. The reach of these organizations was remarkable. In 1820 fewer than 5 percent of the adult males in New York City belonged to the lay boards of Protestant organizations; by 1869, 20 percent did. In that latter year something approaching half of all adult Protestant males were members of at least one church-related association. In 1825 the American Sunday School Union claimed that it enrolled one-third of all the children in Philadelphia between the ages of six and fifteen. In 1829 more than 40 percent of the children in New York City were said to attend Sunday school. Within ten years after its introduction into the United States, the YMCA enrolled more than twenty-five thousand young men.

But the temperance movement had the most far-reaching effects. In the decades leading up to the 1830s, the consumption of alcohol rose sharply. By one estimate the annual per capita consumption of alcohol was 10 gallons in 1829, up from 2.5 gallons in 1790.[23] Respectable Americans were appalled by the results: rowdy urban streets, saloons on every corner, young men showing up for work drunk. In 1829 there was one saloon for every twenty-eight adult males in Rochester, New York, and that city was not atypical.[24]

The temperance movement meant different things to different people. To some it meant moderation, to others total abstinence. Some wanted legal compulsion, others preferred moral suasion. But taken as a whole, the movement embraced almost every strata of society, including the intelligentsia. By the thousands, men were induced to sign temperance pledges and boys were recruited into the Cadets of Temperance and the Cold Water Army. By 1855, thirteen states had passed laws that banned the manufacture and sale of liquor statewide or at the option of cities and counties.

The effect of this effort was dramatic. Between 1830 and 1850 annual per capita alcohol consumption for persons aged fifteen and older fell from 7.1 gallons to 1.8 gallons.[25] What effect this had on behavior, especially criminal behavior, is impossible to say, but most people at the time believed that it made a difference for the better. And in retrospect we know that crime rates declined far faster than one would have predicted by knowing only the aging of the population. Some places were unaffected, of course. The Tenderloin districts of New York and other big cities remained riotous, boozy neighborhoods. But social pressure, police enforcement, and the absence of cheap and convenient transportation kept the rioters and the boozers in their place, a place that respectable folk rarely visited except on missionary errands.

Whatever effect these associational activities had, it was as much from the routine moral training and social pressure they produced as from the religious convictions they imparted. This is pure conjecture since we do not have—and can never have—any measure of either religiosity or habituation. But the conjecture is consistent with what we know about the development of character in people. Aristotle argued that the moral virtues, unlike the intellectual ones, are the product of the regular repetition of right actions. We are habituated to temperate and moderate behavior by routinely acting in temperate and moderate ways.[26] Developmental psychology has confirmed this insight by showing through countless studies how children who are the object of regular, consistent, and appropriate discipline acquire a habitual tendency to control their impulses, take into account the distant consequences of present acts, and attend to the feelings of others.[27]

Both the public schools and the Sunday schools had a moral object: the production of better children. The object was sought by precept as well as practice, but from everything we now know of child rearing, practice is more important than precept. In England and the United States the Sunday schools were staffed by working-class teachers who sought to inculcate values as well as to increase literacy. Both were achieved by rote, that is, by the steady repetition of exercises designed to make habitual behavior that would otherwise be episodic, whether the behavior was recitation of the alphabet and Biblical verses or the observance of the rules of punctuality and good order. By these means, as Thomas W. Laqueur was later to write, "the bourgeois world view triumphed in the nineteenth century largely through consent, not through force." The middle class established a "moral hegemony."[28]

Religion played a role in this but more as an animating force than as a moralizing precept. Religious sentiments inspired many of these social movements; churches supplied the institutional catalyst for many of these voluntary associations; church-related societies provided the continual social reinforcement necessary to sustain participation in the movements and associations. But the associations outlasted their religious inspiration. A spiritual awakening tends to be evanescent, organizations tend to be immortal. The Sunday school, the YMCA, the temperance society—these endured for decades, long after the Great Awakening was but a memory. The Victorians, whether in the United States or England, lived off their capital in more ways than one. They retained "a strong moral consensus long after the decline of the religious faith that had originally sustained that morality."[29]

What was decisive about the religiously inspired movements of the nineteenth century was that they were endorsed and often led by the upper classes. In this respect the American experience was like the British one. In both places the "best people" endorsed a view of right conduct and the path to good character that was accepted by almost all classes. Contemporary Marxist historians are correct in asserting that nineteenth-century schools and associations were used to control the working classes. They are also correct in suggesting that the requirements of the new industrial workplace rewarded those best able to conform to them and thus encouraged schools to teach those personal traits—order, obedience, punctuality—that would equip people to be successful workers.[30] They are wrong only in suggesting that this was done over the opposition, or contrary to the best interests, of those workers. The working classes not only absorbed those lessons and took those jobs, they taught those lessons and sought those jobs.

Changed Attitudes

Today matters could scarcely be more different. Beginning in the 1920s and resuming (after time out for a depression and a war) in the 1960s, the best people were at pains to distance themselves from, and even to denounce, what their counterparts a century earlier had taken for granted. Religious revivals, once led by liberal college students (such as Theodore Weld, a founder of the antislavery society), were later scorned by educated people, who saw such enthusiasms as the atavistic rumblings of rural fanatics. Temperance movements were disdained as the domain of elderly women who wished to bring back Prohibition, which "everybody knows" failed. (In fact it did not fail in one regard: Prohibition did result in a reduction in alcohol consumption by at least one-third and perhaps by one-half.) Saloons that were once condemned as dens of iniquity were now called cocktail lounges and hailed as centers of sophisticated sociability. Cities that were once viewed as the breeding ground of vice and disorder were now hailed as indispensable arenas of personal liberty.

The very phrase "middle-class values" became a term of derision rather than pride. Sigmund Freud was interpreted (wrongly) as having blamed mental disease on the suppression of natural human instincts by artificial social conventions. Margaret Mead became a best-selling anthropologist in large measure on the strength of her claim (now much disputed) that Samoans were happy because they enjoyed greater sexual freedom. Schools were criticized for their emphasis on rote learning and moral instruction and urged instead to foster self-discovery and self-directed learning among their pupils.

These changes in attitude probably affected childrearing practices, but not much can be said with confidence on this matter. We can observe how people talked about child rearing; whether what they said mirrored what they did is another matter. In the mid-nineteenth century mothers were advised by the ladies' magazines of the supreme importance of inculcating moral and religious principles. Corporal punishment even then was subject to criticism, but the goal of obedience was not. In 1890, 1900, and 1910, one-third of the child-rearing articles published in a sample of articles from the *Ladies Home Journal, Women's Home Companion,* and *Good Housekeeping* were about character development; in 1920 only 3 percent were.[31] Personality development had taken its place.

When parents in Muncie, Indiana, were asked in 1924 what traits they most wanted to see in their children, 45 percent said "strict obedience" and 50 percent said loyalty to the church. When the same question was put to Muncie parents a half century later, 76 percent gave "independence" as the desired quality (47 percent said "tolerance"). Only 17 percent now mentioned obedience.[32]

Today Victorian morality and even the era to which that queen gave her name are known to most of us only as symbols for prudery, hypocrisy, repression, and conformity. There were elements of all of these things in nineteenth-century England and America, but there was something else as well: the maintenance of a reasonable degree of social order, without extensive government repression, in the face of massive economic and demographic changes.

The Invention of Adolescence

Between 1860 and 1960 elite opinion underwent a sea change, from advocating self-control to endorsing self-expression (or, as it was quickly understood, self-indulgence). Society's fundamental task has always been to socialize its youth, especially during the tumultuous teenage years. Never an easy task, it was in the nineteenth century easier than it is today because adolescence—that recognized interregnum between childhood and adulthood—did not exist. As soon as children were physically able to work, they worked, usually on the farm but sometimes in grim, satanic mills and mines. Moreover, there was a cultural consensus about what constituted right conduct, a consensus strong enough to follow and to envelop young men and women when they left the farm to work in the growing cities. Today we live in a world in which an intellectual invention—adolescence—has become a practical reality. Large numbers of young people are expected to be free both of close parental control and of the discipline of the market. They live with parents but not under them, they work in the market but not from necessity. They are free to seek mates, not under the old (parent-defined) rules of courtship but under the new (peer-defined) rules of dating. It is obviously a status both privileged and precarious, one that is well managed only by those young people who have already been set on a proper course by virtue of a sound constitution and responsible parents.

What is remarkable about the social invention of adolescence is that by itself it leads to no great harm. The vast majority of teenagers grow up to be perfectly ordinary and respectable adults. A large fraction of the boys (in Philadelphia, London, and Copenhagen, one-third) will be arrested by the police at least once, but the great majority of these will not be arrested again.[33] The reason is that most parents do a very good job of setting their children on the proper course. As Joseph Adelson has reminded us, most adolescents are neither enraged nor disengaged; they are, on the contrary, much like their parents and usually turn out to be something of which their parents approve.[34]

But the existence of adolescence and of a youth culture puts some young people deeply at risk because they have, by virtue of a defective constitution or inadequate parenting, been set on an uncertain or disastrous course. The embarrassment many adults feel at correcting teenagers, the belief inculcated by higher education and the youth culture itself that freedom and self-realization are the supreme goods, the scorn in which Victorian morality is held—all these deprive the at-risk adolescents of the kind of moral instruction the adult world once provided and enforced.

Adolescence by itself is hardly a threatening social invention (Japanese adolescents are not seen as a social problem); the ethos of radical individualism and commitment to self-expression of educated elites is by itself not especially worrisome (nineteenth-century England was filled with the respectable followers of John Stuart Mill). But the two in combination—that is troublesome.

The two coincided in the United States during the 1960s. There ensued a dramatic increase in teenage pathologies: delinquency, drug use, suicide, eating disorders, and teenage pregnancies. The pathologies afflicted only a minority of all adolescents, to be sure, but the minority totaled several million people.

We are not entitled to be surprised. If we set several million teenagers free from direct parental or market supervision, knowing that a fraction of them lack a strong moral compass; if we expect those young people to learn from what they see and hear about them; and if what they hear is a glorification of the virtues of individualism and self-fulfillment, then we ought to be thankful that any adolescents are left intact.

In the 1930s, when marijuana first come to public notice, it was routinely condemned by elites who associated it, often wrongly, with Mexican immigrants. Marijuana use did not spread widely.[35] When it reappeared in the 1960s, it was praised as a liberating or at least legitimate experience and associated with creativity and musicality; its use spread like wildfire. Peyote and other naturally occurring psychedelics were used by Indians for generations without much notice; when Aldous Huxley, Timothy Leary, and Alan Watts, among others, endorsed the consciousness-expanding properties of LSD, its use spread rapidly. When cocaine was first introduced in this country, it was thought to be a harmless stimulant, and Coca-Cola put it into its soft drink. When elite opinion turned against it, its use shriveled. When cocaine returned to public awareness in the 1970s, it was advertised as being consumed at the best parties attended by the most fashionable people; other people could not wait to try it.

Moral Habituation

I do not wish to blame widespread drug use on the glitterati, but I do wish to point out that all kinds of ideas—not just Marxism or Keynesianism or capitalism—have consequences. Young people do learn from older people; at-risk young people learn from the most self-indulgent older people. As Richard Herrnstein has pointed out, morality must be learned just as surely as the multiplication tables and the rules of grammar. And like multiplication and grammar, morality is largely learned by rote. That form of learning is now in disrepute, partly because rote learning is wrongly seen as the enemy of creativity and individuality and partly because the elites who must inculcate the learning disagree about what is to be inculcated.[36]

This reduction in routinized moral habituation probably affects everyone to some degree, but for most people the effect is minor because their parents and peers have intuitively rewarded decency and punished selfishness and because these people have entered markets and neighborhoods that reinforced the lessons of their early training. But some lack either the earlier training or the later environment, and so become especially vulnerable to the self-indulgent tone of modern elite culture.

Black Americans have been especially vulnerable in this regard. Roger Lane has described how black homicide rates in Philadelphia rose from the mid- to the late-nineteenth century, roughly doubling at a time when, as we have already seen, the overall homicide rate was falling.[37] Other immigrant groups, notably the Irish and the Italians, had high murder rates when first settling in that city, but soon their rates began to fall.[38] Lane attributes the black increase to their systematic exclusion from the economic life of the city, an exclusion that placed the black middle class in a hopeless position: its commitment to respectability was threatened both by whites (who refused to reward respectability with legitimate economic advancement) and by other blacks (who scorned respectability by creating profitable and status-conferring criminal enterprises).

No doubt exclusion is an important part of the story, but it cannot be the whole story because even sharper increases in black crime rates occurred later, in the 1960s, when the barriers to entry into legitimate occupations were falling rapidly. Adult unemployment rates for blacks and whites were declining when age-adjusted crime rates started increasing. The other part of the story, to which Lane's excellent study offers important support, is that the culture of respectability was itself precarious, such that its reach was limited to a minority of the black minority.

William E. DuBois, the leading black scholar of his time, was himself the exemplar of the respectable Negro: intellectual in his manner, puritanical in his views, and reformist in his politics. His book about Philadelphia blacks in the 1890s was at once a revelation of the extent of racism and segregation and a plea for self-help based on a strong family life, steady work habits, and the strict control of crime.[39] But the message was not institutionalized or routinized, and so did not reach those most in need. The folk culture of urban blacks, as many observers have noted, was and is aggressive, individualistic, and admiring of semiritualistic insults, sly tricksters, and masculine display. [40] This popular culture may have been a reaction against the repressive and emasculating aspects of slavery; whatever its origin, it was not a culture productive of a moral capital off which people could live when facing either adversity or affluence. The contrast between black popular culture and that of other repressed minorities—Asian-Americans and Hispanic-Americans—has often been remarked. This may help explain why, as Lane notes, black crime rates are higher than Hispanic ones, even in cities where black income is significantly higher than Hispanic income.[41] Glenn Loury has complained of the continuing failure of middle-class blacks to provide visible moral leadership on issues such as crime, teenage pregnancy, and single-parent families.[42] While one can appreciate the desire of black leaders to avoid giving ammunition to racists by publicly discussing the moral decay of some parts of the black community, in the long run silence will be self-destructive.

Some critics of liberal democracy argue that the sea change in elite opinion from self-control to self-indulgence was caused by the democratic spirit. I disagree. Nothing in democratic theory leads inevitably to a warped elite ethos. Democracy is, after all, only a system for picking rulers. *Liberal* democracy is a more complicated matter, for "liberal" implies that it will be the goal of democratic rule to enhance liberty. But the liberties the better democracies have secured (and on which their perpetuation depends) are the traditional liberties to life, conscience, and property. The United States functioned democratically (except for the denial of the vote to women and blacks) from about the 1830s on. Removing the barriers to female and black participation did not change matters fundamentally; women, especially, voted much as men had always voted. Yet for about a century after the adult white male franchise was universal, after virtually every office one can imagine was placed under popular control, and after a Civil War had begun the emancipation of blacks, the United States did not experience, on an age-adjusted basis, a sharp increase in criminality during times of prosperity—until the 1960s.

Changes in Culture

Some may argue that the extension (in my view the bending) of the constitutionally protected freedom of expression to include not merely political and artistic speech but also pornography and nude dancing has fostered an ethos that harms youthful socialization, but I am not convinced. Scarcely any society consumes more prurient material than does Japan, yet this has not worked any obvious corruption of Japanese character. One might also argue—with considerably more force—that the multiplication of restrictions on the police has made certain aspects of the culture of self-indulgence, notably drug use, harder to bring under control. That is true up to a point. But it is not yet clear how much would be gained by reducing the constraints on the police. In New York City, they made 90,000 drug arrests in 1988; in Washington, D.C., nearly 13,000; yet only a small fraction of these arrests resulted in a jail term. Whether the fallout is the result chiefly of legal barriers to conviction or of a public unwillingness to pay for prison space, I do not know.

If not liberal democracy, what is the culprit? One possible answer is affluence. Only an affluent society can afford an adolescent class; in poorer societies everyone, including the young, must work. Only an affluent society can have a middle class large enough to produce dissidents from the orthodox culture in sufficiently large numbers such that they constitute a critical mass. Only in an affluent society can people afford to buy large quantities of heroin, cocaine, LSD, PCP, and crack. Only an affluent society can have enough consumer goods so that feelings of injustice are sufficiently aroused to lead everybody to believe they are entitled to everything and to arouse feelings of injustice if they do not get it.

But we have enjoyed affluence before (though never quite on the scale of the past three decades), yet affluence has not before been associated with so great a commitment to hedonism and self-indulgence. The reason, as I have argued, is that in the past, when freedoms were expanded and economic opportunity enhanced in ways that threatened to free young people from the constraints of conventional morality, the defenders of that morality redoubled their efforts to maintain and extend those constraints. Sometimes, as in the Second Great Awakening, religiosity inspired the effort, but at other times (perhaps one can place the 1890s in this category) the religious impulse was less important. In the contemporary world the adult reaction to enhanced adolescent freedom has not been to control the adolescents but to emulate them. Once upon a time young boys waited impatiently until they were old enough to dress like their fathers; today fathers try to dress like their sons. Today one can imagine the graduates of our best universities leading almost any cause save one designed to instill orthodox morality.

What has changed has been the culture. That change can be described as the working out of the logical consequences of the Enlightenment. The Enlightenment meant the acceptance of skepticism and individualism, coupled with a recurring assertion of the possibility of infinite social progress and human perfectibility. This change brought with it extraordinary social benefits: freedom from religious intolerance

37

and sectarian fanaticism, the development of the scientific method and modern technology, and the intellectual foundation of capitalism and thus of affluence. Man was knowable, authority was suspect, society was malleable.

So summary a statement cannot do justice to the several stages and many variants of Enlightenment thought. The founders of the eighteenth-century Anglo-Scottish Enlightenment—David Hume and Adam Smith—certainly embraced reason over religion (Hume's great *Treatise of Human Nature* was subtitled "An Attempt to Introduce the Experimental Method of Reasoning into Moral Subjects"), but they believed that the scientific study of morality would explain why mankind accepted the same virtues—justice, benevolence, temperance, modesty, chastity— that earlier philosophers derived from natural or divine law. Radical individualism came later and might be thought of as the romantic heresy: reason is an imperfect or wholly unreliable guide to understanding man and the universe. Virtue, if such there be, can only be apprehended directly, spontaneously, aesthetically, and individually. Reason can at best discover what is useful; only feeling can discover what is beautiful, and beauty is superior to utility. All that is left of the Enlightenment is individualism.

It is another matter for another day to discuss whether the seeds of their own decay were contained in the naturalistic moralities of Hume and Smith, whether, that is, championing reason and science as against revelation and prescription inevitably meant freeing the individual to pursue his own self-expression to the point of self-indulgence. My provisional view is that it was not intellectually inevitable, although it may have been historically so.[43] If an eighteenth-century Scotsman asserts that virtue derives from sentiment, he should not be surprised to discover that an eighteenth-century Frenchman (or a twentieth-century Englishman) concludes that sentiment is more important than virtue— *any* sentiment, so long as it is "authentic" or "natural."

However the Enlightenment may have been altered beyond the intention of its founders, it is clear that wrenched loose from its moorings in the virtuous habits of eighteenth-century Edinburgh or Victorian London, it came to mean the triumph of skepticism and individuality. As received, the Enlightenment that honored freedom contained within it no principle by which to define the limits to freedom. The skeptical reason that challenged religious, scientific, or political orthodoxy challenged every rule by which one could defend moral orthodoxy. The individualism that unleashed the material accomplishments of capitalism was insensitive to the moral preconditions of capitalism.

The Enlightenment has been institutionalized in the university and there has become the public philosophy of the millions of people who each year pass through those ivied halls. Fortunately for most of these people, their philosophy does not much affect their lives. Having been habituated to goodness by those very processes—adult authority, rote learning, and the maintenance of appearances—that the university teaches them to distrust, they absorb the ethos without changing their habits. But their public philosophy alters how they define the proper policy for others. It is an "enlightened" philosophy: people should be left alone to do their own thing, historical lessons should be subordinated to immediate needs, utility should be maximized but authority distrusted. For two centuries we have been enjoying the benefits of having supplanted revelation with reason. Most of us will continue to enjoy those benefits for centuries to come. But some will know only the costs, costs imposed on them by well meaning people who want only to do the right thing.

4

Character and Biology

After the appearance in 1985 of Crime and Human Nature, *I found myself defending before academic audiences the finding, made by many scholars, that a propensity to crime has in many cases and to some significant degree a genetic or biomedical origin. It was a curious experience: audiences composed of people who by virtue of their (largely) inherited intelligence and their (partially) inherited temperament had acquired or were acquiring degrees at elite universities were challenging the proposition that heredity had anything to do with behavior. It then occurred to me that some people mistakenly thought that if a tendency toward aggressiveness or impulsiveness had some biological source, that tendency was immutable and the afflicted party beyond help. In lectures in 1990 at Loyola University of Chicago and Louisiana State University, I tried to correct this misunderstanding.*

Character is shaped in part by constitutional factors, including genetic (that is, heritable) ones. If a concern for character strikes you as conservative, a concern for genetic endowments may strike you as reactionary. It is not. Quite the contrary: it is hard to find a significant human behavior (with the possible exception of rooting for the Boston Red Sox) that does not reflect to some degree endowments that have a genetic component. We recognize this readily when we observe that some people are much better than others at playing the violin, carrying a tune, doing calculus, playing chess, or hitting a curve ball. Parents notice that their children differ in temperament at birth: one is shy, the other bold; one sleeps through the night, the other is always awake; one is curious and exploratory, the other reticent or even passive. These observations are about differences that cannot be explained wholly or even largely by environment, a conclusion most of us have little difficulty in accepting.

But this commonplace observation suddenly becomes controversial when someone suggests that it also applies to adult character. No matter how often the speaker proclaims that a predisposition to good or bad conduct reflects a complex interaction of biology and environment, the assertion that nature plays any role at all in shaping that proclivity produces among many listeners, especially in academic audiences, narrowed eyes and whitened knuckles. The person who, when young, had little doubt that she was doing better in school than her classmates because she was smarter, better organized, and more strongly motivated than they, and who took for granted that these traits could not be wholly explained by having taken Flintstone vitamins, upon attending college suddenly accepts the view that now, at age eighteen or nineteen, the human personality is formed wholly by environmental factors. Such a view implies a radical discontinuity in human experience: while both nature and nurture play a role in the early years, only the latter plays any role later. We do not believe that about our talents (for music, chess, or baseball); why do we believe it about our personality?

One reason is that college, as I argue in chapter 9, is the chief institution through which we acquire in systematic fashion the legacy of the Enlightenment. One part of that legacy is the argument of John Locke that there are no innate ideas or by extension innate traits; the child is, in the phrase attributed to Locke, a tabula rasa, a blank slate, on which experience writes what it will, unconstrained by nature. That claim was an important part of the seventeenth-century effort to discredit the justification for a natural aristocracy and in particular for a divinely anointed king. It became an even more important part of the eighteenth- and nineteenth-century belief in progress. Man could progress without limit to the extent his environment could be altered without limit. If infinite progress was possible, it was because man was transparent, that is, entirely knowable and wholly changeable. That view, as I suggest in the following pages, has not kept up with science. I know of no reputable professor of child or developmental psychology who believes today that the child's mind is a blank slate, although there are important differences among these academics as to which childhood traits persist into adulthood. But scarcely a year passes without our seeing new evidence that teenage or adult behaviors we once believed to be wholly the product of adolescent or mature experiences have in fact biological or early childhood roots.

The Lockean view might be more readily abandoned and the Enlightenment belief in unlimited progress more quickly modified were it not for another, more pressing concern. Statements about character are, or should be, statements about morality; saying that someone has a good character is fundamentally different from the assertion that someone can hit a good curve ball, play a good chess game, or sing a Mozart aria. In the first case we assert that a person is good; this implies a strong claim (that the person deserves respect) and a strong prediction (that the person can be trusted). We do not expect good people to be kept after class, to lose out in the competition for jobs, or to wind up in jail. If these things happen anyway, we are suspicious that they may have been treated unfairly. In the latter cases we assert that a person is talented; this implies a weaker claim (that the person deserves attention) and a weaker prediction (that the person is likely to earn good money and social status). If baseball players, chess masters, or gifted singers are kept after class, lose out in the struggle for jobs, or wind up in jail, we do not automatically suspect that an injustice has been committed. There are, alas, lots of crooked ball players, screwy chess masters, and egomaniacal vocalists.

In short, admitting that biological factors are involved in shaping adult character seems tantamount to saying that some people are born bad and are irretrievably bad; they are in the grip of a destiny that will lead them straight to economic failure, social ostracism, penal servitude, or eternal damnation. A good consequence of the broad acceptance of the Enlightenment is that most of us refuse to accept the doctrine of predestination.

Biomedical Roots of Behavior

In the remainder of this chapter I want to adduce evidence that biology is not predestination. On the contrary: a candid admission that biological and even genetic factors are an important part of the complex process by which our character is formed creates opportunities for change that should warm the heart of even the most devoted adherent of the Enlightenment. Opportunities for change are also opportunities for well-meaning mistakes and even wicked manipulation. How we use the knowledge that is now accumulating will depend on our intelligence—and our character. But to foreclose the opportunity by denying the knowledge is an even greater failure of intelligence and character. Indeed, it contradicts a central teaching of the Enlightenment: if one believes that the environment is decisive, how can one ignore (or among some radicals, block) changes in that environment, namely, growth in scientific knowledge?

I take as my case criminality, by which I mean not an occasional violation of the law but a persistent and high rate of participation in illegal or disorderly actions. Criminality in this sense refers to a personality disposition—a character trait—that makes some people less likely than others to resist the temptations presented by criminal opportunities, less likely because they are impulsive or self-centered.

The evidence of a biological, possibly a genetic, factor in criminality is quite strong. When we compare the criminal records of identical and

43

fraternal twins, we find in virtually every study (and there have been more than a dozen) that identical twins are much more alike in their criminality than fraternal twins. Identical twins have identical genetic endowments; fraternal twins are no more alike than any other pair of siblings. Some may say that the greater similarity in behavior among identical twins arises out of the fact that their parents are more likely to treat them alike (and that the twins themselves wish to be more alike) than is the case with fraternal twins. But we have good reason for doubting that explanation. For one thing, studies of identical twins reared apart show similarities in personality that are about as great as what are found among twins reared together.[1]

For another, we know that boys put up for adoption have criminal records more like those of their biological parents (whom they never knew) than like those of the adoptive parents who actually raised them. Again one can imagine problems in making inferences from adoption studies. Suppose, for example, that the adoption agencies tried to match boys from criminal fathers with similar adoptive fathers. But these are mostly imaginary problems. Adoption agencies do not engage in that kind of matching. They often do not know anything about the criminal records of the biological parents either because the record is not available or because the parents have not yet started committing crimes. Adopted boys tend to have crime records more like those of their biological parents even when those records began after the boy is adopted. Taken together, twin and adoption studies provide hard-to-ignore evidence that some constitutional factors increase the probability that a person will be at risk for criminality.[2]

Even people who may accept this evidence still find it troubling because it strikes them as suggesting that people are born criminal or are beyond help. Nothing could be further from the truth. There is no crime gene; there are genes that affect our personality (especially, it appears, our tendencies to be impulsive) and our intelligence, and these, combining in as yet poorly understood ways, can make us more vulnerable to familial and social factors that reduce rather than strengthen impulse control or lessen rather than heighten our willingness to take into account the well-being of others.

Contrary to what some critics suggest, the scientific investigation of the biomedical roots of human behavior has widened, not narrowed, the opportunities for helping people. Once all slow learners in school were regarded as dumb or lazy; then science learned that heritable learning disorders, such as dyslexia, prevented even bright and eager children from achieving to their potential. As a result these children no longer sit in the corner wearing dunce caps, they enroll in special education programs that teach dyslexic children to read. Once alcoholism was regarded as a moral failing to be managed by religious instruction or penal servitude; then science learned that a heritable predisposition to alcoholism makes perfectly upright people unable to control their alcohol consumption. As a result these people can be taught that they have a disease, that coping with that disease requires abstinence, and that friends and family members can help them cope. Once schizophrenia was thought to be madness induced by sin or misconduct; then science discovered that a genetic factor contributes to, if it does not wholly cause, this ailment. As a result there are new opportunities for finding chemical means for controlling and perhaps even eliminating the schizophrenic disorder.

Biomedical research offers hope for dealing with those characterological disorders that contribute to criminality. If feasible, this will enlarge the possibilities for coping with at least some of these problems.

I will go further: unless we investigate the biomedical as well as the social bases of criminality, we will never understand the most obvious and important facts about criminality. Males commit more crimes than females, young males more crime than older males. These age and gender differences dwarf all other factors associated with individual variations in criminality (for example, ethnicity and social class). We have theories and data in abundance that purport to explain class differences in crime rates but scarcely any well-supported explanations for why boys are far and away the most common offenders.

Some people think that there is an explanation—namely, boys are raised in ways that emphasize aggressiveness. If boys and girls were treated the same way and played with the same toys, this theory predicts, most if not all of the gender differences in criminality would disappear.

No doubt parents do treat boys differently from girls. No doubt that treatment has some effect, perhaps a large one, on male aggressiveness. But the most careful surveys of the available studies—and there are many—leave little doubt that a significant portion of male aggressiveness has a constitutional origin: it arises from a temperament that predisposes boys as young as two or three years of age to behaviors that in their milder forms we describe as roughhousing, assertiveness, and independence and in the more extreme forms we characterize as hostility, conduct disorders, and antisocial personality.[3] These studies should remind us that parents do not treat male children in a certain way just because they are male but also because male children behave in distinctive ways. If biology played no part in male criminality, then surely there would be some society somewhere in which women committed more crimes than men. But we find no such society.

Age poses the same challenge. The peak years for crime—and fighting, recklessness, and risk-taking—are those of late adolescence. A review of data spanning 150 years in four countries shows that teenagers

45

are more likely to be offenders than any other age group.[4] The age distribution of crime looks pretty much the same no matter how society is organized—regardless of its laws, political system, family structure, economic status, or ethnic composition. Of course the total amount of crime varies greatly from one society to another, but not the association of criminality with age and gender.

If we are to understand the formation of character, we must know more than we now know about how males enter and pass through childhood and adolescence. Such knowledge may do more than enhance our understanding; it may also improve our competence. We may better handle undercontrolled aggression if we know more about its sources. That knowledge must begin with the constitutional endowments of male infants and how those endowments interact with the environment.[5]

New Lines of Inquiry

Let me mention six examples of lines of inquiry that suggest possible new ways of viewing, and reducing, high-rate criminality: (1) hormones, (2) enzymes, (3) fetal drug syndrome, (4) low birth weight, (5) toxins, and (6) addiction. Let me stress in advance that we do not know whether changing these biomedical conditions will affect criminality, although in each case the presumptive evidence for a connection cannot be ignored. Nor should anyone assume that science will discover a pill or vaccine that will reverse these conditions in a lasting way. Altering human predispositions is a complex and chancy process that even when successful has its own legal and ethical perils. All that I wish to assert for the present is that biomedical research, even into factors that have genetic origins, is not a threat but an opportunity; it is not reactionary but liberalizing.

Hormones. Surely one of the most striking findings in the study of conduct disorders and delinquency is that whatever the adversity, be it biological or environmental, it has a greater effect on boys than on girls. Low birth weight, maternal drug use, child abuse, marital discord, and insecure infant-mother attachment all seem to cause greater behavioral problems among boys than among girls. So pronounced is this difference that one scholar has referred to females as the "buffered" sex.[6]

Yet boys are not all alike. There is some evidence that high levels of circulating testosterone are associated with physical and verbal aggressiveness, impulsivity, and lack of tolerance for frustration. The studies are not entirely consistent, are based mainly on adult subjects, sometimes rely on suspect measures of behavior, and often involve small samples. The study by Dan Olweus and others is one of the few that uses multiple measures to assess antisocial conduct among a large sample of adolescents.[7] They found that blood testosterone levels were strongly related to self-reports of aggression in response to provocations and threats, moderately related to self-reports of impatience and impulsivity, and unrelated to peer ratings of aggression.

There is evidence that testosterone levels are higher in prisoners with violent rather than nonviolent criminal histories, among those labeled dominant rather than nondominant, and among the most violent compared with less violent rapists.[8] Conversely testosterone levels are not significantly correlated with fighting among prison inmates.[9] An important recent study suggests that rule-breaking behavior among males was associated with higher levels of unbound testosterone.[10] Studies of primates consistently show that prenatal androgen levels are associated with rough or aggressive play.[11] If hormones cause impulsive or aggressive behavior, it is most likely the result of differences in the exposure of the fetus and the young infant to androgens rather than from day-to-day changes in testosterone within a grown individual. This suggests that monitoring such levels in infancy may provide useful clues to the development of delinquency.[12]

Enzymes. Monoamine oxidase (MAO) is an enzyme that affects the way in which nerve cells communicate with each other by means of neurotransmitters. After a chemical messenger has done its work, it either returns to the original neuron or is flushed out of the system by an enzyme. That enzyme is MAO. Although the process is much more complex than what I have described and although there is a good deal of uncertainty as to the effects of having too little MAO, there is reason to believe that people who have abnormally low amounts of MAO experience inappropriate activity of their nerve cells, leading to impaired judgment, overexcitement, and impulsiveness. The nerves are working at the wrong time and in response to the wrong stimuli. How much MAO we have and how active it is seem to be genetically determined. Moreover how much we have depends in part on how high a level of hormones, especially androgens, we have. Whatever the mechanism, we know that men with low levels of MAO are more likely to be aggressive, defiant, impulsive, and delinquent.[13] If we understood why some people, especially young males, had abnormally low levels of MAO, we would better understand (and perhaps could modify) individual differences in delinquency.[14]

Fetal Drug Syndrome. Women who drink heavily or abuse drugs place their fetuses at serious risk for emotional and intellectual impairment. For reasons we do not fully understand, male fetuses are more likely to be harmed by these chemical insults than female ones. The worst case consists of crack babies: infants born after they have, so to speak, suffered a stroke while in the womb, a stroke induced by the mother's use of crack cocaine. Though perhaps less dramatic, there are more numerous cases of babies afflicted by the mother's heavy use of alcohol and tobacco.

Low Birth Weight. Premature babies born with low weights compared with babies carried to term and born at normal weights are on the average less cuddly, more demanding, and slower learners. Being less easily managed, they are more likely to stimulate in some parents neglect or abuse. Being slow learners, they are less likely to do well in school. Neglect, abuse, and poor school performance in varying degrees contribute to conduct disorders that in turn seem to be associated with the emergence of serious delinquency. Again male infants seem to suffer the greatest harm from low birth weight.[15]

Toxins. The body tissues of many violent criminals seem to have unusually high levels of certain metals (such as lead, cadmium, and manganese) and unusually low levels of others (such as zinc). We have always known that lead poisoning produces serious behavioral problems; it is becoming clearer that for some people even moderately high levels of lead have adverse affects on learning, emotional stability, hyperactivity, and violence.[16] Preventing this may prove to be more complicated than simply altering diets or cleaning up the environment (by, for example, removing lead from gasoline and paint). All of us are exposed to these metals; arc welders and target shooters are exposed to high levels of them. But most of us, even most arc welders and target shooters, do not become criminals. Those who do are those who, for unknown biochemical reasons, cannot handle (by, for example, converting them into harmless compounds) the metals absorbed by their bodies. These unbuffered metals seem to operate directly on the nervous system with serious consequences.

Addiction. Some people drink alcohol in moderation; others, if they drink at all, do so to excess. Some people experiment with drugs and become addicted; others either never touch them or, if they experiment, do not become dependent. We do not know why these individual differences exist, although we do know that susceptibility to alcoholism has a genetic basis. (So far no genetic determinant of drug abuse has been found, although researchers at UCLA have recently identified a gene that accounts for some vulnerability to addiction.) Science is rapidly gaining more knowledge about the biochemical aspects of drug dependency. It seems to have learned that stimulants (for example, cocaine) interfere with the normal workings of neurotransmitters (for example, dopamine) such that these chemical messengers send exaggerated pleasure messages along the brain's pathways. What science can learn it can change. If one chemical overstimulates a neurotransmitter, another chemical can normalize it. Or so one would hope.

This brief and incomplete tour by a rank amateur through the immensely complex world of neuropsychology is not meant to be a guide to the future much less a prescription for action. It is intended to suggest an important truth: biology is not destiny, although our destiny is shaped in part by our biology.

Each of the possibilities I have suggested may offer a greater opportunity for society to help improve character and reduce criminality than do many of the more prominently discussed (and in polite intellectual society, easily tolerated) social possibilities. There can be little doubt, for example, that early childhood experiences affect the likelihood of delinquency. Children who form a weak attachment to their parents and are the objects of unreliable affection and inconsistent discipline are the children whose conduct is most likely to be first disorderly and then delinquent. If that were the whole story, what would we do? How could we change at a reasonable cost the child-rearing practices of tens of thousands of incompetent or uncaring parents? Skilled therapists at such places as the Oregon Social Learning Center (see chapter 5) have shown that it is possible to help, at great cost and with great effort, some parents. Their work is a monument to what can be achieved by intelligence and dedication. But the OSLC enrolls at any one time a few dozen clients. Could it ever enroll hundreds or thousands? Could this organization be reproduced in fifty states, a hundred cities? It seems unlikely, although it is worth a try. And even if it is enlarged, how many parents of unruly, at-risk youngsters will enroll and, if enrolled, stick it out? A lot, one hopes, but these are wistful hopes.

Or take schooling. School failure is associated with delinquency. How best to improve schools is the topic for another lecture. But even if improved, how well can they be expected to handle children who are out of control by the age of eight? Or take job training programs. Many high-rate criminals are unemployed—at least at legitimate jobs. Despite heroic efforts, such as those of the Manpower Development Research Corporation, we have not learned how to convert in large numbers eighteen-year-old boys who have failed at six jobs and have been in trouble with the law countless times into young men who will stick it out in the seventh job and stay clear of the police.

Many of our best intentions have foundered on one or both of two hard facts: if we start early, we have to change families, and then we discover that we do not know how; if we start later, we have to change fully formed personalities, and we discover not only that we do not know how but that many of those personalities prefer not to be changed. To succeed, we must start early but with strategies that require of us something less heroic than repairing families.

Whether any of the possibilities I have listed will make our task easier, I do not know. But they are possibilities—possibilities that depend on our doing the kind of research that some regard as intellectually dubious and others as politically wrong.

Character Formation in Children

We want to know how character is formed among children. Some people think they already know, and they may be right; after all, hundreds of millions of parents have produced generations of decent children, all without any help from professors. As Dr. Benjamin Spock said to mothers reading his popular baby-care book, you know more than you think you know. But surprisingly, we do not know how character is formed in any scientifically rigorous sense. We believe that early family experiences are important, but we also have reason to think that such experiences are not the whole story; otherwise the behavior of fraternal twins raised in the same family would be more alike than it is, and the behavior of identical twins raised in separate families would be less alike than it is. There is obviously some interaction between infant temperament and family life, but I am not aware of any social scientist who can give an accurate account of it.

Why is this important? It is important because efforts to improve character that are not grounded on knowledge, as opposed to opinion, are likely to prove at best ineffectual and at worst harmful, especially since serious interventions require us to trespass onto the most intimate precincts of life: the pregnant woman, the young infant, the family circle. We can try to tiptoe around this matter by acting as if we can change in important ways the behavior if not the character of young adults through schooling, the labor market, or mass communications, but I must insist that except for some small-scale, hard-to-repeat successes, we do not know how to do this. At the margin the criminal justice system can deter some would-be offenders; under propitious circumstances rehabilitation programs can reduce the criminality of some delinquents; in isolated cases an inspired preacher or sympathetic friend can hand a lifeline to a desperate man. In general, however, few propositions in criminology are better established than this: the younger the age at which a boy (or occasionally a girl) embarks on delinquency, the greater the likelihood of that boy becoming a high-rate criminal and the less the prospect of his later reform.[17] As the twig is bent . . . .

What then bends the twig? If you have studied the work of John Bowlby, Mary Ainsworth, and L. Alan Sroufe, you will be convinced that it is the success the mother has in forming a strong emotional bond with her infant.[18] Securely attached children are less likely to have conduct problems than insecurely attached ones. But if you have given equal care to the writings of Jerome Kagan, Jay Belsky, and Carroll Izard, you are not so certain.[19] How well a child is attached to his mother may importantly depend on the temperament of the child, and temperament, as we have seen, is to some significant degree determined by constitutional factors. A sensible view—one shared by most of the scholars I have mentioned during the occasional moments when they are not emphasizing their differences—is that infant temperament and maternal bonding are both important.

But if character is shaped by two factors rather than just one, the uncertainty surrounding the effect of these causes grows exponentially. And if you then imbed the infant's temperament and the mother's bonding in the context of family stresses—a drunken father, an uncertain income, an unexpected illness, a poor school—then the full depth of our ignorance becomes so obvious as to scarcely require comment. To exaggerate only slightly, when a complex mother-child interaction occurs in the midst of a host of complicating environmental factors, we really have no idea as to what intervention will make any lasting difference.

Not that there are no promising leads. I have already mentioned family therapy programs run by the OSLC. We hear even more about preschool education. Hardly a state in the Union has not been affected by the discovery in Ypsilanti, Michigan, that twelve hours a week of preschool experience for underprivileged three- and four-year olds increases the proportion of them completing school and reduces the proportion reporting (even at ages fifteen and nineteen) that they had engaged in serious misconduct.[20] The Ypsilanti experiment is a ray of hope, one that is being pursued, but it remains only an attractive glimmer. Unfortunately, overly eager policy makers, in their rush to do something, have magnified that ray beyond what is reasonable. We do not know why or how the Perry Preschool Program helped these sixty children in Ypsilanti or what would happen if sixty thousand youngsters in a dozen states were exposed to similar programs. It would be worth finding out, but the zeal for progress is often the enemy of progress, and so hardly any comparable new experiments are planned.

James Coleman and his colleagues have given us ample reason to believe that the ethos of the high school has a major effect on what is learned there.[21] A constructive ethos is one sustaining a good learning environment, free of disruptions, harassment, and violence. It turns out that such an ethos is more easily maintained in private and parochial

51

schools than in public ones. Does that mean that all schools should be privatized? Possibly; John Chubb and Terry Moe have enlarged on Coleman's findings and given us a concrete plan for putting them to work.[22] Some cities are trying these choice plans but not in an experimental cast of mind.

All of these findings offer tantalizing snapshots of what society might do to improve character and those things that depend on character, such as school achievement and law-abidingness. But we lack a systematic motion picture that shows a group of children growing up, from birth through the early school years, in a large American city. Such a continuous record would enable us to assess at frequent intervals the social, biomedical, and familial factors at work on the child and his parents so that we can better understand how character is formed or deformed and can more accurately identify those critical points at which planned interventions—medical, educational, or economic—might make a difference.

Despite all the talk about teaching ethics, expanding opportunities, and ending oppression, we do not know—as opposed to have an opinion about—how children grow up in our society. Because of that lack, we are not any better prepared to cope with crime today than we have been in the past.

I have advised, formally or informally, four presidents on what this nation's policy should be toward crime and drug abuse. Only a few of my recommendations have made matters worse; it is conceivable—though probably unlikely—that a few may have made matters better. But through that experience I have learned that scholars were not substantially better prepared to advise President Bush in 1990 than they were to advise President Johnson twenty-five years earlier. Crime rates in general were declining during the late 1970s and early 1980s. But that decline will not last and in some cities has already been replaced with an increase. The children of the baby-boomers of the 1960s are now entering the crime-prone years, and doing so in numbers large enough to drive crime rates up, just as their parents drove those rates up in the 1960s and 1970s. Each new wave of young people always seems to be accompanied by a new fad in drug use: LSD, speed, and heroin in the 1960s and 1970s, crack cocaine in the 1980s. As a result, each new wave consists of youngsters who on the average are more inclined to criminality than were predecessor generations. It is not a happy prospect.

What to do? For some years now I have been part of a loose association of scholars who are determined to stop this cycle of ignorance followed by crisis followed by bad advice. We are working to begin one or several major longitudinal studies, from birth through adolescence, that will tell us, using the best and most comprehensive array of biomedical, social, and familial measures, how children grow up in our society and how they respond to interventions, planned and unplanned, in their lives. The case for that research agenda is set forth in chapter 13.

I am too old to do the research myself; it is a task for younger legs and quicker minds. But I hope to nag the next generation of scholars about this and to protect them, insofar as I can, from the groundless charges that caring about character is philistine or investigating biology is reactionary. What I cannot protect them from is the possibility that we shall in the end learn that character formation is an ineffably mysterious process, knowable to intuition but not to science. Even should this be the outcome, it will have been a journey worth taking.

5

Character and Families

Biology is not the whole story; families make a difference. Nowhere is that difference made more vivid than in those clinics where parents with problem children are taught better ways of raising their offspring. My visit in 1983 to the Oregon Social Learning Center in Eugene, Oregon, made a lasting impression on me, not only because of the extraordinary skill and dedication of the staff under the direction of Dr. Gerald Patterson but also because, unlike many clinicians, Patterson systematically tested his techniques to see whether they really worked. They do.

"When I met him, he was six and a half years of age. There was nothing about his appearance that identified him as the boy who had set the record." The words are those of Gerald R. Patterson, a family therapist at the Oregon Social Learning Center, in Eugene. The record to which he referred was the frequency—measured with painstaking care by the Learning Center's staff—with which Don, a small boy, displayed rotten behavior. Nearly four times a minute while in his home Don would whine, yell, disobey, hit or shove. When he was not at home, telephone calls from teachers and merchants would mark his progress through the neighborhood: "He left school two hours early, stole candy from a store, and appropriated a toy from a neighborhood child."

Don had "a sleazy look about him," Patterson wrote, "like a postcard carried too long in a hip pocket." His violent outbursts were frightening; any simple request or minor provocation would trigger obscene shouts, attacks on other children, or assaults on the furniture. His mother was tired, depressed, and nearly desperate as a result of coping unaided with this monster—no babysitter would take on the job of minding Don, whatever the pay. She nevertheless persevered, changing his wet sheets, bathing and dressing him, even feeding him, all the while talking to him in tones that vacillated between cajolery and scolding, murmurs and shouts. When her seemingly bottomless patience was at last at an end, she would threaten or hit him with a stick. That produced only temporary compliance. When the father was home, things were not much different.

The shouting and fighting between Don and his younger brother continued, occasionally punctuated by the father's slapping both children.

Children like Don are the youthful precursors not only of difficult teenagers but sometimes of delinquents and adult criminals. The progression from violent, dishonest youngster to violent, dishonest teenager is not automatic, but it is common. Although child psychologists disagree about the extent to which personality in general is shaped by early childhood experiences, there is not much dispute over the fact that male aggressiveness tends to be stable from the early years on. Donald West and David Farrington, of Cambridge University, followed 411 London boys from childhood to adulthood and concluded that those who were hostile or aggressive at the ages of eight or ten were likely to be hostile or aggressive when sixteen or eighteen. A Norwegian psychologist, Dan Olweus, reviewed this study and many others and concluded that there is a great deal of continuity in male aggressiveness and misconduct. Aggressiveness tends to appear early, often by the age of three, and to persist for many years in ways that are clearly reflected in the reports of parents, teachers, and police officers and even in the reports of the young men themselves.

What is remarkable about this persistence is that it occurs despite the fact that aggression is often punished. Don's parents hit him; we can safely assume that his teachers scold him; and it is likely that in time the police will arrest him. Some explain this persistence with the argument that punishment actually causes aggression: young men and women who are hit or abused learn to hit or abuse in return; they model themselves on the behavior of others, which leads to a cycle of violence. Others believe that children bring to families some constitutional dispositions, acquired by heredity or from the accidents of prenatal or birth traumas, that not only cause them to behave more aggressively than others but cause parents to treat them differently from their brothers and sisters. Still others think that it is not punishment that causes aggressiveness but punishment poorly conceived and badly executed. Whatever the case, contemporary research, by Patterson and by scores of others, has placed the family at the center of any effort to explain and reduce unruly or violent behavior.

The role of the family in producing such behavior seems to be a greater mystery to social scientists than to parents. If one asked the average citizens why some people are more likely than others to misbehave, they would likely blame family experiences. If one then asked why children from the same family differ in their behavior, they would probably say that because children have different temperaments, they react differently to the same treatment or are treated differently by their parents.

When Sheldon Glueck and Eleanor Glueck, at Harvard Law School, published in 1950 the results of their ten-year study of delinquent boys in the Boston area, they concluded that if one held age, race, neighborhood, and (roughly) intelligence constant, delinquency appeared to be the result of an interaction between certain constitutional traits (body type and temperament) and a family environment in which one or both parents were indifferent or hostile and followed lax or erratic disciplinary practices.

There were criticisms of the Gluecks' research. Some suggested that the observations of the boys may have been colored by the observer's knowledge of whether a boy was delinquent. Others noted that some of the factors thought to be most important in producing delinquency, such as the degree of affection and the disciplinary practices of the parents, were not observed directly but inferred from statements by the boys and their parents. Still others objected to the Gluecks' efforts to predict who would become delinquent given a certain family background; such predictions, it was argued, might unfairly label a decent boy a troublemaker.

But if the only problems with the Gluecks' findings were these and similar methodological difficulties, one would have expected better studies to be mounted to test their conclusions more rigorously. Few such studies were done. The reason, I suspect, is that the beliefs of social scientists about what constituted the appropriate objects of research changed. By the mid-1950s the family was no longer the major unit of analysis in criminological research, having been supplanted by the gang and the social system.

Owing in part to an apparent rise in gang violence in the 1950s and in part to the advent of a newer group of criminologists, various theoretical perspectives that assigned a less prominent role to the family (and no role at all to constitutional traits) became dominant. One view held that children naturally conform to the values to which they are exposed; delinquents are simply exposed to values different from those the rest of us learn. The social class of the family or of other boys on the street is an especially important determinant of what values boys accept. Lower-class boys may come to disparage the conventional ethic of success and embrace instead the values of toughness and immediate gratification.

Another view, first formalized in 1949 by Robert K. Merton, of Columbia University, held that man is governed by the relationship between his aspirations and the means available to achieve them. Families may encourage boys to want a good car and social respect, but if society denies the boys legitimate means for obtaining them, they might react by stealing to get the car and committing violent acts to earn the respect. Richard A. Cloward and Lloyd E. Ohlin, both then at Columbia University, applied this view to delinquency in 1960 by asserting that economically disadvantaged adolescents turn to crime as a way of achieving material goods and avoiding the shame that accompanies economic failure.

Other writers claimed in the 1950s and 1960s that delinquency was less the result of having learned from peers to commit crimes or of being driven to crime by frustrated expectations than the result of being arbitrarily labeled a criminal by society and its institutions. Young people who violate some arbitrary social convention are called criminals; once treated as criminal, they become criminal.

Travis Hirschi, of the University of Arizona, observed that these perspectives sought to explain crime not by reference to manifestly wicked influences but by reference to supposedly good ones. Whereas an older generation of criminologists, of which the Gluecks were very much a part, thought that evil causes evil (for example, bad families produce bad children), many members of the newer generation were attracted to the idea that good—for example, the desire for achievement, the class structure, the economic order, or the decisions of the police and judges—produces evil. This view was most clearly implied by Merton: "A cardinal American virtue, 'ambition,' promotes a cardinal American vice, 'deviant behavior.'"

The critical stance of many criminologists was reinforced by reformist impulses that led them, implicitly or explicitly, to explain social problems by reference to those factors that are, or appear to be, susceptible to planned change. The 1950s was a period of worry about gang violence, the 1960s one of attention to civil rights and economic opportunity. It was natural to assume that if one wished to deal with these problems, one had first to make them the focus of one's analysis. Gangs, race, social class, and criminal justice were concepts that seemed close to the crime problem and amenable to change. By contrast the family was given less attention because of two defects: it was not on the public agenda, and it was not clear how its practices might be altered.

The study of the family did not stop, but it did begin to lose its connection with the study of crime. Research on child development, for example, was a vigorous enterprise but one not much concerned with crime (although it was concerned with behavior such as hostility and aggression, which we now know to be strong indicators of later criminality). There were exceptions: the sociologists William McCord and Joan McCord continued to trace well into adulthood the unhappy effects on later behavior caused by the discordant families in which a group of Cambridge and Somerville, Massachusetts, boys had been raised in the 1930s and 1940s.

Family as the Focus

The family was placed once again near the center of criminological attention by the masterful study of Travis Hirschi, published in 1969 under the title *Causes of Delinquency*. It began, as do most path-breaking works, by showing how we had been asking the wrong question. Most criminologists had been trying to explain how a naturally good person, or at least a naturally compliant one, might be led by social forces—gangs, schools, the police, labor markets—to commit crimes (or "deviant acts," a phrase used by those criminologists who were anxious to avoid giving the impression that "crime" was anything more than the label middle-class society attached to behavior it did not like). Hirschi argued that the first question is not why men break the law but why they obey it: conformity, not deviance, is what is most in need of explanation.

His answer was that people obey rules to the extent that they form a bond to society. That bond is composed of four elements: attachment, chiefly to the family; commitment, by which Hirschi meant a prudent regard for the costs of wrong actions and the benefits of right ones; involvement in conventional activities, such as school; and belief in the moral validity of society's rules. Hirschi tested his theory against the predictions that could be derived from rival theories by gathering information about the delinquent acts and personal backgrounds of several thousand junior and senior high school children living in and around Richmond, California.

The number of delinquent acts, as reported by the children themselves, was powerfully influenced by the children's attachment to their parents. The closer the mother's supervision of the child, the more intimate the child's communication with the father, and the greater the affection between child and parents, the less the delinquency. Even when the father held a low-status job, the stronger the child's attachment to him the less the delinquency. Other factors also contributed to delinquency, such as whether the child did well in and liked school, but these factors were themselves affected by family conditions. Hirschi's evidence supported his theory of social control of the sources of delinquency better than it supported any alternative theories, such as those that say delinquency results largely from the influence of peers or the social class of the child: after one takes into account the bond with the parents and achievement in school, the contribution of parental class nearly vanishes and that of delinquent friends sharply drops.

A large body of data has demonstrated beyond much doubt the powerful effect on aggressiveness and delinquency of being raised in a family that is discordant, lacking in affection, or given to inappropriate disciplinary practices. The best studies followed a group of boys while they were growing up. The longest-running inquiry was the Cambridge-Somerville one, which began in 1937; data from it are still being published. From these industrial communities, 650 boys were selected to participate in a program designed to prevent delinquency. Half were chosen because teachers or social workers thought they were likely to become delinquent, the other half because they were thought to be normal boys. They entered the program at age eleven on the average, well before most had committed any delinquent acts. The object was to test the efficacy of a counseling program in preventing delinquency, and to that end the boys were randomly assigned to treatment and control groups. There is little evidence that the counseling worked, but that is not what interests us here. Rather the study is valuable because of the relationship it found between family background—as reported by counselors, teachers, social workers, and doctors—and behavior.

In 1955, eighteen years after the program began, William McCord and Joan McCord analyzed the voluminous records of these boys blind, that is, without knowing in advance which boys had been convicted of crimes and which had not. Thus whatever biases may have existed in the Gluecks' research, owing to their prior knowledge of who was delinquent, could not have affected the McCords' investigation. The McCords found that the delinquent boys were about twice as likely as the nondelinquent ones to come from homes where parental disciplinary practices had been rated as erratic or lax. Delinquents were also much more likely to come from homes with a quarrelsome rather than an affectionate or cohesive atmosphere. The combined effect of these two factors—warmth (or its absence) and consistent discipline (or its absence)—was powerful: *all* the boys from quarrelsome families with erratic discipline, but only one-fourth of those from cohesive families with consistent discipline, were convicted of a crime.

Lest someone suppose that the courts were more likely to convict boys from unhappy than from happy homes, the McCords analyzed separately the backgrounds of those boys who were described by counselors or others as aggressive but who had not officially been called delinquent. They found that these aggressive boys had essentially the same family backgrounds as the convicted delinquents.

It is possible that these differences in family background reflect how the boys were originally selected for inclusion in the study; children chosen because they appeared especially good or especially bad might differ more in family circumstances than would a random sample of boys. Indeed it is possible that some of the boys were chosen because of what the teachers or others already knew about their families. There is not much evidence in the Cambridge-Somerville project that this was the case, but it cannot be ruled out entirely. Fortunately another long-term study, this one in England, was carried out in ways that eliminate this potential source of bias. West and Farrington followed the careers of 411 boys chosen at random from a working-class section of London, starting at age eight and continuing for seventeen years. The boys were given batteries of tests and interviews, and their parents were interviewed about once a year until the boys were teenagers. West and Farrington gathered information about self-reported, as well as officially recorded, delinquency. By the time they reached the age of twenty-five, a third of the boys had criminal records. About thirty of the boys became persistent repeat offenders; in fact those thirty accounted for more than half the convictions of the entire group.

The delinquent boys were more likely than the nondelinquent ones to have low IQs and to have parents who were cruel, neglectful, or passive. Boys described as aggressive by teachers or by themselves had the same background as the officially reported delinquents. Parental behavior could not explain all of the observed delinquency, however. If the father had a criminal record, this materially increased the chance that the son would be delinquent, independent of family income and parental behavior. In all, five factors seemed to play the largest role in predicting which boys would become delinquent: low intelligence (as measured by both verbal and nonverbal tests), large family size, parental criminality, low family income, and poor child-rearing practices.

What is indisputable in the London study is the impact of adverse child-rearing practices. West concluded:

> A particularly noticeable characteristic of the parents of many of the delinquents in the study was carelessness or laxness in matters of supervision. They were less concerned than other parents to watch over or to know about their children's doings, whereabouts and companions, and they failed to enforce or to formulate fixed rules about such things as punctuality, manners, bedtime, television viewing or tidying up.

The Family and Crime

All this may strike the average parent as so obvious that it seems hard to believe that so much time and money had to be spent to establish it. Before making exasperated comments about professors' reinventing the wheel, however, a parent reading this should be aware that there are at least three other possible explanations for the observed connection between family circumstances and youthful criminality. One is that delinquency is caused by the labels society attaches to children. A youngster from a discordant home is more likely, in this view, to be arrested and charged with a crime than a child from a happy (or an influential) home, who would be released in the custody of his parents. No doubt different kinds of children are treated differently by governmental institutions. There is evidence, for example, that a delinquent from a broken home is more likely to be incarcerated than one from an intact home. But the labeling process cannot explain away the influence of families on misconduct generally, because, as we saw in the studies mentioned so far, the connection between discordant or unaffectionate families and delinquency exists even when our only knowledge of the delinquent act comes from the child himself (Hirschi; West and Farrington) or from counselors instead of police officers (the McCords).

A second explanation for the link between family life and criminality rests on the possibility that the child may have inherited some cognitive deficiency or temperamental predisposition that causes aggressiveness. In this view the discordant family is not so much the cause of the misconduct as either a reaction to it (a mother slaps or yells at children who since birth have been fussy or irritable) or irrelevant to it (the delinquent is born, not made). There are good scientific grounds for believing that the child is not a blank slate on which families, friends, and society can write at will. There is some constitutional, possibly genetic, predisposition to certain forms of misconduct, as shown by elaborate studies in Scandinavia and elsewhere that reveal a connection between the criminality (or the alcoholism) of the biological father and the subsequent criminality (or alcoholism) of the son, although the son was adopted at an early age and raised by noncriminal foster parents. Important as these constitutional factors may be, their exact operation is not well understood, nor do they account for all of the individual differences in criminality that we observe. Familial factors play an important role.

A third explanation is that discordant or unaffectionate parents cause aggression by their use of punishment, especially physical punishment. One famous study, by Robert Sears, Eleanor Maccoby, and Harry Levin, concluded that "the more severe the punishment, the more aggression the child showed." Barclay Martin, after reviewing the evidence about how young (aged two to five) children go about seeking attention from their mothers, noted that the studies suggested that punishing attention-seeking behavior seemed to increase rather than decrease the frequency of the children's demands. The clear implication of such findings is that the use of punishment is at least as likely to teach children, by their observations, to be aggressive as it is to teach them, by being conditioned, to be pacific.

But as Martin and others have pointed out, there are some reasons to be skeptical of such conclusions. First, most are based on the mother's report of the child's behavior and of her discipline; both may be seriously in error. A mother trying to raise a difficult child may overstate how often punishment is used while a mother raising an easy one may understate how often it is used; these reporting errors would create a false positive correlation between punishment and aggression. Second, most such studies neglect the way the child is predisposed to behave. An active, restless, fussy child may be punished more frequently than a placid, easygoing one. The greater punishment of the former may in fact reduce the rate of such misconduct, but because that rate is already high, it can appear that more frequent punishment causes more frequent aggression.

Most important, the effect of punishment (or affection) on behavior will depend not on how *much* is used but on *how* it is used. For a reward or a penalty to have significant effect on behavior, it must be used in a consistent and contingent manner. Suppose a child who nags his mother for attention often gets her attention but on occasion is slapped instead. The child will come to believe that he can usually get his mother's attention by nagging, although he is sometimes slapped. Sometimes he wins, sometimes he loses, but if he values her attention enough, or if he gets his way more often than he gets slapped, he will redouble his nagging. If nagging does work often, the amount of it can be great, and thus the number of times he gets slapped can be great as well. This can cause the unwary observer to conclude that slapping has caused the nagging.

Or the parent may slap the child without regard to whether he has broken a rule because the parent is grouchy, or irritated by behavior that ordinarily is permitted, or acting under the erroneous belief that a rule has been broken. Such punishment, not being clearly contingent on behavior defined by some rule, is not likely to produce adherence to any rule; on the contrary, to the extent that it is random or erratic (in the child's view), it may lead him, just as social-learning theorists argue, to believe that violence is a normal and acceptable method of expressing one's feelings.

Changing Behavior

Speculating about all these possibilities is no substitute for directly observing children's behavior and trying to change it. Family therapists have been doing this, in one way or another, for decades. In the 1950s, and to some extent today, a therapist presented with an aggressive, sneaky, or hostile child would assume that the youngster was aggressive because he was anxious or frustrated or because he had a weak ego, often as a result of the parents' neuroses. The therapist would use individual psychoanalysis or counseling to cure the parents and, sometimes, nondirective play therapy to help the child, or would perhaps stage a psychodrama that involved the parents and the child simultaneously. In general, little of this seemed to make a difference, although there were individual success stories.

Beginning in the 1960s, a new approach was tried. Owing to the rising influence of behavioral psychologists, foremost among them B. F. Skinner, family therapists began looking at a child's behavior as learned on the basis of the rewards it received. A young boy would engage in rotten behavior if he found it useful. If he got what he wanted from his parents and teachers by yelling, shoving, and hitting, no one should be surprised to discover that he would continue to yell, shove, and hit. A variant of this approach, pioneered by Albert Bandura, held that a child would also learn to yell, shove, or hit when he saw other people doing this and getting away with it. The clear implication of these theories was that the therapist should try to reward the child for doing the right thing instead of the wrong thing. There was already evidence that such alleged sicknesses as bed-wetting, stuttering, and fear of snakes could sometimes be cured by rewarding the opposite behavior; why not reduce aggression by rewarding obedience?

Soon the principles of behavioral psychology were being applied in schools, foster homes, juvenile institutions, and even adult prisons. This application came to be called "behavior modification," a term that fell into some public disrepute because a few such programs used drugs or electric shock to punish—and, it was hoped, extinguish—undesirable behavior. But the great majority of these programs sought chiefly to reward desirable behavior by, for example, giving a person a valuable token every time he did something right. (Such programs were called "token economies.") Other methods were employed as well, all having in common the effort to affect behavior by changing its consequences.

There have been countless demonstrations of the fact that applied behavioral psychology can change the behavior of individuals in schools, clinics, and prisons. Students have been induced to study harder, children to throw fewer tantrums, and prisoners to obey institutional rules. But in the great majority of cases these changes disappear soon after the individual has left the institution. While behavior modification was an effective way to make life easier for people running the institutions, there was not much evidence that it was doing anything to protect the community.

Perhaps the best known of these programs tried to improve the behavior of delinquent or troublesome youths by placing them in foster homes run on behavior-modification principles. The idea was to use psychological theory to construct a better family life for children who had an unsatisfactory natural home. Achievement Place, in Lawrence, Kansas, is a foster home led by two professionally trained foster parents, in which six to eight delinquent adolescents live. Through instruction reinforced by a token economy, the leaders of Achievement Place hope to teach the delinquents to take care of their living quarters, study hard in school, improve their social skills, become punctual, and otherwise display self-control and conformity to rules. Since its inception, the Achievement Place strategy, now called the "teaching-family model," has been followed in many parts of the country; by 1982 there were about 170 such group homes in operation, staffed by foster parents trained at six regional centers. Moreover the system has been used not only for delinquents but for autistic or emotionally disturbed youths, the mentally retarded, schizophrenic adults, and even the aged. The bibliography of books, articles, and dissertations written about the teaching-family model runs to nearly fifty single-spaced pages.

There seems to be little doubt that the teaching-family system improves the behavior of even serious delinquents while they are in the group homes. But according to a comprehensive review of the system, completed in 1981 for the National Institute of Mental Health by Richard R. Jones, Mark R. Weinrott, and James R. Howard, there is little evidence that it alters the rate at which the youths commit offenses one year after their release from treatment or that it has any greater effect on delinquency than do other community-based programs.

The reason is obvious. When delinquents leave the foster home and return to the discordant family and the criminal street life, most of the rewards they receive will once again reinforce, or fail to discourage, impulsive, aggressive, or illegal activity. The key to breaking this unhappy cycle is to improve life in the delinquents' natural home. Since the late 1960s, there have been a number of efforts to do this.

Various programs have been established to teach the parents of troublesome youths to be better parents. Among the first was one carried out in Tucson, Arizona, by Roland Tharp and Ralph Wetzel and reported on in 1969. Believing that the parents of delinquents often failed to reinforce good behavior and instead denigrated or nagged their off-spring, Tharp and Wetzel tried to persuade parents and children to manage their conflicts more constructively. To make it easier to manage day-to-day affairs with a minimum of discussion and hence of arguments, Tharp and Wetzel designed a behavioral contract that would set forth the rights and obligations of parents and children in a particular family. Instead of arguing over whether he could use the family car, for example, a boy would enter into a contract with his parents whereby he would get the car at stated intervals in exchange for performing certain chores and being home at a specified time. These and other efforts at family contracting, or as it is sometimes called, contingency management, were based on the assumption that rewards should be stably linked to desired behavior on the basis of an agreement that seems fair to both sides. The youths whose families followed a behavioral contract showed a reduction in offenses, an improvement in grades, and an improvement in behavior, but the significance of these changes is hard to assess inasmuch as there was no control group with which the youths in the experimental program could be compared.

A variation of this approach to altering family life was tried in Salt Lake City by James F. Alexander and Bruce V. Parsons, then of the University of Utah. Several dozen boys and girls who had been involved with the juvenile court for various minor delinquencies—truancy, shoplifting, drinking, and running away from home—were referred to a clinic at the university. There the youths and their families were randomly assigned to one of four groups: a behavior-modification program, a conventional group-discussion counseling program, a church-sponsored family-counseling program, and a no-treatment group. The behavior-modification program involved inducing family members to talk more constructively with one another, to tolerate interruptions, and to agree on certain standards of conduct and the consequences of conforming to those standards. Over the ensuing year and a half, the youths who had been in the behavior-modification program were only half as likely to reappear in juvenile court as were those who got no treatment or who were in the conventional counseling programs; moreover the brothers and sisters of the youths in the treatment program were also less likely to get into trouble with the law than were the siblings of the youths in the control groups. The number of families involved was so small and the kinds of delinquencies averted so minor that the Utah project cannot be regarded as settling the question of whether family life can be altered in ways that will reduce serious delinquency, but it provided a promising lead.

Reducing Deviant Behavior

That lead has been most thoroughly explored by Gerald R. Patterson and his colleagues at the Oregon Social Learning Center. Unlike many other therapists, they have concentrated on reducing deviant behavior among preadolescents rather than on rehabilitating teenage delinquents; much of their research suggests that beyond a certain age, changes in the family environment have little, if any, effect on young persons because peer pressure becomes more important than parental rewards. And unlike some programs, the Learning Center's is not based on the assumption that families need to communicate more (or less); what is crucial is the way in which parents define, monitor, and control the behavior of their children in routine settings.

The key to Patterson's approach—and that of several like-minded therapists, such as Robert Wahler, in Tennessee—is the belief that many parents do not know how to raise children. What makes bad families bad is not neurosis or indifference as much as incompetence. When parents have an unruly, violent, sneaky kid on their hands, it is not because they like him that way or because they do not care how he behaves or because they have failed to solve his Oedipal conflict; it is because they fail to tell him clearly how he is expected to behave, fail to monitor his behavior closely to ensure that he behaves that way, and fail to enforce the rules with appropriate rewards and penalties, promptly and unambiguously delivered. The child may actually suffer from a weak sense of self, but such a subjective state is not readily changed directly. There is little good evidence that therapists can change the behavior of Don, or of children like him, by first changing their attitudes; indeed it would be a miracle if they could get so hostile and violent a child as Don even to listen to a discussion of his attitudes. Instead one changes behavior first and hopes that changes in underlying attitudes will follow.

Between the mid-1970s and 1983, the Learning Center treated more than 250 families whose children, ranging in age from three to fifteen, had been referred to the clinic because most of them had set fires, stolen property, picked fights, or upset their teachers or parents; some were victims of child abuse. In the child's home the therapists carefully measured all that occurred between the child and the parents or siblings every six seconds for nearly an hour. About half of the child's possible ways of behaving were termed "aversive," meaning unpleasant; these included whining, yelling, teasing, and hitting.

Their central conclusion was that the families of problem children differed from those of normal children not so much in whether they punished too much or too little as in whether they know *how* to punish. The parents of antisocial children both used more punishment (scolding, shouting, threatening) than did the parents of normal children and failed to make their use of penalties contingent on the child's behavior. More precisely, these parents were less likely than others to state clear rules, monitor compliance, and punish violations. Instead they nattered at the child, occasionally and unpredictably interrupting the nattering with a slap or a loss of privileges. Patterson and his colleagues suggested that nattering instead of effective discipline occurred in part because the parents were less attached than other parents to their children, in part because they did not know how to control behavior effectively, and in part because they felt overwhelmed by a succession of minor problems that cumulatively amounted to a crisis. The irritable parent who does not use discipline effectively tends to produce aggressive children; the indifferent and ineffective parent tends to produce larcenous ones.

The notion that there is a defect in parental skill, as opposed to personality, mental health, or economic resources, that accounts for failures to socialize young children may not be a surprise to many normal parents, but it is a revolutionary conclusion in the field of family psychology. As Patterson observes in his recent book, *Coercive Family Process,* some psychologists, confronted by a young person who becomes violent or criminal, have sought explanations "at least as dramatic as the phenomena they purport to explain," and so we are treated to accounts of a primal instinct for aggression, a lurking Oedipal complex, or a shattering divorce. Rather than "cataclysmic episodes, flood tides of rage, or crumbling defense structures," what in fact is happening, Patterson writes, is the mismanagement of "coercive family processes," processes made up of events that are "inherently banal."

Among these banal events are the routine interactions of parents and children as they convey, by word, tone, gesture, and expression, their approval or disapproval of the behavior of others. Although the literature on family socialization is heavy with discussions of the merits of love versus punishment, most of the socialization process is carried out by the often reflexive display of attention or irritation, interest or disinterest, and approval or disapproval.

The failure of parents to use reasonable reinforcements contingent on steadily monitored behavior places children in a situation in which they come to understand that they cannot control by their own actions what happens to them. When one receives penalties unconnected to one's own behavior, one experiences a kind of stress that Martin E. Seligman has called "learned helplessness," just as when one receives rewards that are unearned, one develops "learned laziness."

The treatment at the Learning Center was to teach these troubled parents how to set clear rules, to monitor behavior, and to make rewards contingent on good behavior and punishment contingent on bad behavior. By rewards the therapists meant not necessarily giving presents in exchange for some major instance of good conduct but routinely responding in pleasant and supportive ways or with points exchangeable for small privileges (such as ice cream for dessert) to pleasant language and helpful behavior. And by punishment they meant not only assessing major penalties for major misdemeanors but promptly and consistently penalizing unpleasant and destructive language and conduct. An especially favored penalty, the value of which was established by repeated trials, was "timeout," that is, being sent briefly, usually for five minutes, into seclusion in another room, usually the bathroom, without recriminations or long lectures.

Teaching these common-sense methods was difficult, but not nearly so difficult as motivating the parents to put them to use. Both instruction and motivation required extraordinary clinical skill and patience, neither of which was easy to sustain. Patterson does not assume that parents will learn how to raise children by reading a book or listening to a lecture. If that were all there was to it, they would not be in trouble in the first place. Benjamin Spock's reassuring advice to young parents—"you know more than you think you do"—is probably correct for most mothers and fathers, but it is not correct for those who, owing to their temperament and personal problems, are parental disasters. These people sense that something is badly wrong with the way they are raising their children, but they do not know what to do about it, or, worse, they often *think* they know, so they persist in trying to control children with vague rules that are frequently changed and erratically enforced. Moreover, many parents do not always share the therapists' enthusiasm for the principles of behavior modification. To these mothers and fathers, "reinforcing socially desirable behavior" sounds too much like bribing kids to do what they are supposed to do anyway, and "relying on positive rather than negative reinforcers" seems to be spoiling the child by sparing the rod.

The only way to convince such parents is to show them that the rules they learn during many hours spent in the Learning Center actually work. I watched videotapes of a woman being trained to cope with her out-of-control young son. The child went to bed only when he felt like it, insisted on sleeping with his mother (she had no husband), rarely obeyed even the most reasonable commands, spread his excrement all over the living room walls, was a terror to other children who tried to play with him, and seemed destined to be a terror to his teachers. The first task was to make the mother realize that he was not minding her in important ways because he was not minding her in small ones. Every day for one hour she had to count the number of times the boy failed to obey an order within fifteen seconds of its being issued and report the results to the therapist. This led the mother to become aware of how many times she was issuing orders and how long she was waiting to get results.

At the second session she was taught how to use rewards to increase the frequency with which her son minded her. Every time he minded within fifteen seconds, he was to get one point; at the end of the day the points were added up and converted into some small but valued privilege, such as a special dessert. Many parents, impatient, want to use big rewards to achieve big, quick improvements in behavior, but this is discouraged: such a strategy debases the currency, fails to inculcate the habit of minding, and does not reduce routine parental nagging.

At the third session the mother was taught how to use timeout as a means of discipline. She was told that whenever her son did something wrong, she should immediately tell him why it was wrong and order him to go to timeout—five minutes alone in the bathroom. She resisted doing this because it forced her to confront all of her son's rulebreaking, and to do so immediately. She preferred to avoid the conflict and the angry protests. She especially resisted using this means to enforce her son's going to bed at a stated, appropriate time; she was a lonely, not particularly attractive woman, and it was clear to the therapist that she wanted her son to sleep with her. In time the woman was persuaded to try this new form of discipline and to back up a failure to go to timeout by the withdrawal of some privilege ("no TV tonight"). As the weeks went by, the woman became excited about the improvement in the boy's behavior and came to value having him sleep alone in his own room. Not long after, she acquired a male friend.

Some parents come to the Learning Center having relied on severe physical punishment to control their children. The staff members do not approve of spanking, but neither do they try to talk parents out of it, unless it is clearly abusive. Instead they show the parents that another method works better: a lesser penalty, such as timeout or a loss of points, given immediately for every minor infraction of the rules. Parents who physically punish their children usually do so only for major offenses that occur at the end of a long sequence of minor ones. These big penalties erratically employed only against major misconduct are less effective than small ones regularly used to control minor misconduct.

The Learning Center double-checks on the progress of the parents by observing the family in action, making frequent phone calls to the home to see how things are going at that moment, and gathering information from teachers. Increasingly the researchers at the center have been testing their own work using the only scientifically sound method— comparing its results with those achieved by other methods applied to similar families. Nineteen families of aggressive children were randomly assigned to either the center's parent-training program or some conventional form of therapy available in the community. In 1982 Patterson and two associates, Patricia Chamberlain and John B. Reid, were able to show that the children in the parent-training program displayed a sharp drop in the frequency of aversive behavior, while those in the conventional programs showed on the average no change.

The limit, it turns out, is the amount of time, effort, and therapist skill at the disposal of the clinic. Before Patterson's group demonstrated what it could accomplish, efforts to prove the lasting value of parent training had produced mixed, and often negative, results. Some programs reported great success, but it turned out that their measure was the parents' own reports that "things were getting better." Parents always like to think things are getting better. Observations by outsiders, such as schoolteachers and therapists, would often show that things were not getting better at all. Other programs produced no benefits, no matter who was reporting, but it would turn out that these programs employed young, relatively inexperienced therapists, usually graduate students, and lasted only a short time. Patterson has been able to show that training parents takes a great deal of time and skill—a family with only minor problems may be in treatment for six weeks, one with moderate problems for sixteen weeks, and an especially troubled one for much longer. The most experienced therapists produce the best results but only if they are continuously supported by a caring and knowledgeable group of colleagues.

The Patterson group is coming to understand how complex is the relationship between the economic circumstances of a family and its child-rearing problems. Most of their clients have low to moderate incomes. Half or more are single mothers. Economic disadvantage, especially when faced by a lone mother, can be a great source of stress, which exacerbates the normal difficulties of raising a child. But the connections among economic circumstance, parental personality, and the child's behavior are not simple or obvious. The mothers in the Learning Center program tend to be maladjusted personalities, as measured by a variety of tests. Their economic and marital difficulties may have contributed to this, or just as likely, their personalities have made it hard for them to succeed in marriage or in the labor market. If their material circumstances improved, the problems of their daily lives would be somewhat reduced, but owing to their personalities, their capacity to manage the child-rearing stresses common to all families would probably remain low.

Changes in Family Life

It is tempting to speculate whether the growth in crime experienced by this and other nations in the past few decades can be explained by changes that have occurred in family life. It is easy to believe that the increase in the number of single-parent families, working mothers, or unattended, latchkey children lies at the root of the increase in disorder and delinquency. It may, although I am struck by how weak or contradictory the evidence is. A review, for example, by Elizabeth Herzog and Cecelia E. Sudia of eighteen studies of the relationship between broken homes and crime carried out between 1950 and 1970 found seven that claimed father-absent homes produced more delinquency, four that claimed they produced less, and seven that came to equivocal conclusions. The Gluecks, among others, claimed that broken homes made a difference; the McCords and Travis Hirschi, among others, claimed they did not. Moreover, even if the rise in American crime rates could be explained by the increase in female-headed families here, the growth in crime in European countries—a growth that parallels ours almost exactly, though beginning from a lower base—cannot be explained this way because these countries have not had a comparable explosion in the number of female-headed homes.

Other things being equal, single-parent families, or two-parent families with working mothers, probably experience greater trouble in raising children than two-parent families in which the mother stays home—but other things are rarely equal. *Why* one parent is absent is surely more important than whether he is absent. As Michael Rutter, of the University of London, notes, based on his own research in England and that of others elsewhere, families that are broken by divorce or desertion are more likely to affect the child's behavior adversely than those broken by the death of one parent. Homes that are broken because of parental discord are unhappy places in which the child experiences not only the stresses associated with separation but those produced by the discord that led to the separation.

Many intact families are also discordant. When New York City families, some living on welfare and some not, were studied by a group of researchers based at Columbia University, it was found that delinquency was best explained among both kinds of families by parental coldness. But this coldness was most strongly associated with delinquency among the welfare families because, as the authors put it, the "welfare child is in double jeopardy"—when there is no father present, the harmful effects of maternal coldness are more serious. Here, as in all aspects of family life, what causes what is never quite clear. A discordant or broken home may harm the child, but a troublesome child can cause some homes to become discordant. Candyce Russell, a sociologist, found that the parents of babies who were more demanding—who cried a lot or had feeding problems—were more likely to experience discord and crises than the parents of quiet infants.

Changes in the structure of the family may have contributed to the growth of crime, although of late crime rates seem to have been stable even as the number of children raised in broken homes has continued to increase. It is more likely that broad social forces—the advent of the baby boom, the increase in personal freedom and mobility, the spread of the ethos of self-expression, and the increases in the net benefits of crime (the value of loot minus the risk of being caught and punished)—have produced both increases in crime and changes in family life.

There is no reason to assume that parents have become less intelligent about how to raise children. For hundreds of years, all over the globe, parents who have never heard of Dr. Spock, much less of

72

behavior modification, have been raising tens of millions of perfectly decent children. If crime and disorder have increased, can it be that parents who once knew how to raise children have forgotten? It seems unlikely. But social changes may have made parents somewhat less interested in being parents and have provided children with more ways to evade parental control. More mothers and fathers may have found children to be a burden as the traditional social and moral supports for family life have become more precarious and the opportunities for distraction and entertainment outside the family have become greater. Parents who once just got by as child rearers now find themselves slipping over the edge as it becomes harder, or less necessary, just to get by.

A National Policy?

Given the deep-seated and poorly understood causes of discord and incompetence among families, it is hard to imagine mounting any national program to deal with the problem directly. One shudders at the thought of developing, as some politicians too eager for the national spotlight have proposed, a national family policy. But at the same time one also wonders whether, starting small and in a frankly experimental mode, we might not do more to prevent the frenzied or apathetic incompetence of so many families from producing monsters like Don.

The fact that much skill and time are needed to change families means that this method of reducing delinquency, like most methods, could not easily be made into a national program or even one that would serve a large city. But it is conceivable that the elements of the program might become part of an effort to prevent bad parental practices from developing in the first place. The principal barrier to success in helping troubled families is that they resist help. It is not the complexity of the parenting techniques that requires so much time and effort to be devoted to therapy—the techniques are simplicity itself, based as they are on common sense. Rather it is the client's resistance to adopting these techniques, or even to confronting the fact that his own practices are disastrous, that requires so great an investment of resources.

But suppose that these techniques were learned by young people before they become parents and enmesh themselves in the vicious cycle of nagging, exasperation, appeasement, and random hitting. Suppose the techniques of scoring behavior from videotapes of actual families in trouble were taught in school, using the same equipment researchers now rely on—the engrossing paraphernalia of hand-held computer terminals and video displays with which the Pac-Man generation has become so familiar. Suppose the changes in behavior that occur as a result of adopting sensible parenting techniques could be seen (on a TV set) by young people. It is conceivable that they might find this experience more interesting and this information more useful than what they often get from lectures they are now obliged to hear on sex education or personal hygiene, to say nothing of courses in civics or woodworking. This suggestion—not yet tried, to the best of my knowledge, anywhere—may turn out to be but another example of misplaced hopes and wishful thinking. But the costs to society of weak, discordant, incompetent families is so great as to make the experiment worth the effort.

6

Character and Young People:
The 1940s

Character is shaped by peers as well as by families. My occasion for reflecting on this was the election of Ronald Reagan as governor of California in 1966. At the time I was a Californian teaching at Harvard University. For all the grief I took, I might as well have been a Muslim teaching in Rome at the time of the jihad. What follows began as an effort to explain to the readers of Commentary *why the election of Reagan (whose candidacy I had not supported) was not just another sign of Lotus Land voters' being gulled by a matinee idol. As I got into the matter, it became clear that neither Reagan nor the election needed explaining, the culture of Southern California did, and beyond that the emerging culture of Middle America in a time of prosperity. In the 1940s and 1950s, when I grew up there, Southern California formed character as it might have been formed on an Iowa farm had farm life not required hard work during bitter winters a long way from the beach.*

I grew up in Reagan country—not Hollywood, but the lower-middle-class suburbs of Los Angeles. It was a distinctive way of life. I think I can still recognize another person who grew up there no matter where I should meet him, just as surely as an Italian can spot a person from his village or region even though they are both now in Queens. I am under no illusion that anyone has the slightest interest in my boyhood (I have next to no interest in it myself), but it may be useful to try to explain what it was like at least in general terms and how what it was like is relevant to what is happening there today.

The important thing to know about Southern California is that the people who live there, who grow up there, love it—not just the way one has an attachment to a hometown, any hometown, but the way people love the realization that they have found the right mode of life. People who live in Southern California are not richer or better educated than those who live in New York; the significant point about them is that they do not live in New York and do not want to. If they did, they—the average Los Angelenos (my family, for example)—would have lived most of their lives in a walk-up flat in, say, the Yorkville section of Manhattan or not far off Flatbush Avenue in Brooklyn. Given their income in 1930, life would have been crowded, noisy, cold, threatening—in short, urban. In Long Beach or Inglewood or Huntington Park or Bellflower, by contrast, life was carried on in a detached house with a lawn in front and a car in the garage, part of a quiet neighborhood, with no crime (except kids racing noisy cars), no cold, no smells, no congestion. The monthly payments on that bungalow—one or two bedrooms, one bath, a minuscule dining room, and never enough closets—would have been no more than the rent on the walk-up flat in Brooklyn or Yorkville. In 1940, with the depression still in force, more than half the population of Los Angeles lived in single-family homes. Only about half of these were owner occupied, but even renting a house was such a vast improvement over renting an apartment that nobody looked back; they only looked ahead to the time they could pick up their own mortgage. San Francisco in the same year was another matter. Only a third of the population lived in single-family homes there, the reason being that there were almost no houses to rent; if you wanted a house, you had to buy it, and not many people in 1940 could afford to buy.

Radical Politics

There has been a good deal of loose talk about radical politics developing out of a rootless, highly mobile population with no sense of place, of continuity, of stability. That may explain radical politics somewhere but not in Los Angeles. The people who voted for Reagan have lived for years, in many cases decades, in Southern California. And they have lived in houses, not anonymous, impersonal apartment buildings.

Indeed during its greatest population growth Los Angeles voted over and over again for Earl Warren, the embodiment (then) of moderation. The explanation is quite simple: truly rootless, mobile people are more likely to vote the way established institutions—newspapers, churches, labor unions, business firms—tell them to vote. Revolutions are never made by the last person to get off the train; they are made by those who got off a long time ago and, having put down roots and formed their own assessment of matters, have the confidence, the long-nurtured discontent, and the knowledge of how to get things done sufficient to support independent political action. (Radical politics follows the same pattern as black riots: contrary to what the McCone Commission asserted but did not prove, the blacks who rioted in Watts—or at least those who rioted violently enough to get themselves arrested—were blacks who had been in Watts for a long time. More than half the teenage blacks arrested had been born in California; more than three-fourths had lived there for more than five years.)

The people who in 1940 lived in those hundreds of thousands of detached and semidetached homes came from all over the country, but primarily they came from the Midwest, the Border States, and the Near South. Almost none came from Europe: about 6 percent, to be exact, had been born in Italy, Ireland, England, Germany, France, Sweden, or Russia; another 2½ percent had been born in Mexico. (In San Francisco the proportion of foreign born was twice as large.) But 28 percent had been born in the American heartland—the dustbowl states (Texas, Oklahoma, Arkansas, Louisiana, Kansas, Nebraska) or the Border States (Indiana, Missouri, Tennessee, Kentucky) and the upper plains (Iowa, Wisconsin, Minnesota, the Dakotas). If you add in the nearby mountain and Southwestern states (Colorado, Utah, Arizona, New Mexico, Nevada), the total proportion rises to over a third. And if you add in the persons whose parents had been born in these states, the proportion no doubt (there are no figures) exceeds a half. Again San Francisco is a contrast—only about a tenth of its people in 1940 were from the heartland states. Between 1920 and 1940, during the depression, more than 400,000 persons born in the heartland moved to Los Angeles. Less than a tenth as many moved to San Francisco.

Except for Arkansas, Louisiana, and Texas, no Southern states are included in these migration figures. This is important to bear in mind—such conservatism as Southern California displays was not imported from the Deep South. Even those who came from Southern states were likely to be from places like West Texas, where Confederate sentiment was never strong.

These migrants were rural and small-town people. And here another popular explanation of Southern California politics takes the stage. These voters are supposed to yearn for the simpler life and the small-town virtues that they left behind. They are reactionary, it is claimed, in the precise sense: seeking to turn back the clock to a day when life was easier, virtues less complicated, and the Ten Commandments a sufficient guide. Perhaps so—there is no doubt some truth in this. But it flies in the face of the fact that these are people who *left* small-town and rural America (millions more stayed behind, after all)—and left it for jobs in big defense plants and large office buildings. I was never aware of any effort to re-create small-town America in Southern California, unless you put in that category the victory gardens people planted to raise vegetables during the war. On the contrary they adopted rather quickly a suburban style of life with its attendant devotion to the growing of a decent lawn (how many farms have you ever seen with a good lawn?). Furthermore,

77

it is not the migrants themselves who on the whole have voted for Reaganism but their children. The migrants voted for Roosevelt and Upton Sinclair and looked on disapprovingly as their children began to adopt the hedonistic mores of Southern California teenage life. There was as much intergenerational conflict among the Okies and Arkies in California as among the Italians and the Irish in Boston or New York. And yet these youngsters grew up, married, moved out to Orange County or to Lakewood, and voted for Reagan and castigated Pat Brown, the last of the New Deal–Fair Deal Democrats. (To be completely accurate, a lot of the older people voted for Reagan too, but they, I imagine, found it much harder to let go of their traditional attachment to Franklin Roosevelt and Earl Warren; the young people had no trouble at all.)

This is not to say that the migrants brought nothing with them. On the contrary they brought an essential ingredient of Southern California life: fundamentalist Protestant individualism. We like to think of the storefront church as being a black invention; not so. I remember scores of white storefront churches—mostly of small Pentecostal and Adventist sects—lining the main streets of Long Beach. Most people went to established churches, but these were only bigger and slightly more orthodox versions of the same thing: Baptist, Methodist, Mormon, Brethren, Church of God, and so on. Church was an important part of life, but hardly any two people belonged to the same one. We were Catholics, and we had to drive out into the dairy farming country (I will never forget the way Sunday morning smelled: incense and cow manure, in equal portions) where there were enough Mexican farmhands and Dutch Catholic dairymen to make up a parish. All my friends sang hymns and listened to "preachin'." And the preaching was evangelical, fundamentalist, and preoccupied with the obligation of the individual to find and enter into a right relationship with God, with no sacraments, rituals, covenants, or grace to make it easy.

The religious character of San Francisco was strikingly different. In 1936 (the last time the government took a census of church organizations) 70 percent of the reported church membership of San Francisco but only 40 percent of that in Los Angeles was Catholic. And of the claimed members of Protestant sects, 40 percent in San Francisco but only 26 percent is Los Angeles belonged to the high-status, non-fundamentalist churches: Congregational, Episcopalian, Unitarian, and Universalist. Both cities had about the same proportion of Jews, but, as will be argued in a moment, the leadership at least of the two Jewish communities was rather different. Los Angeles, and even more its middle-class suburbs, was Protestant and fundamentalist Protestant at that.

Focusing on the Individual

The social structure did nothing to change the individualistic orientation of life. People had no identities except their personal identities, no obvious group affiliations to make possible any reference to them by collective nouns. I never heard the phrase "ethnic group" until I was in graduate school. I never knew there were Irishmen (I was amazed many years later to learn that, at least on my mother's side, I had been one all along) or Italians (except funny organ grinders in the movies, all of whom looked like Chico Marx). We knew there were blacks (but none within miles of where we lived) and Jews (they ran Hollywood and New York, we knew, but not many of us had ever met one). Nobody ever even pointed out to me that I was a Catholic (except once, when a friend explained that was probably the reason I wouldn't join the Order of De Molay, a young people's Masonic group).

The absence of such group identities and of neighborhoods associated with those identities may be one reason for the enormous emphasis on personality. Teenagers everywhere place great stock in this, mostly because they feel such an urgent need to establish an identity and to be liked by others. But in Southern California it went far beyond that—a cult of personality dominated every aspect of life. Everybody was compared in terms of personality; contests for student body office were based on it. To be popular and sincere was vital. In a New York high school, by contrast, personality would have to share importance in such contests with a certain amount of bloc voting among the Irish, Italians, and Jews, or between project people and brownstone people, or even between Leftists and Far Leftists.

Perhaps because of the absence of ethnic and religious blocs, which in turn are associated with certain political positions, perhaps because Southern California (then) was remote from those urban centers where the future of socialism was being earnestly debated, student life in and around Los Angeles was remarkably apolitical. Most people were vaguely for Roosevelt, although a substantial (and growing) group announced defiantly that while their parents had voted for FDR in 1932, and perhaps even in 1936, they were not going to do that anymore. Registered Democrats who voted Republican were commonplace, but after noting that fact, there was not politically much left to be said. (It was different in downtown Los Angeles where the Jews lived; LA High and later Los Angeles State College were political. A considerable Wallace movement flourished in 1948. Many of those people were later in the Democratic club movement.)

Politics for our people came to mean in later years expressing directly one's individual political preferences and expecting them to be added up by a kind of political algebra into a general statement of the public interest. Bloc voting and group preferences were unheard of and, when heard of, unthinkable. And the idea that political parties ought to do anything besides help add up preferences was most heterodox—the worst thing that could be said about it was that it was Eastern. The well-known institutional features of California's political system—weak parties, the extensive use of the referendum to decide policy issues, nonpartisanship—were perfectly matched to the political mentality that was nurtured in Southern California.

That nurturing was distinctive but hard to describe. Rural Anglo-Saxon Protestants have lived in lots of states, but they have not produced the Southern California style of politics anywhere else. One reason is to be found in what it was like, and to a considerable extent is still like, to grow up in Southern California. Everybody, as I have already noted, lived in a single-family house. There was no public transportation to speak of, so that the movement of people within the city followed no set corridors. People moved about freely and in so doing saw how everybody lived. That movement was institutionalized in the Sunday afternoon drive—not to the beach or an amusement park but just "around" to look at homes, to call on friends, or to visit distant relatives. A house was, as a Catholic might put it, the outward and visible sign of inward grace. There was no anonymity provided by apartment buildings or tenements or projects. Each family had a house; there it was, for all to see and to inspect. With a practiced glance, one could tell how much it cost, how well it was cared for, how well a lawn had been coaxed into uncertain life, and how tastefully plants and shrubs had been set out.

A strong, socially reinforced commitment to property was thus developed, evident in how people treat those homes today. An enormous amount of energy and money is devoted to repairing, improving, remodeling, extending, and landscaping. Even in areas with fairly low incomes, such as those where the elderly and the retired live, houses are not on the whole allowed to deteriorate. A family may buy a house for six or seven thousand dollars with for the period a big mortgage and then spend several times that over a generation or two in home improvements. Those who cannot afford it substitute labor for capital. People were practicing do-it-yourself in Southern California long before anybody in the advertising business thought to give it a name. Year-round warm weather made year-round outdoor labor possible—and year-round outdoor inspection by one's critical neighbors.

Much of this labor is cooperative. The Southern California equivalent of the Eastern uncle who can get it for you wholesale is the Los Angeles brother-in-law who will help you put on a new roof or paint the garage or lend you (and show you how to use) his power saw. A vast informally organized labor exchange permeates the region, with occasional trades of great complexity running through several intermediaries—the friend who will ask his brother, the plumber, to help you if you will ask your uncle with the mixer to lay the concrete in front of somebody's sister's home. Saturday sees people driving all over the county carrying out these assignments.

Driving

Driving everywhere, over great distances, with scarcely any thought to the enormous mileages they were logging—a car was the absolutely essential piece of social overhead capital. With it you could get a job, meet a girl, hang around with the boys, go to a drive-in, see football games away from home, take in the beach parties at Laguna or Corona del Mar, or go to the Palladium ballroom in Hollywood. To have a car meant being somebody; to have to borrow a car meant knowing somebody; to have no car at all, owned or borrowed, was to be left out—way out.

Those cars led parents and professional moralists to speak of teenagers and their jalopies. They were not jalopies—not to us anyway. The oldest, most careworn Ford Model A was a thing of beauty. To be sure, the beauty often had to be coaxed out; yet what was life for but to do the coaxing and take credit for the beauty? Beauty meant different things to different boys. For some, it was speed and power; and so they would drop a V-8 block into the A chassis and then carefully, lovingly, bore it out, stroke it, port it, and put two barrels or four barrels on it. For others, beauty was in the body, not the engine, and their energies would go into customizing the car—dropping the rear end, chopping down the top, leading in the fenders, stripping off the chrome (it took Detroit decades to recognize the merits of these changes and then to mass-produce them), and above all painting, sanding, rubbing, painting, sanding, rubbing—for ten or fifteen or twenty coats, usually of metallic paint. Again warm weather made it easier—you could work outside year-round, and if you ran out of money before the job was finished (which was most of the time), you could drive around in the unfinished product with no top, primed but not painted, and no hood over the engine. Tom Wolfe of *New York* magazine discovered car customizing and decided it later was a folk art. It was not folk art in the 1940s; it was life.

The sense of property developed by this activity has never been measured and perhaps never can be; I am convinced it was enormous and fundamental. After marriage, devoting energy to the improvement of a house was simply a grown-up extension of what, as a juvenile, one had done with cars. There is a paradox here: the car was used in great part to get girls. It was a hand-polished, custom-made rolling bedroom, or so its creators hoped. (In this they were as often disappointed as a Harvard man taking a Radcliffe woman into his house rooms during parietal hours; every woman likes to be seen in such places, but a distressingly small proportion are inclined to do anything there.) But the hedonistic purposes to which the car might be put did not detract from its power to create and sustain a conventional and bourgeois sense of property and responsibility, for in the last analysis the car was not a means to an end but an end in itself. Shocked parents never got that point: they saw the excess that the car permitted, they did not see the intensely middle-class values that it instilled.

Low-density, single-family homes, a lack of public transportation, the absence of ethnic neighborhoods, and the use of cars combined to prevent the formation of street-corner gangs, except in central portions of Los Angeles and one or two older cities. The principal after-school occupation of a teenage Eastern boy from a working-class family is to hang out at the corner candystore, at the ice-cream parlor, or in front of the drugstore with class and ethnic compatriots. Having a corner of your own—or having turf, in the case of the ambitious and imperialistic—would have made no sense to an equivalent group of young men in Southern California. The Eastern lifestyle produced a feeling of territory, the Western lifestyle a feeling of property. Teenagers in Southern California hung out together, to be sure, but not in any fixed spot, and where they did hang out tended to be a place reached by a car, with lots of free parking for other cars. The drive-in restaurant was the premier institution catering to this need. But it was also a democratic institution since it was not (and because of its location some distance from one's home, could not become) the turf of any particular gang. Rich and poor, Protestant and Catholic, anybody with a car could get there and, barring a losing fight over a girl, stay there. There were rivalries, but like modern warfare they tended to be between large, heterogeneous, and impersonal rivals—one high school against another, not one ethnic group against another.

Can all this explain why Southern California is so different politically from Northern California—why it, so much more than the Bay Area, supported Goldwater and Reagan? Perhaps not entirely. And yet the kind of people living there and their lifestyles are important, much more important than, say, the presumed influence of the then-conservative *Los Angeles Times*. The *Oakland Tribune* was even more conservative, but the East Bay region it served was more liberal in its voting than LA. And the liberal McClatchey newspapers in the Central Valley did not seem to have turned back the Reagan tide. Conversely, San Francisco has Southern California style suburbs as well, with bungalows and cars and the like, and the people there are not as conservative as their counterparts in the South. But as we have seen, the people who migrated to San Francisco in the 1930s and 1940s were different from those who settled in Los Angeles. And once the different lifestyles of the two cities became apparent, non-Californians must have begun deciding to move to the Bay Area or to Los Angeles on the basis in part of what they had heard about those styles. A small but visible difference in the beginning thus became a large difference in the end.

Political Disorganization

The political institutions and economic character of Southern California reinforced the lifestyle and gave it expression. Politics, as I have said, was nonpartisan, free-swinging, slightly populistic—a direct appeal to the people was to be made on all issues. The major parties for decades were virtually moribund and therefore never performed their customary (and, to my thinking, desirable) task of aggregating interests, blurring issues, strengthening party loyalties, and finding moderate candidates. Not that the people wanted immoderate candidates. So long, at least, as the issues were not grave—before civil rights and welfare and Berkeley and crime— they wanted honest, competent administrators who favored change but in an orderly manner. In Earl Warren they got such a man, and he made sure the regular Republican party, whose fat cats were on the whole considerably to his right, would not have a chance to replace him. He built a personal following outside the regular, and cumbersome, party apparatus. Like most personal followings, however, it made no provision for a transfer of power. Warren's personal following in the state could not be handed to another man, and the party was in no shape to find a candidate of its own. Any man with money and a good smile could take a crack at capturing the nomination on his own, and many did.

Such organization as existed tended to be in the North, rather than the South. San Francisco and Alameda County across the bay had more in the way of party machinery, financed on a steady basis, than the South had, at least until the emergence of the California Democratic clubs. A little organization goes a long way in an organizational vacuum, and the North exercised a disproportionate influence in California politics for some time. The Northern Democrats had some old families—many Jewish—who helped pay the party's bills during the long, lean years.

The South had few such persons—or more accurately it had some rich, self-made men from the oil business and from the vast agricultural enterprises of the Imperial Valley who were conservative Democrats in the well-documented tradition of the American Southwest. They may be more visible in Texas today, but twenty years ago they were more influential in California.

Why? There were Jews in Southern California, tens of thousands of them in and around Los Angeles. (Yet looking back on my high-school days, I can think of only one Jew I was personally acquainted with, and he went to another high school across town. Jews were Hollywood, we all knew.) Many of them were in the movie industry and in command of wealth and great resources for publicity. Why didn't they help to finance and lead the Southern California Democratic party? Some did—or tried—at least for a while. A high point of that influence was the 1950 senatorial campaign of the liberal Helen Gahagan Douglas, the movie actress. It was not George Murphy or Ronald Reagan who put Hollywood into politics, it was Mrs. Douglas, who lost to Richard Nixon. Two years before, many of her supporters had turned in frustration to third-party politics and become important figures in the 1948 campaign of Henry Wallace. It was a disaster. Bolting the party nationally was a far more serious thing than bolting it locally, where it could hardly be said to exist. The Truman Democrats took control in California, and when Communist party influence in the Wallace movement became too obvious to be denied (Wallace himself was to admit it later), they were in a position to treat the Douglas and Wallace Democrats as thoroughly discredited in the eyes of the voters. Shortly thereafter the era of McCarthyism descended upon the country, and in Hollywood involvement in politics was for the time being finished. What Mrs. Douglas had begun, Wallace and McCarthy succeeded in ending (for a time).

But it was not only that Hollywood Jews had lost power, it was also that Hollywood Jews were different from those in other urban centers. The social and economic heights of Hollywood were commanded not by German Jews but by East Europeans; not by old families but by immigrants; not by Wall Street smoothness but by nouveau riche entrepreneurship. Such Hollywood money as went into politics was used much as money was then used in the movie industry—impulsively, by dictatorial men used to having their own way, and on behalf of stars. If the star system worked on movie lots, why couldn't it work in politics? Thus a glamorous figure, a big name, and occasionally a conspicuous nut could get personal backing for a campaign, but there was little or no money for organization, for routine affairs, or for professional (and necessarily bureaucratic) leadership.

Anyway the voter was not much interested in liberalism even if it could be financed. Los Angeles was prosperous, and even greater prosperity seemed just around the corner. The aircraft plants and shipyards had taken tens of thousands of families and given every member, including the mother, a job, thereby putting them, in four years' time, in a wholly different and higher economic bracket. A generation of slow gain was compressed into a few years; progress was not around the corner or something you hoped for for your kids, it was right here and now. War prosperity affected the whole country, but it had a special effect on Southern California—there was more of it because more war industry was located there, and it benefited people who only a few years before had been fighting for survival on a dust-swept farm in the Texas Panhandle. John Steinbeck has told us how those farmers and sharecroppers saw California as the promised land. They had been promised only relief checks from the Farm Security Administration; instead they found overtime checks from Lockheed.

Economic Growth

Next to the kind of people who live there, the rate of economic growth of Southern California—and today of the whole Southwest—is the main key to its political life. Visiting scholars make much of the business domination of Dallas or the presumed influence of the *Los Angeles Times* in Southern California or the chamber of commerce mentality of San Diego. The important thing to understand is that these have not been alien influences imposed from above on the populace—they are merely the more obvious indicators of the fact that business values are widely shared. (Not business control: voters are as quick to resent that, when it is pointed out to them, in Los Angeles as anywhere. Sam Yorty became mayor by running against the *Times* and other downtown interests.) Business values are here meant in the widest sense—a desire for expansion and growth, a high rate of increase in property values, finding and developing mass markets, and keeping capital moving and labor productive. [In the 1980s the progrowth ethos was challenged by an antigrowth movement. Although it took a half-century to develop, that cleavage is now the central political issue of the region.]

No one was immune from this psychology. How could he be? Everyone was buying, or intended to buy, his own home. Many factory workers and salesmen speculated in real estate on the side. A favorite topic of conversation at our dinner table, and I am sure at thousands of dinner tables just like it, was the latest story about the fantastic price a certain parcel had just been sold for and what a shame it was that we passed up the chance to buy it two years ago for peanuts. The purpose of government was to facilitate this growth—open up new land, bring in water, make credit easy, keep the defense plants rolling. Government was not there to keep painfully acquired positions secure by paying out benefits or legislating new regulations. Government was there to help bring in the future, not to protect the past.

Not everyone felt this way. Elderly people who came to California to retire had a different view. They wanted pensions, benefits, regulations. They were numerous and visible, but although they came quickly to mind when one thought back on the shuffleboard and croquet courts at Lincoln Park in Long Beach or on the soapbox orators and bench sitters in Pershing Square in Los Angeles, they were never representative of the local political ethos. They were the butt of countless jokes and the target for much political criticism: they wanted to hold back tomorrow (it was believed), to cash their relief checks, and to lie in the sun. That was wrong, most working families thought. The black, who today is the victim of the antiwelfare sentiment, was actually the second victim; the first was the old folks. They were attacked for moving to California just to get a pension, told to go back where they came from, and fought against in countless welfare issues. (About the only thing they were spared was allegations that they constituted a sexual threat. I cannot recall my father, no paragon of tolerance, ever trying to clinch an argument against a liberal by asking him how he would like it if his daughter grew up and married an old man.)

The old folks fought back, but in California it was a protest movement. George McLain organized the old folks (nobody ever called them "senior citizens"; they did not even call themselves that) and made them a potent force in state politics, but it was a force directed against the two major parties and their candidates. He won concessions for his followers, and now they may be so secure as to be accepted as a political fact of life; what they wanted, however, was never accepted.

Southern California's political culture, including but not limited to what might be called Reaganism, may be characteristic of areas experiencing rapid economic growth and general prosperity, especially if there are few institutions—political parties, churches, labor unions—to frame the issues and to blunt popular instincts. People there are concerned about the growth in the size of the economic pie, not (except for the elderly) in preserving the size of their present slice. The attributes in a person to be admired are those that indicate his ability to enhance his position and to expand his resources, not to conserve his position and to maintain his resources. If I had to cite only one way in which Southwestern politics differ from Northeastern politics, it would be this: the former region is developmental, future oriented, and growth conscious; the latter is conserving, past or present oriented, and security conscious. Note that I say conserving, not conservative; there is a difference. The Northeast by any measure is less conservative than the Southwest, although it is easy to exaggerate the difference. A conservative is usually thought of as a person who favors limited government, minimal administrative involvement in private affairs, maximum free choice. A conserver, however, needs more government to protect present stakes from change, from threats posed by other groups, and from competition.

86

Ideological Idealism

Even more important as a challenge to the general political culture of the region, with its concern for property, propriety, individual responsibility, economic growth, and limited government, is ideological liberalism. By the time McCarthyism was ending and the blacklists were beginning to lose their grip on Hollywood (perhaps because, faced with the competition from television and European producers, Hollywood could no longer afford the luxury of a blacklist), Adlai Stevenson was making his appearance as a force in the Democratic party. The enormous outpouring of support for him in Southern California has been oft remarked upon, as has the vigorous club movement that grew up in the aftermath of his 1952 and 1956 presidential campaigns. The movement activated a wholly new generation of political enthusiasts and provided a new base of operations for some of the leftovers from older forms of liberal and radical politics.

These clubs did not recruit the people I have been describing in earlier pages, nor have they taken hold in the areas in which these people live. The clubs grew up on the northern and eastern periphery of the region: the Hollywood hills, Santa Monica, Beverly Hills, Pacific Palisades, and out into the college towns, such as Pomona, in the interior. Young Jews, young intellectuals, persons transplanted to Los Angeles from the East (by 1940 about 10 percent of the population had been born in New England, New Jersey, or Pennsylvania), and older California radicals flocked into the clubs. But the clubs never really took root among the working-class and middle-class bungalows of Long Beach, Inglewood, or Redondo Beach, to say nothing of Orange County to the southeast. The Democratic clubs initially had little interest in Southern California; they were interested in national and international issues. (The civil rights movement soon changed that; the clubs became deeply involved in such matters locally.) They had at the outset no real program for California (although they had one for just about everything else), and thus there was no necessary conflict between what they wanted and what those who later voted for Reagan wanted—no necessary conflict, perhaps, but conflict nonetheless. And the most intense kind of conflict, for what was at stake were large and symbolic issues: Red China, capital punishment, world peace, and civil liberties. The Southern California electorate quickly became deeply polarized.

The polarization is not immediately evident in voting statistics. In the aggregate, Southern California elects a mixture of liberals and conservatives much like any other region and, on many of its famous referendums, votes for and against public expenditures about like other areas. But these aggregate figures conceal the real symptoms of polarization—several Democrats (not all) are as far to the left of their party as is possible; several Republicans (not all) are as far to the right of their party as possible. And on referendum issues—especially those involving such matters as open occupancy in housing—the returns and the polls suggest that Southern California has both the most intense proponents and the most intense opponents (the latter outnumbering the former: the region as a whole was against fair housing by a considerable margin; in San Francisco the vote was both less lopsided and, I suspect, based on less intensely polarized views). This is not the same thing as saying that Southern California is more bigoted than the Bay Area. Because of the way the issue was framed, people were asked to vote for the right to sell their property to whomever they chose. In Southern California property rights are vital and freedom in their exercise staunchly defended. There have been, I would guess, fewer attacks on black families seeking homes in white neighborhoods in Southern California than in, say, Pennsylvania, Ohio, or Illinois. The housing issue was fought out at a more general level—not over whether one was for or against blacks but over alternative conceptions of what freedom requires. And the polarization of opinion on this issue, as on most, was most intense among persons of higher status. The educated, affluent Easterners and intellectuals (who worked in law firms or the communications media or the universities) are more inclined than their less well-off fellows to support the Democratic clubs and liberalism; the educated, affluent sons and daughters of the Midwestern migrants (who worked as engineers and accountants in aerospace and petroleum industries) were more inclined than their less well-off fellows to support Goldwater and Reagan.

A Spreading Political Style

Is Southern California's culture unique? Not really—it is but the earliest, most publicized, and most heavily populated example of a pattern now to be found throughout much of the Southwest. It appeared first in Southern California because more people went there and because California's political institutions gave almost immediate expression to it. In other states the party structure constrained its free expression for a time; the ambitions of rival politicians and factions in Texas and Arizona made the ideology less evident, at least for a while. Barry Goldwater's easy victory at the 1964 Republican convention indicates how widespread are certain aspects of that culture—in fact, it overstates it, because Goldwater himself overstated many features of that culture. The Southern Californians about whom I have written want limited government, personal responsibility, basic education, a resurgence of patriotism, an end to chiseling, and a more restrained Supreme Court. They are not quite so certain that they want an adventurous foreign policy. No doubt the militant Goldwater enthusiasts wanted such a policy, but they must have mistaken what the rank and file would support. Reagan did not make the same mistake—he took Goldwater's views, stripped away the foreign policy (except for general statements) and references to turning back the clock on social security (after all, he wanted a coalition between the elderly and the young).

But Goldwater, however badly managed his campaign, won the convention and won it by methods and with supporters who, in whatever state they were found, could easily have been found in Southern California. Amateur political clubs, impassioned volunteers, appeals to highly moral and symbolic issues—the Republican party professionals had, to their profound irritation, to put up with all of it, just as party professionals in California, Democrats and Republicans alike, have been putting up with it since the early 1950s.

The Southern California political style is spreading; it seems to be, at least in the Western part of the United States, the concomitant of the American success story. There millions of people are realizing their ambitions. They are not rootless or yearning for small-town simplicity or profoundly irritated by all the hustle and bustle; they are acquiring security, education, living space, and a lifestyle that is based in its day-to-day routine on gentility, courtesy, hospitality, virtue. Why then are they so discontented? It is not with their lot that they are discontented, it is with the lot of the nation. The very virtues they have and practice are in their eyes conspicuously absent from society as a whole. Politics is corrupt—not in the petty sense, although there is that—but in the large sense; to these people it consists of deals, of the catering to selfish interests, of cynical manipulation and doubletalk. The universities are corrupt—children do not act as if they appreciate what is being given them, they do not work hard, and they are lectured to by devious and wrongheaded professors. And above all, everywhere they look, somebody is trying to get something for nothing and succeeding.

These views may not be confined only to the political culture in which they are now articulated. Surveys I have taken, and others I have read, indicate that the single most widespread concern of middle-class Americans is over the decay of values—evidenced by crime in the streets, juvenile delinquency, public lewdness, and the like but going much beyond these manifestations to include everything that suggests that people no longer act in accordance with decent values and right reason. In many places, especially in the Northeast, our political institutions have not allowed such views to play much part in elections. Parties, led by professionals, instinctively shun such issues, feeling somehow that public debate over virtue is irrelevant (what can government do about it?) and dangerous (nobody can agree on what virtue is or that your party has more of it). Powerful nonpolitical institutions tend also to keep such issues out of politics or to insist that they be matters of private conscience. For one, the Catholic church, which draws the religious and moral interests of its followers inward, toward the sacraments and the educational and religious facilities of the church, which must be maintained and served. For another, large labor unions, which have never mistaken a stamp-out-smut campaign for a fifty-cent increase in the minimum wage. And a self-conscious intelligentsia with common ties to prestigious centers of liberal-arts education has in many regions, especially the East and the Bay Area, an important role to play among local elites. They use their access to the mass media and to officialdom to make certain that other, nonmoral issues predominate—after all, the major function of the schools they went to was to induce them to rebel against middle-class morality, which in the modern parlance is a hang-up.

Regional differences will never disappear entirely, and thus the political culture of Southern California will never be the political culture of our society. But the strength of all those institutions that resist it is waning, and thus we are likely to have more of it in more places. Morality is important, and those concerned about it are decent people (after all I am related to a sizable number of them). But I fear for the time when politics is seized with the issue. Our system of government cannot handle matters of that sort (can any democratic system?), and it may be torn apart by the effort.

7

Character and Young People:
The 1960s

In 1969 Harper's *asked me to go back to Long Beach to see how, if at all, my home town had changed since I grew up there. I spent a week at my high school, half hoping and half fearing to find the celebrated youth culture of the 1960s. Both hopes and fears were groundless. The character-forming process of adolescent life was changing, but slowly and as a working out of deeply held values that were acquiring a fuller, but not significantly different, mode of expression.*

North Long Beach, where I grew up, is one of the many communities in the Los Angeles basin that, blending imperceptibly into one another, seem to be neither city nor suburb. It is also a community that has reached maturity and begun to show its age. The period of rapid growth of the 1930s and 1940s is at an end and has been for some time. Even in the 1950s the population increased only by about 7,000 to a 1960 total of 48,000. An area of single-family houses, it has for many years seen little new construction of this sort; instead the few remaining vacant lots, as well as the backyards of existing homes, are being filled in with small apartment buildings, two or three stories high, having little open space and catering to older persons, young couples without children, or singles. Long Beach was never the center of whatever youth culture Southern California may have—if any age group in the city received special attention and concern, it was the old folks to be found near the public shuffleboard courts—and now with the population changes young people are even less at the center of gravity. North Long Beach has begun to change from being an outlying area in which child rearing was the focus of life to a place out of which young couples move in search of larger or newer homes.

In 1969, as twenty years before, the area is neither affluent nor squalid—it combines in a way unfamiliar to Easterners a suburban lifestyle (single-family homes, neat gardens) with a working-class and lower-middle-class population. Driving north on Atlantic Avenue from downtown Long Beach, one passes through Bixby Knolls, now, as in the past, a prosperous neighborhood bordering the Virginia Country Club and with an attractive, off-the-street shopping center. North Long Beach begins abruptly as one passes under the Union Pacific railroad tracks and encounters, on each side of the street, small, semidetached stucco storefronts, painted various pastel shades and cluttered with a patchwork of neon signs. The street is broad, wider than many big-city thoroughfares, but the shops are almost all one-story, and together they convey no clear sense of line, mass, or color. Things seem strangely out of scale and slightly out of focus—the stores are too low for the width of the road, and the muted green, beige, and pink colors offer no sharp contrast with the hazy, often smog-filled sky. Even the low-income public housing project on county land near the railroad tracks is distinctively Southern Californian. Although built before 1949, it is set back off the main street and consists of one- and two-story buildings surrounded with grass and vegetation and painted the same yellow, green, and coral shades as private housing. Most of the few black families in North Long Beach have moved into this area, although many of the tenants are still white.

David Starr Jordan Senior High School, which I attended, first appears along Atlantic Avenue like an oasis. Towering palm trees border the well-kept park adjacent to the school, and the campus itself has tall eucalyptus trees that impart a sweetly pungent smell to the walks. In my student days it was filled with children born in the depression. For many, the bungalows of North Long Beach were their first nonfarm homes, or at least their first taste of a city of any size. Although the war had just ended and many parents had saved a good deal of money from wages earned at the Douglas aircraft plant or in the Long Beach shipyards, there was not yet much to spend it on (the new postwar cars were eagerly awaited) and little inclination to hand it over to the kids. Many people spent what they had to pay off as much as they could on their house. Accordingly, there was little exotic clothing, with few expensive hobbies—surfboards, for example, cost more than anybody I knew could afford. The young people were mostly Protestant and Midwestern, and all white.

In 1969 the young people look much the same, only more prosperous. They are still Protestant, but now they are Californians, not Okies, Arkies, and Missourians. By 1968 eighteen black students had entered the high school, but a majority lived outside North Long Beach. Many indeed were transferred to Jordan High from other schools for disciplinary reasons, a system that may not augur well for the development of friendly interracial contacts among the students.

The young people, especially the girls, are better dressed (and I think better looking, although I cannot trust my judgment on that) than in 1948, when I graduated. But their general style is much the same—*really* or *real* is for them, as probably for all adolescents, still the standard, all-purpose adverb ("Gee, that's real great!"), and *ya know* still serves as a kind of oral punctuation ("I think, ya know, he's all right, ya know?"). Big or difficult words are still avoided, even by bright students, because they convey ostentatious intellectuality; as one girl told me, "In class, I've gotta talk in words of one syllable, or the guys will think I'm a kiss-up" (that is, teacher's pet).

Names have changed, at least for the girls. It is almost as if their parents, symbolizing the greater security and prosperity they felt as compared with their parents, wished to bestow first names that conveyed fashion and what they took to be urbanity. In the class of 1948, my yearbook tells me, girls' names were simple, straightforward: Patricia, JoAnn, Barbara, Shirley, Mary. One Darlene and a few other stylish names were the exception. Many boys had rural names: LaVerne, Dwayne, Dwight, Verlyn, Delbert, Berl, Virgil, Floyd. In the class of 1968 the girls had blossomed out with unusual names and unusual spellings of familiar names—no fewer than eight Sharons, six Cheryls, two Marlenes, two Sherrys, two Charlenes, and one each of Melodee, Jorjana, Candy, Joy, Cherry, Nanci, Carrolyn, Cyndi, and Darlene. Mary may be a grand old name, but it is no longer a common one.

Social Structure and Behavior

In a school where ethnic and class distinctions are either nonexistent or invisible, the social structure is organized around differences in behavior. There are distinct social groupings, complete with names, at Jordan High, although there is no agreement that they are hierarchically arranged, and little agreement as to the membership of each group. Most students, of course, belong to no particular group at all. Three that have names are the soshes, the surfers, and the cruisers. *Sosh* is a word with a double meaning—pejorative for someone who is snobbish, aloof, or preoccupied with matters of dress and appearance, and descriptive for the well-dressed, personable young people who get elected to most of the student offices, are active in the clubs, and support the school. They are great favorites of the teachers and the administrators, though they are also fearful of being thought kiss-ups. Because the term has two meanings, no one with these attributes likes to apply it to himself, but for better or worse the obvious nonsoshes use the label frequently and with respect to a clearly visible group.

Surfers may or may not be people who actually surf—indeed, most do not, although they all like the beach. The term applies not so much to what they do as to what they look like. Unlike the soshes', their hair is long (at the extreme, and in few cases at Jordan, the surfers fade into the hippies) and blond as a result of inheritance, sun, or chemicals. Compared with the soshes, they are more casual in dress and less deferential to teachers (though hardly rude). Cruisers (sometimes called "Northtowners") are the rough group oriented to automobiles and with little interest in studies. The boys wear their hair neither short (as do the soshes) nor long (as do the surfers) but in modest pompadours or otherwise waved. Their pants are tight, their shirts untidy (and whenever they can get away with it, out of their pants), and their shoes run toward suede, sharp-toed, elevator-heel boots. Their girlfriends are called hair girls because they wear wigs or have their own hair arranged in fantastic creations rising precariously almost a foot above their heads and held in place with a hair spray that must have the adhesive power of epoxy cement. During compulsory physical education classes, all girls turn out for softball or other games dressed in regulation blue gym suits designed, no doubt intentionally, so as to make a Sophia Loren look like something out of Louisa May Alcott. The hair girls will be out too, their towering creations waving unsteadily as they run about. A softball hit into one of those hairdos would have to be called a ground-rule double since it could not possibly be extracted in less than half an hour.

Cruisers cruise. The accepted routes are Atlantic Avenue and Bellflower Boulevard: the accepted cars are the ones that have been lowered, equipped with mag wheels (sometimes fake), and their windows decorated with a tasseled fringe and a hand-painted slogan ("Midnight Hour"); the accepted driving style is slowly, with the driver slumped down in his seat until only the top of his head shows and his hand draped casually out the window. Pinstriping, metallic paint, and other car fashions described by Tom Wolfe are no longer much in evidence around high schools (partly no doubt because customizing has become expensive). And sadly the classic hot rods of the 1940s, with exposed, reworked engines, straight pipes, and minimal driver comfort are rare. Perhaps they have been taken over by adults whose nitromethane-fueled supereliminators make a conventional hot rod look now like what it once emphatically was not: kid stuff. Or perhaps no one in North Long Beach knows how to make them anymore or perhaps the parts are unavailable or perhaps no one cares.

Casual observation of the campus conveys chiefly an impression of sameness—middle-class Wasp students preoccupied with social life, school activities, and class work. But the students themselves see differences where adults see similarities, and although the differences might be narrow indeed on a scale that included all teenagers in the country, they are nonetheless important. I suspect the differences may be even more important in 1969 than twenty years earlier, and that there are now fewer uniformities in behavior and manner. In 1948, for example, styles of dress were more or less standard (simple skirts, sweaters or blouses, and white Joyce shoes for girls; jeans or cords, and T-shirts and lettermen's sweaters for most boys); twenty years later, though scarcely radical by the standards of contemporary fashion, clothing is more varied, reflecting in part the freer choice that comes from prosperity and in part the emergence of more distinctive subgroups with which students consciously identify.

Dress regulations have always been a major issue in the high school and a not infrequent cause of disciplinary action. The rules are set by a citywide committee of students and teachers, subject to administrative approval, and revised annually. The effort to define what constitutes an acceptable miniskirt has been abandoned as dress lengths have steadily risen, an inch or two ahead of the regulations every year. In resignation the rulemakers have retreated into comfortable ambiguity, saying only that "skirts must be of reasonable length and appropriate for school wear." My close study of the situation suggests that the meaning of "reasonable" is not self-evident—some skirts come almost to the knee, some remain defiantly (and gloriously) at midthigh. For the boys, clothing must "avoid extremes," hair may come down to the collar but not below it, and sideburns and moustaches (but not beards) are all right. A few young men display long hair (thereby becoming surfers even if they do not know how to swim), but going beyond modest deviance is risky. As one football player and student officer told me, "The guys don't like hippies much. One of the guys walked up to a fella with hair down to his shoulders and just hauled off and hit him. A lot of guys will say something to the hippies, sort of challenge them, and if they answer back, then it can get rough."

One might suppose, to judge from the breathless accounts given by a mass media fascinated by youth culture, that teenagers in 1969 thrive on individuality, independence, and fancifulness—each person doing his own thing. Although this state of nature may prevail in some places, it is not found in North Long Beach or, I suspect, in most communities. Young people of course are always struggling to rebel against adult authority, but precisely because of that they tend to place even greater stock in the opinion of their peers. Teenagers draw together, discovering themselves in the generalized opinion they form of each other—seeing themselves reflected, as it were, in the eyes of their friends. What is surprising is not that their life tends to a certain uniformity in manners and dress but that there is any heterogeneity at all.

95

Social Values

The chief social values of the young people to whom I spoke (and whom I remember from the late 1940s) are friendliness and, above all, sincerity. Anything smacking of a pose, a front, or phoniness is hotly rejected. The emphasis in media youth culture on love, honesty, communication, and intense self-expression is not a reaction against traditional youth values but only an extreme expression of these values. Affluence, freedom, and rapid social change produce more exaggerated statements of the enduring concerns of young people (or, for that matter, most people) than a repudiation of those concerns. Of course to a true hippie or young political radical, the Jordan High School student is at best a square—the embodiment of tradition, philistinism, and middle-class preoccupation with property, dating, and boosterism. Although in behavior and ideology the hippie and the square could not be more different, the animating impulse in both cases is similar—a deep concern with honesty in personal relations. For the square, honesty is simply not so complex a value as for others.

Among surfer and sosh alike, as well as among the mass of unaffiliated students, the strongest criticism voiced about the behavior or attitude of others is that it seemed snobbish or phony or that the individual was part of a "clique." The most popular students are not those one might imagine if one remembers the Hollywood musical comedies about campus life; they are not the socially aggressive big men on campus. They are instead rather quiet persons who are socially at ease but who also embody in greatest degree the quality of being sincere. The student body president said little in meetings I attended of student leaders, but when he spoke, he was listened to respectfully—perhaps precisely because he did not chatter or try to be a wise guy and because he seemed to think carefully about what he wanted to say, and when he spoke, he was neither flustered nor bombastic.

Still I detect sharper cleavages among the social groupings of the students, sharper, that is, than I would have expected knowing merely that young people seek to find a place where they can belong and a circle they can join. One new factor, almost unknown to my generation of students, helps explain these wider distinctions: drugs. There is no doubt whatever that at Jordan, as (according to the police) at all Long Beach high schools, illegal drugs (marijuana, barbiturates, amphetamines) are widely used. During the fall semester preceding my arrival on campus, twenty-six drug cases came to the attention of the school authorities. Every student I spoke to knew of persons who used drugs, several implied (without quite admitting) that they had used them, two or three told me they could make a purchase for me within the hour if I wanted. (I did not.)

Students were concerned about this and aware that certain social groupings were heavily populated with dopies. (The term connotes more than it should. No one believes there are any addicts, or users of physiologically addicting drugs, among the students; drugs—"reds" and "whites"—are used much like alcohol, on weekends and at parties and occasionally at school.) Many kids are worried about drugs because of fears over health or acquiring a police record, and leery of groups or parties where the dopies gather. For the city as a whole, police arrests of juveniles in cases involving marijuana increased between 1962 and 1968 from 18 to 186; cases involving pills rose from 12 to over 650. For a student, being a user—or worse, being caught as a user—intensifies normal social cleavages.

For some boys, athletics is seen not only as fun but as an absorbing activity that increases one's chances of staying away from a social life involving dopies. One player told me that "if it hadn't been for football," he probably "would have wound up where the guys I used to hang around with are"—in trouble with the school and the police. Conversely the same young people reject as phony many of the materials they see in class designed to warn them of the dangers of drug use. One complained that "the stuff they show you in those movies about dirty old men hanging around school trying to push dope—that's all pretty stupid, that's not the way it is at all. Anybody who wants to buy drugs can get them easy."

Perhaps because social groupings are more sharply defined, perhaps for other reasons, most students complained that there was not enough school spirit and that many of the formal student organizations were meaningless or ineffective. "Nobody cares about the school," one girl said. "There are no cheers at the pep assemblies." Many students think student government is a waste of time (only a third of the students voted in the previous election), and most of those in student government worry about the same thing—organizations seem weak, spirit is flagging.

If the football team could have a winning season, this all might change, but it had not for some time, mainly, it appears, because it was playing over its head in a league composed of several larger schools with more and bigger talent to draw on. But nobody is convinced that a losing record in football is the whole reason. One girl (labeled by others a surfer although she herself, as everybody else, refused to accept any label) said that students want to be "more individual," not "try to act just like the soshes," but then complained of the absence of school spirit. I asked her whether more intense individualism was incompatible with school spirit; she puzzled over it a moment, and then said she guessed that was right.

Issues That Matter

The formal student organizations cut across the informal social group-ings, and that may be one reason for their weakness. More than thirty clubs exist in a student body of 2,200, chiefly to serve social, vocational, or hobby interests. The Shutterbugs enjoy camera, the Rooks play chess, the Thespians participate in drama, the Girls' Rifle Team drills. There are chapters of Future Teachers of America and Future Medical Leaders of America. Music produces the most organizations, partly because many grow directly out of elective classes—the Concert Band, the Orchestra, the Marching Band, the Military Band, the String Quartet, A Capella, the Girls' Choir, the Mixed Chorus, the Choraliers, the Straw Hatters. An important way in which the community reaches into the school is through the sponsorship of student organizations by business and civic associations—the Kiwanis sponsors the Key Club, Rotary sponsors Interact.

Because the formal organizations crosscut, rather than coincide with, informal groupings, their vitality is compromised (except those that pursue a clear activity, such as the music organizations). Social organizations are not, and under school rules cannot be, exclusive as to membership, and thus a number of unofficial, "secret" organizations flourish. These are mainly fraternities and sororities that have no (and want no) approved adult sponsor, and thus are illegal. The administra-tion struggles against them but with little success. Students differ as to the importance of the secret organizations; some members feel they have declined in recent years, but all members compare them favorably to the official clubs with open memberships, no hazing, adult sponsors, and thus no fun.

One official organization that has both a large number of followers and considerable respect is Campus Life, a quasi-religious group begun by members of the Youth for Christ movement. It holds a number of dances during the year and in addition has education programs featuring, for example, films about LSD or other controversial subjects. The popularity of Campus Life is one current indication of an enduring feature of community and school: the extraordinary importance of churches. The area from the first had many storefront Protestant sects, and the more successful of these have become large, active organizations. The local Brethren church, for example, has a huge physical plant, including a school, and runs a number of well-attended youth activities. Mormons for decades have accounted for a sizable fraction of the student population, and Baptists, Methodists, and Presbyterians are also numerous. It is difficult to assess the religious significance of the strong and clear church affiliations, but their social and institutional importance is unmistakable.

The most striking aspect of organizational life, however, is the complete absence of any group devoted to questions of public policy, world affairs, or community issues. Only one club, Cosmopolitan, touches matters external to the school (it organizes and raises money for an exchange-student program that brings one foreign student to campus each year and sends one Jordanite abroad). In the years of slowly fading optimism following the Second World War, the World Friendship Club was an active organization, sponsoring an annual World Friendship Day and meeting regularly to study international events with heavy emphasis, as I recall, on the Chinese government of Chiang Kai-shek and especially on the views of Madame Chiang. Neither the club nor the day remains, and no new policy area has generated any substitutes.

I asked various groups of students what questions other than personal or campus matters concerned them, but other than one boy who mentioned the draft, I got no clear answers. To be sure, if I had asked them whether they were interested in, say, civil rights or the Vietnam War, many would have said they were. And most issues of this sort are discussed, often heatedly, in their classes. But what is impressive is that no general question, couched in broad terms, elicited any strong feelings or active, spontaneous concern. The issues that they did volunteer were wholly campus-oriented—the students had argued with the principal over the date of the senior prom, there was some indignation about a fence that had been erected between the school and the adjacent park (not, it seems, to keep the kids in but to keep the undesirables out), and some complaints about the tight control the administration was believed to exercise over the contents of the student newspaper. Some students noted wistfully that another high school in the city had an underground newspaper but almost in the same breath said they did not like the recent efforts of a group of older men, perhaps college students, to distribute such a paper on the Jordan campus.

In an era of aroused youth preoccupied with relevance, why should the young people of North Long Beach be neither aroused nor relevant? It is easy, too easy, to think of explanations, some plausible but none convincing. The students are middle-class, they are Wasps, they live in a sheltered community, there are few Jewish students on campus, North Long Beach is not a central city, they are all part of Southern California and probably just another crop of young backlashers. And of course their parents were not radical; no Jordan student could be a red-diaper baby. Some explanations, especially the last one, have partial significance, but none satisfies me. What is perhaps equally important, none would even be intelligible to the persons described. To them almost everybody is middle class; extremes of wealth or poverty are outside their experience. Some may know what *Wasp* means, but the term is still an Eastern invention, largely marketed in the East. Long Beach is to them neither sheltered nor noncentral—to them it is highly central. ("We've got everything around us here," one said. "The beach, the mountains, LA, Hollywood, Disneyland. It's really great.") As for the idea that families have a tradition of liberalism or radicalism, they can scarcely imagine it. And they would be embarrassed to hear anyone speak of the influence of Jewish culture on social change—it's "not nice" to speak of a person's religion, you "shouldn't generalize" about other people, and besides the Jews are supposed to be just like everyone else.

The most important fact about these students is not their class, ethnicity, religion, or location; the most important thing about them is their age. They are sixteen years old, give or take a year or two. They are coming to grips with problems of identity, sex, career, and adult authority. Their responses to these central concerns produce the social groupings we see—the soshes, with their ready acceptance of adult values, especially the virtues of work, service, neatness, neighborliness; the cruisers, with their rejection of those values, their open pursuit of girls as objects of conquest, their contempt for studies that signifies either rebellion or despair; the surfers, who are reevaluating standards, suspending judgments, and above all resisting a premature commitment to the adult world or any abandonment of values of individuality, which they greatly prize. When one is sixteen, the larger world does not touch one, except in crisis or because one's parents make involvement in that world a central adult value. In a profound sense community or world issues are irrelevant to the focal concerns of the students, and not vice versa.

Now, as when I was in that world, young people have great natural idealism, but the objects of that idealism are principally personal relations (friendship, the team, the crush) or else distant and lofty goals (religiosity, human brotherhood in some ultimate sense, world peace). There is rarely any middle ground (again, except when circumstances provide it) of public policy toward which one acts or about which one thinks with much intensity. When an issue from the middle range intrudes, an effort is made to translate it into simpler human values. One student leader spoke critically of the demonstrations on college campuses because they showed a "lack of respect for other people"; another (in a classroom discussion) was critical of de Gaulle's policies toward the United States because he had displayed neither gratitude nor fairness; a third, in a class report on pornography, concluded that censorship would not work but that we must be careful, as parents, to inculcate "the right moral values" in our children.

There is less aversion to classroom discussion of controversial issues than when I attended Jordan but the same tendency to evaluate or resolve those issues by reaffirming traditional values. It would have been most unlikely that, in 1949, a girl would have given an illustrated report on pornography, much less gather material for that report by attending (with her brother) a skin flick and patronizing a downtown dirty book store. Had the discussion occurred, the boys in the back of the room would have nervously snickered over the (rather mild) illustrations and concluded that the girl must not be nice and thus fair game. There were no snickers, nervous or otherwise, the discussion was matter of fact (and rather quickly branched off to include student use of marijuana and drugs), and the girl was obviously nice. The teacher played almost no role in the uninhibited discussion that followed, but despite this a general agreement on the importance of morality and family training was quickly reached. At this point several girls spoke disapprovingly of the looseness of the younger generation, by which they meant their ten-year-old kid brothers. "They are learning too much, too soon," one said. "You'd be amazed at the words and things they know already! It wasn't like that for me."

Race

The one major issue that has touched their lives, and that they speak about frequently though still in guarded tones, is race. No blacks attended Jordan when I was a student there, and scarcely any lived in the area. Although Compton, which is two-thirds black, is just across the city line and Watts not far away, almost no black families have yet moved into North Long Beach—apparently because no one has been willing to sell to them. In time that line will break (there is a great deal of housing in the area within the buying power of the blacks) and Jordan High School will face what for it will be a crisis, unless the district lines are redrawn. Such a strategy is conceivable since a new freeway under construction runs east and west across North Long Beach just south of the Compton line, thereby providing a natural barrier to immigration.

The young whites with whom I spoke are obviously torn between two standards that they think ought to be consistent but when applied to what they see as the black problem, produce incompatible judgments. One is that people ought to be judged as individuals, fairly, and without regard to skin color; the other is that people ought to have a common standard of behavior, and in the adolescent world this includes not being ostentatiously cliquish and not occupying a place of special favor in the adult-managed authority system (not, as they put it, being able to get away with something by reason of privilege rather than cunning). The two standards are familiar enough—liberty and equality—and the tension between them gives rise to the same problems for young people as for older ones.

101

The Jordan High whites spoke approvingly of a few blacks whose behavior did not produce any dilemmas—who could be judged as individuals because they were like everybody else. Liberty tended toward equality in these cases, and the blacks involved were singled out for special praise: "he is real boss," "one of the guys," he "goes around with a bunch of white guys." They spoke critically of others who were a "clique" and "got away with murder" because "the teachers are afraid to do anything about it." One white claimed she had seen a black girl "crowd in line in the cafeteria and a teacher who saw it just stood there." A boy said he thought some of the blacks had stolen ballots in the student body election, again without penalty. "If you say anything to them, they say you're picking on them because they're black."

"Them"—when the standard of equality is violated (in white eyes), the violators are set apart as outside the school's social system and given a collective label. Soshes, surfers, and cruisers all resist and resent the labels given them and struggle to show that they do not really fit, each person insisting that he is an individual (valuing liberty but unwilling to accept its price, which is inequality—at least in the mind of the beholder). But the blacks, being black, cannot escape or argue about the collective label, and with growing racial pride they now understandably flaunt it.

It would be easy to stigmatize the racial views of these white youngsters by putting in their mouths a phrase I never heard them use, perhaps because they are aware that it has become a symbol of complacent bigotry—"some of my best friends are Negroes." Whatever they may become as adults, few are now complacent bigots by any means—their sense of fair play is much too strong for that precisely, I would argue, because they are adolescents. When a black did act like "one of the guys," there was no visible resistance or resentment. At a Friday night dance at the Canteen, a popular youth center run by the city recreation department and located in the park next to the school, I saw two black high school boys dancing with white girls. Nobody paid any attention. I asked one of the more conservative students (he had told me earlier of his outrage at the "disrespectful" attitude of college students who "rioted and demonstrated" at their campuses) if anybody cared about the interracial dancing, and he said, in some surprise, "No, they're good guys." He then said that the previous year a black boy had married a white girl after graduation, and there had been "no fuss." A Canteen official said there had not been any racial problems with the young people but that she imagined some of their parents (whom she thought "less honest" than their children) might be upset.

With the growth in numbers of black students at the school, it will be increasingly difficult either for many blacks to be "one of the guys" in white society or for the whites to continue to apply individual tests of worth in the face of increasing collective differences. One white girl who liked a black boy and was seen with him frequently on campus reported growing undercurrents of criticism from both blacks and whites.

When I asked some white student leaders if there was anything they thought should be done about the black students, they strongly reasserted the value of equal treatment. "Everybody should be treated the same," "no special favors," "the rules ought to apply to everybody equally" were the common views. Teachers and administrators were criticized sharply for not (in the students' opinion) acting this way. They were "afraid" to enforce the rules on the blacks, students said. If blacks stayed together, it was because of "self-segregation." (Some students dissented, however. One came up to me afterward and said he thought blacks needed extra help and "some breaks," but he clearly did not feel he could push this view too hard in a public discussion.) The administrators of course had a more complicated view of the situation, concerned as they were about avoiding friction and forestalling an incident, but what to school officials may have been prudence was to the students inequity.

Such racial tension as exists, however, is at a low level. Most of the black students live out of the school attendance area, and thus there is little after-school contact. Nor are there many community problems that would provide fuel for racial conflict—there are no teenage gangs, delinquency is (in police eyes) no more than what might be expected in a middle-class area, and church and civic groups are influential. It is an area of almost numbing wholesomeness.

Unchanging Social Life

The social life of Jordan students remains much as it was in the late 1940s. The most important events are the Friday night dances at the Canteen, at which four or five hundred boys and girls regularly turn out to enjoy bands picked by student officers of the Canteen; as always, far more girls than boys are interested in actually dancing. On Saturday night there are movies, perhaps a church dance, cruising, working at the Kentucky Colonel Fried Chicken shop, or hanging around the A&W Root Beer stand. A big date means a trip to Melodyland or Disneyland or occasionally to the Shrine for a rock show. The secret fraternities and sororities will have an annual dance at the Elks Club or a nearby veterans' hall. Parties at homes are less common than formerly, apparently, as one girl said, because the "boys get too wild and wreck the place or steal things." During Easter Week those with access to cars (and a little money) will drive to Palm Springs or Balboa; during the Christmas vacation many go to Big Bear in the mountains.

The sexual revolution, like youth culture, has not had the radical effect its middle-aged chroniclers (and admirers) sometimes suggest. Teachers and counselors with many years' experience at Jordan find no evidence of a dramatic increase in premarital sex but a good deal more candor about what actually does occur. An unmarried girl who got pregnant used to be whisked off in shame to some distant relative to have the baby; now she is likely to stay in town and be given a shower by her friends. The chief restraints on libertinism remain what they have always been: the conflict between a boy's desire for action and a girl's quest for commitment, together with each other's fears of rejection and embarrassment.

The opportunities that money and automobiles are supposed to have provided adolescents generally have long since been available in Southern California. The perimeter of youthful social life—Hollywood to the north, Big Bear and Palm Springs to the east, Balboa to the south—is far-flung, but it has always been so, and there is therefore little sense of newfound freedom or heady experiences. Perhaps like children in European families who grow up familiar with wine, Southern California teenagers take their environmental stimulants pretty much for granted.

Within that perimeter they are highly mobile, but the world beyond is still known primarily by hearsay. Other than those young people who make a summer pilgrimage back to their grandparents' home in Kansas, Missouri, or Iowa, few Jordan students know anything at all of the East and rather little of the urban Midwest. Students frequently asked me "what's it like" at Harvard, or in New England. I asked them what they thought it was like, and they said that New England was "really cold" and Harvard has a lot of "rich snobs who are big brains." I tried to assure them that Boston temperatures do not preclude all forms of life, that Harvard students are on the whole not rich, and those who are rarely are smart, but I could see in the eyes of my questioners that nothing I could say would dispel the mystery of the East.

Nobody I spoke to knew anyone who had gone away to college in the East, and no one intended to go himself. A survey of Jordan's class of 1968 showed that 52 percent had gone on to college full- or part-time, but the vast majority of these (more than 80 percent) attended the two-year Long Beach City College and a large but unknown proportion dropped out in their first year. The record college enrollments around the country, and especially in California, conceal the fact that for most students formal education ends with high school or within a year or two after graduation. Few (only about 7 percent at Jordan) go directly on to a four-year college or university; most go to tax-supported institutions located in the immediate area.

Even though California State College at Long Beach, a four-year school, is located just a few miles from the Jordan campus, few seniors (perhaps 16 of more than 700) go even that far away. One reason is transportation—even a few miles in Southern California, given the state of public transportation, is a big distance if one does not have a car (Cal State has few dormitories). But the more important reasons are probably social and cultural—Cal State is a big place (more than 25,000 students), it is overcrowded with large classes, and there are a lot of weird people there (during my visit it was convulsed by a conflict over a black-studies program). City College, by contrast, is nearby, familiar, and attended by all one's friends. As one girl said, "It's like a high school with ashtrays."

Cost is also a factor. Jordan students are keenly aware that their parents cannot afford everything and probably cannot afford even the cost of UCLA, much less a private school. Jordan has its share of bright students (one represented Southern California at a youth science conference in Chicago), and some of these will get scholarships, but most will think wistfully that while it might be nice to go to UCLA or Santa Barbara, it is easier to enroll in LBCC. Even among the academically talented members of the class of 1968 included in the survey, the furthest east one had gone was to the University of Redlands—seventy miles away.

Measuring Change

Jordan High School, like North Long Beach, has not changed in any fundamental way. New buildings of green and pink stucco have replaced the wooden bungalows in which I attended class, but the social structure and the values of the people are essentially the same, modified perhaps by the influence of higher incomes and the settled sense of being a Californian rather than a migrant. So striking is the continuity one finds in North Long Beach that one is tempted to describe it under a pseudonym and then let the reader guess where it is actually located. Many will suppose, even as I might have supposed, that it is an isolated backwater of the nation—a small town in Iowa, perhaps, or a suburb of Omaha. But it is not: it is near the center of one of the most populous, affluent, mobile, media-conscious areas in the United States, part of a state where Robert F. Kennedy and Eugene McCarthy met head-on in a bitter, closely watched primary election, and near the place where, in August 1965, the "black revolt" is thought to have begun. At one nearby university, two Black Panthers were shot and killed; at two others a fraction of the student body was in open revolt.

The Jordan students are aware of the turmoil but not seized by it. How it has affected them will probably not be apparent for years. Already of course the older teachers lament that the work ethic has been eroded: "They just don't seem to work as hard in class as they used to," one told me. "There's no real discipline problem, but it seems as if they want to be entertained more, they want to know what they'll get out of it if they do an assignment." Another veteran teacher agreed but thought the reason was not in broad social changes or in student values but in the school itself: "Increasingly, the emphasis here is on college preparation, but when you get right down to how many actually go to a four-year college, the answer is damned few. For the rest, we're not preparing them for much of anything. Some shouldn't even be here—they ought to be out learning a trade, but the law says we have to keep them here until they're sixteen."

It is hard to evaluate such comments. Men in their fifties are bound to see young people somewhat differently than the same men in their thirties. At the end of one's career, students may not seem as bright or as hard-working or as exciting as they did when one first started teaching. But there is another possibility: the great increase in the proportion of students going on to college, even if only to City College, as a result of both parental pressure and their own assessment of career needs, has undoubtedly placed great strains on the normal social processes of the high school. The new definition of success—college and a good job, rather than immediate marriage and any job—represents simultaneously a school norm, an adult expectation, and an adolescent hope. The normal (and normally minor) symptoms of youthful rebellion against those adult expectations that seem excessive, unreal, or unrelated to their own needs and opportunities may have been intensified by these newer and more demanding expectations which have made high school seem less fun, less responsive to adolescent interests, and more a system to be beaten by doing what is necessary but doing it without zeal. Even the elusive school spirit that students find so lacking may be in part the victim of a process that has made the high school less an end in itself and more a means to a larger and more equivocal end: career success.

Underlying the continuity of manner and style, there may thus be deeper changes at work. But it is unlikely they arise from what, in our intense preoccupation with the immediate crises of race and peace, we imagine—not from the issues and fashions of the moment but from a fundamental restructuring of the ways in which one enters society and the labor force, and thus of ways in which one grows up.

8

Character versus Intellect: Habits of the Heart

I doubt that higher education has much to do with character; college presupposes character among its members, and usually that presupposition is warranted. When it is, there is no happier or more fulfilling place to spend one's days than on a campus. But as everyone knows, decent people often behave indecently when in a mob, and alas universities occasionally are mobs. My college, the University of Redlands, was rarely the scene of mob behavior; when I was invited to deliver the commencement address there in 1988, I did not have to scold anybody and could use the occasion to speak of what higher education could not do for young people. My title, "Habits of the Heart," was chosen to invite comparisons between my understanding of Alexis de Tocqueville's famous phrase and the understanding of the authors of a highly regarded book that had recently appeared under the same title.

My title comes from Alexis de Tocqueville, the great and perceptive French observer of American democracy, who wrote at the time of Andrew Jackson. He wanted to explain how Americans managed to maintain a democratic republic. He noted the advantages Providence had bestowed upon us: a vast and rich land. But many nations of Latin America have a land nearly as vast and just as rich, yet democracy appears there only fitfully. Tocqueville observed that Americans have devised an ingenious Constitution that separates the powers of government, preserves local rule, and creates an independent judiciary. But many nations, such as the Philippines, have faithfully copied our Constitution and laws, yet the people of these other countries are rarely free of tyranny. What distinguishes America from other nations are the customs of its people: the habits of their hearts.

Commencement speakers often suggest that higher education is a great bulwark of a free and democratic society. Statesmen often demand that higher education be made more widely available (although it is

107

already more widely available here than anywhere else in the world). Yet if this is so, how can we account for the fact that over 150 years ago, when Tocqueville sought to explain the persistence of democracy in America, scarcely anyone had gone to college? Indeed, few had gone to anything resembling a high school. If college is the final step in the preparation for good citizenship, then we must not have had many citizens until quite recently.

When we look at the world around us, the puzzle deepens. The revolutionary movements that have brought to power dictatorships of the Left or the Right have been led, to a disproportionate degree, by college graduates and college students. The greatest tyranny the world has known—the Soviet Union—was designed, installed, and defended by intellectuals. Wherever we see impassioned armies of religious, ethnic, or political zealots, we often see intellectuals at their head.

Perhaps college is not such a good idea after all. That is not the conclusion I wish you to draw. Besides, it is too late to apply for a tuition refund. I wish you only to observe that higher education is an incomplete education, for it chiefly tends to shape the habits of the mind. Other things shape the habits of the heart.

Aristotle explained to us several centuries before Christ that there is an important difference between the intellectual virtues and the moral virtues. Intellectual virtue owes its birth and growth to teaching, while moral virtue is the product of habit. One intellectual virtue is scientific knowledge. It is the opposite of superstition, prejudice, and ignorance. It is acquired by study. Another intellectual virtue is art: skill at fashioning beautiful things out of commonplace ones. Art is learned by practice and precept, by apprenticeship to someone who is already an artist. Art and science can be learned in universities (although they can be learned in other places as well).

Moral Virtue

A moral virtue is not the product of formal instruction or even of mental reflection. The moral virtues include courage, moderation, fidelity, and good temper. Moral virtue is the product of habituation. "Ethics" comes from the Greek word "ethos," which means habit. Aristotle described the process as follows: "We become just by doing just acts, temperate by doing temperate acts, brave by doing brave acts." Moral virtue is the same as a good character, and a good character is formed not through moral instruction or personal self-discovery but through the regular repetition of right actions. These habits are chiefly formed in the family.

As some will note, I am distancing myself from the views of certain well-known public figures. I share their general concern for character,

108

but I do not believe that character is formed by praying in public schools, listening to uplifting lectures about the life and words of Abraham Lincoln, or contemplating one's inner self to discover true peace, rock music, and the benefits of organic gardening.

What is the relationship between moral virtue and a college education? Often, none at all. Occasionally they are enemies. Sometimes—I hope most of the time—they are uneasy allies, like a mouse and a cat that have grown up together and so live peacefully together, albeit not without some anxiety on the part of the mouse.

Intellectual Benefits

The great benefit of college is not that it builds character, much less that it helps one make money or find a mate. The great benefit is that it stretches and enlarges the mind and helps one see the larger world beyond oneself more clearly and more fully. The individual derives the true benefits of college not from an ability to pass the law school admission test but from those occasions—I hope they have occurred to you—when one discovers the intense and unique pleasures of intellectual excitement: when one feels, after reading a poem, moved to a new level of self-awareness; when after conducting an experiment one says, "Aha! So that is how it works!"; when after hearing a lecture on philosophy or history one says, "Now I understand" or "That can't be right—I must find out how things really are."

The formal and deliberate pursuit of knowledge, which the university exists to foster, can greatly enrich society. Examples from science, medicine, and technology come readily to mind. Let me mention two less obvious examples.

The free market, which is the greatest instrument yet devised for satisfying the material needs of society, was invented and given its best defense by a professor named Adam Smith. In 1776 he published *The Wealth of Nations*, a book that began to free man from his natural tendency to avoid and suppress competition. Make no mistake about it: there is little in man's nature or in the exercise of his moral virtues that would lead him to embrace so revolutionary a doctrine. Politicians, business people, and professors may say they like competition, but the not-so-secret truth is that every politician hopes his opponent will be indicted, every business person hopes his competitors will go bankrupt, every professor hopes his critics will be struck mute. It may be natural for man to barter and exchange, but it is also natural for him to conspire. A persuasive defense of a free market required a great mind to show how the present pains of competition would provide future gains in abundance. The current demand for protectionist trade policies and the endless effort of business firms and labor unions to seek special subsidies are ready reminders of how unnatural—which is to say, how learned—is our support for free markets.

Human tolerance was also defined and defended in the academy. Man's natural tendency to conspire is matched by his instinctive readiness to oppress. We naturally prefer our own kind: our family, our village, our tribe, our religion, our nation. To an important degree, this preference is desirable, for the loyalties it inspires reinforce our necessary obligations to those who depend on us for their livelihood or from whom we have acquired our identity. But these loyalties often tend to run amok. The principal cause of war, terrorism, and pitiless bloodshed is not the desire for new markets or larger territories but the desire to crush those who are different: Arab against Jew, Muslim against Hindu, Shiite against Sunni, black against white. Like the defense of the free market, the defense of the idea of human tolerance required thoughtful people to persuade us of something that went against our grain. Those who persuaded us and who helped fashion the instruments—laws, constitutions, courts—by which to make that tolerance secure were intellectuals, people for whom freedom is especially important because their existence depends on it. The persuasion of course has been incomplete and temporary and needs constant renewal—even in universities, where there has of late arisen a dangerous tendency to exclude, shout down, or "disinvite" speakers expressing views that we do not happen to like.

The university, or more accurately the life of the mind, has in these and other ways benefited mankind. It is to understand these benefits and the arguments behind them that we go to a university or join in the life of the mind. Some of us go to the university to learn a skill, to find a mate, to throw off a restraint, or to make a contact. But these are the subsidiary and nonessential benefits of higher education. The core benefit—which I hope you have tasted—is to see the world whole, in a long perspective, and in its fundamental aspects.

These ambitions of the mind coexist uneasily with our habits of the heart. In the process of expanding our horizons, a university can tear loose our moorings. Consider the family: If millennia of evolutionary experience had not produced it, no college professor would have invented it. Imagine primitive man employing professors to design a way of rearing children.

If the job were given to an economist, he would probably create a market—a kind of marital stock exchange—in which people would bid for mates. Women would bid for the services of men in conceiving and raising children, men would bid for the affections and companionship of women. Once a merger was arranged, the couple would estimate the discounted present value of having children. Since children always cost more than they are worth in monetary terms, only shortsighted couples would have any, and many of those who had them would sell the more attractive children to other investors.

If the job were given to a professor of law, he would draft a contract for a nuclear family consisting of seven persons: the mother, father, and child; a judge to hear claims alleging breach of contract; two lawyers to represent each side in the dispute; and an appellate judge to overturn the decision of the first judge.

If the job were given to a professor of philosophy, he would tell us that the word "family" is itself meaningless, an empty abstraction that conceals the reality of many kinds of human linkages. Moreover the idea of producing a good family is mere emotion, a personal preference no better and no worse than any other preference.

If mankind had depended on intellectuals to invent the family, it would have died out in two generations. Sometimes I think that if we depend on them to solve the present problems of the family, we will die out in one generation.

Moral Character

The moral virtues of mankind are fashioned by social processes created by experience and evolution and held together by the most subtle bonds of affection and duty. We all know this of course, but often we take it so for granted that we forget how fragile this process of familial habituation can be.

In acquiring moral character through familial habituation, we learn self-control. When we go to college, we learn self-expression. Now men and women need both self-control and self-expression, but self-expression—letting go, doing your own thing—is more fun, especially when you are young. When entering the University of Redlands in 1949, I learned about self-expression with a vengeance. I believe that until this day, no university official has known for certain that it was I who late one night led the group that took all the furniture from our dormitory lobby and put it in the middle of the quadrangle.

Educated people are for the most part the product of familial arrangements that have produced in them sufficient self-control and regard for others so as to make not only college pranks but artistic license and political activism tolerable and even useful exercises. But some college-educated people who have benefited from the character-forming processes of their families come to think ill of those processes, regarding them as stultifying or even repressive. They take for granted their own habitual civility even while deriding its source. The effect of this attitude on others can be devastating.

111

Consider the case of drugs. With few exceptions the most dangerous drugs have first been taken up by affluent and educated people. Heroin, cocaine, LSD: initially all were promoted by intelligent, liberated people as exciting ways to achieve peace, self-discovery, and self-expression—"better living through chemistry." Of course self-discovery soon turned into self-destruction. But the experimenters, being affluent and educated, had access to treatment programs and support systems that gave them a good chance of finding their way back to normality.

But to many less advantaged people, the promise of self-expression was seen much more clearly than the reality of self-destruction. The lure of an easy path to Nirvana proved irresistible to millions of people who lacked the personal character or the family help to cope with the lure and its consequences. What began as a clever experiment for affluent Americans quickly became a living nightmare for disadvantaged Americans. Drug use has not spread because drug pushers have forced it on us but because the apostles of unconstrained self-expression, many of them the best and the brightest college could produce, celebrated the values of self-indulgence.

Even now when the dangers are well understood, many educated people still discuss the drug problem in almost every way except the right way. They talk about the costs of drug use and the socioeconomic factors that shape that use. They rarely speak plainly—drug use is wrong because it is immoral, and it is immoral because it enslaves the mind and destroys the soul. It is as if it were a mark of sophistication for us to shun the language of morality in discussing the problems of mankind. When we have lost our ability to speak of morality, our habits of the heart have been subverted by the ambitions of the mind.

But now I am beginning to preach, and that is the last thing you want to hear on this joyous occasion. For four years you have had to sit still and listen to middle-aged people lecture at you about middle-age things. No more. I am at the end of my remarks just as you are at the beginning of your lives. I wish you all the best, confident that four years at this college have left the habits of your hearts strong and enduring, and I thank your parents for paying for that college experience and for providing that family life that will enable you to sustain the delicate balance between humanity and intellectuality.

9

Liberalism versus a Liberal Education

If college cannot build character, it can certainly provide opportunities for people to display a lack of character. An even more disturbing possibility—that something about higher education under certain circumstances can harm character—was suggested to me by the tumult at Harvard between 1969 and 1972. We are accustomed to seeing colleges make students politically more liberal. I have no fundamental objection to that. But some part of that transformation as it is now practiced seems to supply some students with a perverse kind of liberalism: not a principled set of beliefs but a strong desire to give passionate expression to imperfectly understood rages. (There are many unprincipled conservatives as well, of course, but for various reasons colleges produce them in smaller numbers.) The source of this perversion is to be found in the interaction of the tenets of the Enlightenment (skeptical reason, radical individualism, and social progress) with the inclinations of the adolescent temperament (a concern for authenticity, sincerity, and abstract benevolence). In a word, liberal education, badly done, leads young people not to sober Enlightenment but to rootless Romanticism. Colleges always begin with Francis Bacon and Isaac Newton but sometimes end with Jean Jacques Rousseau—and worse, not Rousseau the philosopher but Rousseau the man.

My title will strike many readers as paradoxical, even absurd. Liberalism, far from being the enemy of a liberal education, is widely regarded as being the product of it. For better or worse, the liberal creed has been nurtured and propagated on the college campuses, and although not all students become its disciples, almost all are affected by it, and some dramatically so.

At one level that is all true enough. We know that those who are college educated are the most tolerant of unpopular opinions, are most prepared to endorse measures to advance civil liberties and civil rights, and are least willing to support antidemocratic regimes. Indeed one of the watershed discoveries of political sociologists writing in the 1950s was that democratic values were least secure among the working class and most secure among the college-educated, upper-middle class. That finding was sharply challenged, though never successfully disproved, by those few scholars who retained during the 1950s and the early 1960s the conviction that the upper-middle class was characterized not by civic virtue but by the ambition for power and animated not by democratic values but by economic ones. Yet even those who offered a radical critique of society found their allies and followers not among the workers but among fellow college students and college graduates. Dissent, in this country as in all countries, in this era as in almost all eras, has been chiefly the province of the intelligentsia.

Among the intelligentsia those who have studied the liberal arts—especially the social sciences and the humanities—have displayed the most liberal attitudes. Students of engineering, of applied sciences, and of agriculture are all much more conservative. And as Seymour Martin Lipset has shown, not only do the liberal arts stimulate liberal views, but the most able, distinguished, productive, and (presumably) highest-paid professors of the liberal arts are the most liberal in their orientation. In short, higher education stimulates the liberal impulse, a liberal arts higher education stimulates it even more, and the best (or at least the most expensive and prestigious) liberal arts higher education stimulates it most of all.

How then can I suggest that a liberal education is at all inconsistent with liberalism? I suggest it quite simply by pointing to the fact that within higher education one finds today many but not all of the most serious threats to certain liberal values: the harassment of unpopular views, the use of force to prevent certain persons from speaking, the adoption of quota systems either to reduce the admissions of certain kinds of students or to enhance the admissions of other kinds, and the politicization of the university to make it an arena for the exchange of manifestoes rather than a forum for the discussion of ideas.

The liberal values that have become precarious in the very institution that once defended them are those of civility, free speech, equality of opportunity, and the maintenance of a realm of privacy and intimacy safe from the constant assaults of the political and the societal. These are not, as I shall point out, the only elements of the liberal faith, but they are important ones and they are much in jeopardy. I realize that the vast majority of faculty and students do not approve of acts that jeopardize these values; from time to time they even say quietly that they deplore them; yet the vast majority also have created a communal setting and institutional culture that permits such acts to continue. The imperiled values have not been repudiated so much as they have been subjected to benign neglect.

The evidence that such a state of affairs exists is not as readily available as my confident generalizations might lead one to suppose. For some reason, no organization monitors the state of freedom on the campus, or none has the resources and persistence with which, for example, the American Civil Liberties Union monitors attacks on civil liberties off the campus. But if one works at or visits a major university, one will find the history of that sorry procession of episodes that has produced not mounting horror but wordless acquiescence and weary resignation.

During my adult life I have been part of five institutions: the Catholic church, the University of Redlands, the United States Navy, the University of Chicago, and Harvard University. If I were required to rank them by the extent to which free and uninhibited discussion was possible within them, I am afraid that the Harvard of 1972 would not rank near the top. Since 1969, the list of subjects that cannot be publicly discussed there in a free and open forum has grown steadily and now includes the war in Vietnam, public policy toward urban ghettos, the relationship between intelligence and heredity, and the role of American corporations in certain overseas regimes. To be sure, certain points of view about each of these matters can be, and are, discussed, but a serious discussion of all sides of these issues is risky, if not impossible. To be specific: a spokesman for South Vietnam, a critic of liberal policies toward the ghettos, a scientist who claimed that intelligence is largely inherited, and a corporate executive who denied that his firm was morally responsible for the regime in South Africa have all been harassed and in some cases forcibly denied an opportunity to speak.

Some of those who have not been able to speak at all, or to speak only under mental and social duress, have views I disagree with; others have views I agree with; still others have views that I have not made up my mind about. Regarding the last it is not clear that I am going to have a chance to make up my mind for it is not clear whether the speakers involved are going to feel that the personal costs of public statements are worth the gains in educating me and others.

These problems have not been unique to my university, and their emergence has been frequently deplored. I am not interested here in adding any rhetorical flourishes to this discussion: the matter is too important for either declamation or recrimination. I do wish to dispute, however, the view that because the organized New Left has lost stature and influence of late, the problem has ceased to exist. The tumult has subsided a bit (although as I write the president's office at Harvard is occupied by demonstrators, and the Center for International Affairs was recently sacked) and a mood of business as usual is now displayed by

115

most faculty and students. But a decline in tumult and a return to self-interest are hardly equivalent to a reaffirmation of liberal values or of any other values for that matter. The legacy of the campus flirtation with authoritarian politics is still with us, not in the continuance of militant action but in the absence of democratic convictions. The New Left may have repudiated itself by its extremism, but it also weakened the institution that gave birth to it by casting doubt on the legitimacy of the university and of the principles of free discussion that support it.

My thesis is that the atmosphere that nurtures certain kinds of illiberality is in part a product of liberal education itself. This is not to say that a liberal education teaches disdain for civil liberties or tolerance for violence; quite the contrary. Nor is it to say that only a liberal education contributes to this attitude; certain persons by family origin and the political socialization it provides are more likely to display both liberality and illiberality than others. It is to say that among the consequences of a liberal education is a set of sympathies that lead many, though not all, persons in a university to acquiesce in the uncivil acts of a small minority.

Relevant Definitions

It is time I offered some definitions. By "liberalism" I mean a loose set of values that emphasize the protection of civil liberties, the support of equal political and economic opportunity, the melioration of the lot of the disadvantaged, and the enhancement of the area of personal self-expression. Liberalism, thus defined, is a tendency that both liberalizes and liberates; that is, it calls both for generosity and open-handedness in the treatment of others and for a minimum of restraint or bondage on the actions of one's self. The modern father of liberalism remains John Stuart Mill: as he explained it, the polity should be organized to ensure both the liberty of the citizens and the liberality of the government; the social principle should be the greatest good of the greatest number and the legal principle should be the greatest freedom of an individual consistent with the freedom of others.

A "liberal education" is thought to mean schooling in subjects that broaden one's cultural and historical sensibilities and strengthen one's critical faculties. The purpose of a liberal education is to induct a student, however partially and briefly, into the world of the intellectual. That world in turn places a high value on the exercise of criticism, the display of originality, and the understanding of what is unfamiliar, ancient, distant, and problematic. The application of critical faculties to political and social practices means displaying suspicion toward what is formally and conventionally thought to be true in favor of what the initiated believe is actually and informally true, challenging beliefs about the purposes and legitimacy of institutions, and comparing existing practices with real or imagined alternatives. The critical thrust of liberal arts education is invariably directed against the conventional wisdom, and as new conventions succeed old ones, the process of criticism is repeated ad infinitum. The object is to acquire new and esoteric knowledge to replace popular or conventional opinion. The criteria for what constitutes knowledge are often not clear, being sometimes the outcome of the scientific method and sometimes merely the ability to be original, daring, or shocking. The critical faculties, for example, when applied to American government would emphasize not constitutions but power structures, not public opinion but the social determinants of opinion, not official statements and legal enactments but bureaucratic empire-building and legislative special interests.

The other part of the world of the intellectual is that which enlarges the perceived range of conduct, thought, and opinion by the sympathetic portrayal of what is remote, forgotten, unusual, deprived, obscure, or precarious. This aspect of the intellectual world stresses the development not of criticism but of cosmopolitanism. The variety of aesthetic, political, and cultural experiences is portrayed, and by being portrayed in neutral or even sympathetic tones, that variety is made to seem if not desirable, then at least legitimate. This aspect of liberal education is directed not so much against conventional opinion as against conventional morality, which is to say, against bourgeois morality. We learn from this experience to know and to appreciate the secret worlds and despised habits of those persons who, before we began our liberal education, were beyond our ken or unpalatable to our taste. We are led, for example, to read sympathetically the works of authors and poets who have stood outside the main cultural stream; we are informed of the life and plight of those who have been disadvantaged in the prevailing distribution of political or economic resources; and we encounter the different lifestyles of other tribes, cultures, and epochs.

Now there is obviously a close relationship between liberalism and liberal education. The exercise of the critical spirit requires the maintenance of political and intellectual freedom. An interest in deprived or despised groups leads to a concern for them, and this in turn tends to imply public and political generosity toward them. It is no surprise that liberal arts students and professors should become liberals.

Defense of Liberty

How then can a liberal education ever be the adversary of liberalism? The answer is that while the critical faculty requires the existence of civil

117

liberties, it also erodes the bases of authority and legitimacy of those institutions that define and defend those liberties. Criticism is relentless and accepts no bound; it may prosper when discourse is free and unconstrained, but the price paid for that intellectual prosperity is the unceasing assault on those political and legal practices that have produced such freedom. And in the case of Herbert Marcuse, the critical faculty even comes to doubt the value of the freedom itself. Freedom exists because a certain kind of social order first existed, maintained and defined by laws, governments, and authority. Freedom cannot exist outside some system of order, yet no system of order is immune from intellectual assault.

Intellectual criticism would have bounds if there were a widely accepted principle of authority or theory of human nature on which certain political institutions could rest immune from eroding questions. At various times there have been. Thomas Jefferson believed, or wrote as if he believed, that political and civil liberty were among the natural rights of men. But the concept of natural rights, I need hardly add, has been among the first principles to be criticized, for it implies by its use of the term "natural" that something exists beyond man's invention and thus beyond man's revision. Reinhold Niebuhr offered a different defense of democracy: man's nature is good enough to make it possible but bad enough to make it necessary. Stated differently, we grant civil liberty because we cannot trust anyone to decide the truth. But that notion is no better suited to resist the critical impulse; it also is based on a theory of human nature and thus implies that there are aspects to our lives that are beyond the capacity of society to understand or to alter. Finally, according to the theory of consent, we have freedoms because we have agreed to have them. But if we have agreed to have freedom, we might also agree not to have freedom. Consent is a weak theory of legitimacy, and intellectuals sense it: their own privileges, if granted simply by democratic vote, could be revoked by democratic vote, and from time to time society has been inclined to do just that.

When one presses an intellectual to supply a defense of liberty, it tends to be some variant of a single argument: utility. Liberty is good because it is useful: it enables society to discover the truth or to find by discussion the best policies or the wisest leaders. Under ordinary circumstances that defense is probably good enough: liberty is useful or at least more useful than the alternatives. But in extraordinary times, such as in 1972, the argument is not decisive. Persons who feel strongly that an injustice should be corrected or a condition alleviated are likely to be impatient with, and even actively hostile toward, those who wish to say that the injustice does not exist or the social problem is the fault not of society but of those who display the symptoms. Efforts will be made to silence such persons. The majority will not participate in such efforts, but if they believe the doctrine being silenced is sufficiently odious, they will take no active steps to oppose the censorship. They will be all the more reluctant to oppose it if it is being imposed by members of the community whom they greatly value and on whose esteem they substantially depend.

Here the cosmopolitan aspect of liberal education becomes important. When one has cultivated an especially keen regard for the plight of some group, one is especially reluctant to continue a critical discussion of the merits of the case. The commitment to the object of concern ought to be expressed. The ways in which that priority is stated are familiar enough: "Following rules ought not to interfere with doing what is right," and "It is wrong to prefer form over substance."

A Theory of Benevolence

Let me state in more grandiose terms what I am suggesting. Liberalism, at least as it is conveyed by higher education, is less a theory of justice than a theory of benevolence. By "justice" I roughly mean treating equals equally and by rules known in advance and applicable to all. By "benevolence" I mean a disposition to treat someone in a generous way, to serve his perceived interests and desires. Liberalism imparts a commitment to certain rules and practices that are very much a part of a theory of justice—the rule of law, equality of opportunity, democratic voting—but these rules and practices, being abstract and justified on grounds of utility, cannot easily or for long withstand an aroused sense of benevolence. Benevolence after all is motivated by sentiments of compassion and a belief in the worthiness of some person or group. A natural, or at least easily stimulated, sentiment is usually more powerful than a belief in a rule or practice.

It is sometimes suggested that students are idealists and that this explains much of their political behavior. If the view I have developed here is correct, the word "idealist" is not the proper one, for it implies a concept of an ideal world or the existence of an ideology or an attachment to the importance of ideas. None of these connotations has been in my experience descriptive of the behavior being explained. A more accurate account would stress the fact that students, and young persons generally, have a larger and more active sense of compassion and a more easily aroused instinct of benevolence. The emotions of the young lie close to the surface; they are quickly stimulated and highly volatile. The current style that favors coolness should not blind us to this fact. The best evidence for it is found in the personal relationships that characterized the young: sudden attachments, romantic love, a concern for sincerity and openness. The communal tendencies of students have been far more visible and will probably be far more enduring than their ideological ones.

A liberal education provides a new or enlarged range of objects for those sentiments: the poor, the black, the ancient, the aesthetic, the distant, the natural. And a liberal education supplies a set of reasons for the neglect or disadvantage that these favored objects must bear. Those reasons are, in the most general version, the callousness of spirit, selfishness of interest, and the smallness of mind of society, its governing institutions, and, above all, its dominant class. At least in the modern period a liberal education has tended, with varying degrees of success, to challenge the values of prevailing society and to set students apart from it. What Lionel Trilling has found to be true of modern literature is true of modern education generally:

> Any historian of the literature of the modern age will take virtually for granted the adversary intention, the actual subversive intention, that characterizes modern writing—he will perceive its clear purpose of detaching the reader from the habits of thought and feeling that the larger culture imposes, of giving him a ground and a vantage point from which to judge and condemn, and perhaps revise, the culture that has produced him.

In its extreme form the concern with authenticity as opposed to conventionality leads to a preoccupation with pure emotion, the unconscious, and even the occult and supernatural. "Authenticity," to quote Trilling again, is an object of almost obsessive concern both "as a quality of the personal life and as a criterion of art." In its extreme form this concern may be new, but at root it is as old as man. It once was called "sincerity" or "passion," and it has always characterized the social world of the young. The young are no longer simply a biological category, they are virtually a social class, at least insofar as they are college students, and thus their concerns have become ours.

The personal concern for sincerity, feeling, and authenticity becomes, when displaced onto society, a concern for benevolence and compassion. That this displacement should occur in the way it does is a consequence of modernity; that is, it is a consequence of the fact that we now live in a secular society. Religion and God once served as objects for passion; to a limited degree they may be returning; but in general only society can today supply the extrapersonal object for passion and benevolence. The decline of religion as a focus for emotion has been underway for decades, but it became dramatically evident in the early 1960s. During the 1950s theology emphasized the depravity, corruption, and imperfection of human nature and the consequent need for social restraint and legal authority as a way of preventing political and social fanaticism. But by the 1960s, as Daniel Bell has noted, an astonishing reversal had occurred: God was dead, society rather than man was the problem, social restraint was insufferable, and activism was the only form of purity. Karl Barth, Paul Tillich, and Niebuhr were replaced by Thomas Altizer and Harvey Cox. A secular theology became a fervent ally of political liberalism.

Thus, almost the only source of ultimate value that could maintain a sense of justice against the rush of benevolence gave way. The delicate balance that must be maintained between form and substance, between rule and action, was seriously disturbed. Liberating oneself, and aiding in the liberation of deserving others, became the single end. How this was done was less important than the fact that it was done.

Benevolence and Balance

But benevolence can never be the sole principle of human action. At a superficial level benevolence often tends to be perceived by its objects as busybodyness, even paternalism. At a more profound level benevolence risks rejection or failure: what if those aided do not improve, or if for some reason personal efforts are not followed by institutional commitments? Benevolence, when frustrated, often turns to rage, and those who once celebrated the virtues of compassion may come to indulge sentiments of hatred.

In 1962 an organization of students produced a document that read in part as follows:

> We regard *men* as infinitely precious and possessed of unful-filled capacities for reason, freedom, and love. . . . Men have unrealized potential for self-cultivation, self-direction, self-understanding, and creativity. . . . The goals of men and society should be human independence: a concern with . . . finding a meaning of life that is personally authentic, . . . one which has full, spontaneous access to present and past experiences. *Human relationships* should involve fraternity and honesty.

Within a few years this organization, including many of those who signed this statement at Port Huron, was attacking universities, harassing those who disagreed with them, demanding political obedience, and engaging in deliberate terrorism. Nothing could have been more liberal than the 1962 statement of the Students for a Democratic Society; nothing could have been less liberal than its subsequent history.

For most of us, choices are never this stark. A sense of balance almost always asserts itself so that neither the stern and unyielding principles

121

of justice nor the heedless sense of compassion dominates our actions. A liberal education is at its best when it strikes this balance: when it makes one aware that principles must ultimately be justified by something more than mere utility, that liberty is as worth preserving when it is attacked by a group one admires as it is when assaulted by a group one detests, and that the bonds of civility upon which the maintenance of society depends are more fragile than we often admit.

When properly conducted, there is an inevitable and desirable tension in a liberal education: developing only the critical faculties produces universal skepticism, even about those new worlds of the mind that are discovered in a college, while heightening one's sensibilities and enlarging one's powers of compassion tend to suppress the exercise of criticism. Among the best students and teachers, that tension is evident: they are educated up to that delicate point where they can be neither true believers nor utter skeptics.

And so it should be with liberalism or indeed any other political faith. The commitment to fair rules and procedures often inhibits the solution of certain problems, just as the commitment to social action can subvert the maintenance of those rules. Living with such partially incompatible goals requires ultimately the preservation within oneself of a realm of inner privacy into which neither politics nor society can reach and where quietude and imagination do gentle battle for the loyalty of our spirit.

10

Character and Community: The Problem of Broken Windows

Cities have helped shape the character of millions of immigrants from America's farmland and from foreign shores. Cities have never done this easily or without casualties; life in many parts of New York or Philadelphia in 1900 was as tempestuous and brutalizing as it is in those same places today. But part of the present-day deterioration in the quality of urban life has been caused not only by the familiar economic and social forces shaping our cities but by a change in the legal order and the rules by which that order is enforced. The agencies charged with maintaining public decency and order have been placed under the control of a new doctrine: public coercion may be used only to constrain criminal behavior and may do so only by following carefully defined procedures. This has left them little guidance and no legitimacy as they go about the problem of trying to maintain right standards of conduct in public places when the violation of those standards does not constitute a clear breach of a well-understood criminal statute. My friend George Kelling first called this problem to my attention with research he and others were doing on the use of foot patrol by police in big cities. What follows is the essay we wrote in 1982 to draw out the larger implications of that research.

In the mid-1970s the state of New Jersey announced a safe and clean neighborhoods program designed to improve the quality of community life in twenty-eight cities. As part of that program, the state provided money to help cities take police officers out of their patrol cars and assign them to walking beats. The governor and other state officials were enthusiastic about using foot patrol as a way of cutting crime, but many police chiefs were skeptical. Foot patrol in their eyes had been generally discredited. It reduced the mobility of the police, who thus had difficulty responding to citizen calls for service, and it weakened headquarters control over patrol officers.

Many police officers also disliked foot patrol but for different reasons: it was hard work; it kept them outside on cold, rainy nights; and it reduced their chances for making a good pinch. In some departments, assigning officers to foot patrol had been used as a form of punishment. And academic experts on policing doubted that foot patrol would have any impact on crime rates; it was in the opinion of most little more than a sop to public opinion. But since the state was paying for it, the local authorities were willing to go along.

Five years after the program started, the Police Foundation, in Washington, D.C., published an evaluation of the foot patrol project. Based on its analysis of a carefully controlled experiment carried out chiefly in Newark, the foundation concluded, to the surprise of hardly anyone, that foot patrol had not reduced crime rates. But residents of the foot-patrolled neighborhoods seemed to feel more secure than persons in other areas, tended to believe that crime had been reduced, and seemed to take fewer steps to protect themselves from crime (staying at home with the doors locked, for example). Moreover, citizens in the foot patrol areas had a more favorable opinion of the police than did those living elsewhere. And officers walking beats had higher morale, greater job satisfaction, and a more favorable attitude toward citizens in their neighborhoods than did officers assigned to patrol cars.

These findings may be taken as evidence that the skeptics were right—foot patrol has no effect on crime; it merely fools the citizens into thinking that they are safer. But in our view, and in the view of the authors of the Police Foundation study (of whom Kelling was one), the citizens of Newark were not fooled at all. They knew what the foot patrol officers were doing, they knew it was different from what motorized officers do, and they knew that having officers walk beats did in fact make their neighborhoods safer.

Disorder and Violent Crime

But how can a neighborhood be safer when the crime rate has not gone down—in fact may have gone up? Finding the answer requires first that we understand what most often frightens people in public places. Many citizens of course are primarily frightened by crime, especially crime involving a sudden, violent attack by a stranger. This risk is real, in Newark as in many large cities. But we tend to overlook or forget another source of fear: the fear of being bothered by disorderly people—not violent people nor necessarily criminals but disreputable or obstreperous or unpredictable people: panhandlers, drunks, addicts, rowdy teenagers, prostitutes, loiterers, the mentally disturbed.

Foot patrol officers elevated, to the extent they could, the level of public order in these neighborhoods. Although the neighborhoods were predominantly black and the foot patrolmen were mostly white, this police function of order maintenance was performed to the general satisfaction of both parties.

One of us (Kelling) spent many hours walking with Newark foot-patrol officers to see how they defined "order" and what they did to maintain it. One beat was typical: a busy but dilapidated area in the heart of Newark, with many abandoned buildings, marginal shops (several of which prominently displayed knives and straight-edged razors in their windows), one large department store, and, most important, a train station and several major bus stops. Although the area was run down, its streets were filled with people because it was a major transportation center. The good order of this area was important not only to those who lived and worked there but also to many others who had to move through it on their way home, to supermarkets, or to factories.

The people on the street were primarily black; the officer who walked the street was white. The people were made up of regulars and strangers. Regulars included both decent folk and some drunks and derelicts who were always there but who "knew their place." Strangers were, well, strangers and viewed suspiciously, sometimes apprehensively. The officer—call him Kelly—knew who the regulars were, and they knew him. As he saw his job, he was to keep an eye on strangers and make certain that the disreputable regulars observed some informal but widely understood rules. Drunks and addicts could sit on the stoops but could not lie down. People could drink on side streets but not at the main intersection. Bottles had to be in paper bags. Talking to, bothering, or begging from people waiting at the bus stops was strictly forbidden. If a dispute erupted between a businessman and a customer, the businessman was assumed to be right, especially if the customer was a stranger. If a stranger loitered, Kelly would ask him if he had any means of support and what his business was; if he gave unsatisfactory answers, he was sent on his way. Persons who broke the informal rules, especially those who bothered people waiting at bus stops, were arrested for vagrancy. Noisy teenagers were told to keep quiet.

These rules were defined and enforced in collaboration with the regulars on the street. Another neighborhood might have different rules, but these, everybody understood, were the rules for this neighborhood. If someone violated them, the regulars not only turned to Kelly for help but also ridiculed the violator. Sometimes what Kelly did could be described as enforcing the law, but just as often it involved taking informal or extralegal steps to help protect what the neighborhood had decided was the appropriate level of public order. Some of the things he did probably would not withstand a legal challenge.

A determined skeptic might acknowledge that a skilled foot patrol officer can maintain order but still insist that this sort of order has little to do with the real sources of community fear, that is, with violent crime. To a degree, that is true. But two things must be borne in mind. First, outside observers should not assume that they know how much of the anxiety now endemic in many big-city neighborhoods stems from a fear of real crime and how much from a sense that the street is disorderly, a source of distasteful, worrisome encounters. The people of Newark, to judge from their behavior and their remarks to interviewers, apparently assign a high value to public order and feel relieved and reassured when the police help them maintain that order.

The Theory of Broken Windows

Second, at the community level, disorder and crime are usually linked in a kind of developmental sequence. Social psychologists and police officers tend to agree that if a window in a building is broken and is left unrepaired, the rest of the windows will soon be broken. This is as true in nice neighborhoods as in run-down ones. Window breaking does not necessarily occur on a large scale because some areas are inhabited by determined window breakers whereas others are populated by window lovers; rather one unrepaired broken window is a signal that no one cares, and so breaking more windows costs nothing. (It has always been fun.)

Philip Zimbardo, a Stanford psychologist, reported in 1969 on some experiments testing the broken window theory. He arranged to have an automobile without license plates parked with its hood up on a street in the Bronx and a comparable automobile on a street in Palo Alto, California. The car in the Bronx was attacked by vandals within ten minutes of its abandonment. The first to arrive were a family—father, mother, and young son—who removed the radiator and battery. Within twenty-four hours virtually everything of value had been removed. Then random destruction began: windows were smashed, parts torn off, upholstery ripped. Children began to use the car as a playground. Most of the adult vandals were well-dressed, apparently clean-cut whites. The car in Palo Alto sat untouched for more than a week. Then Zimbardo smashed part of it with a sledgehammer. Soon passersby were joining in. Within a few hours the car had been turned upside down and utterly destroyed. Again the vandals appeared to be primarily respectable whites.

Untended property becomes fair game for people out for fun or plunder and even for people who ordinarily would not dream of doing such things and who probably consider themselves law-abiding. Because of the nature of community life in the Bronx—its anonymity, the frequency with which cars are abandoned and things are stolen or broken, the past experience of no one caring—vandalism begins much more quickly than it does in staid Palo Alto, where people have come to believe that private possessions are cared for and that mischievous behavior is costly. But vandalism can occur anywhere once communal barriers—the sense of mutual regard and the obligations of civility—are lowered by actions that seem to signal that no one cares.

We suggest that untended behavior also leads to the breakdown of community controls. A stable neighborhood of families who care for their homes, mind each other's children, and confidently frown on unwanted intruders can change in a few years or even a few months to an inhospitable and frightening jungle. A piece of property is abandoned, weeds grow up, a window is smashed. Adults stop scolding rowdy children; the children, emboldened, become more rowdy. Families move out; unattached adults move in. Teenagers gather in front of the corner store. The merchant asks them to move; they refuse. Fights occur. Litter accumulates. People start drinking in front of the grocery; in time an inebriate slumps to the sidewalk and is allowed to sleep it off. Pedestrians are approached by panhandlers.

At this point it is not inevitable that serious crime will flourish or violent attacks on strangers will occur. But many residents will think that crime, especially violent crime, is on the rise, and they will modify their behavior accordingly. They will use the streets less often and when on the streets will stay apart from their fellows, moving with averted eyes, silent lips, and hurried steps: "don't get involved." For some residents this growing atomization will matter little because the neighborhood is not their home but the place where they live. Their interests are elsewhere; they are cosmopolitans. But it will matter greatly to other people whose lives derive meaning and satisfaction from local attachments rather than worldly involvement; for them the neighborhood will cease to exist except for a few reliable friends whom they arrange to meet.

Such an area is vulnerable to criminal invasion. Although it is not inevitable, it is more likely that here, rather than in places where people are confident they can regulate public behavior by informal controls, drugs will change hands, prostitutes will solicit, and cars will be stripped. The drunks will be robbed by boys who do it as a lark, and the prostitutes' customers will be robbed by men who do it purposefully and perhaps violently. Muggings will occur.

Among those who often find it difficult to move away from this are the elderly. Surveys of citizens suggest that the elderly are much less likely to be the victims of crime than younger persons, and some have inferred from this that the well-known fear of crime voiced by the elderly is an exaggeration: perhaps we ought not to design special programs to protect older persons; perhaps we should even try to talk them out of their mistaken fears. This argument misses the point. The prospect of a confrontation with an obstreperous teenager or a drunken panhandler can be as fear inducing for defenseless persons as the prospect of meeting an actual robber; indeed to a defenseless person the two kinds of confrontation are often indistinguishable. Moreover, the lower rate at which the elderly are victimized is a measure of the steps they have already taken—chiefly, staying behind locked doors—to minimize the risks they face. Young men are more frequently attacked than older women, not because they are easier or more lucrative targets but because they are on the streets more.

Nor is the connection between disorderliness and fear made only by the elderly. Susan Estrich, of the Harvard Law School, has recently gathered a number of surveys on the sources of public fear. One, done in Portland, Oregon, indicated that three-fourths of the adults interviewed cross to the other side of a street when they see a gang of teenagers; another survey, in Baltimore, discovered that nearly half would cross the street to avoid even a single strange youth. When an interviewer asked people in a housing project where the most dangerous spot was, they mentioned a place where young persons gathered to drink and play music, despite the fact that not a single crime had occurred there. In Boston public housing projects, the greatest fear was expressed by persons living in the buildings where disorderliness and incivility, not crime, were the greatest. Knowing this helps one understand the significance of such otherwise harmless displays as subway graffiti. As Nathan Glazer has written, the proliferation of graffiti, even when not obscene, confronts the subway rider with the "inescapable knowledge that the environment he must endure for an hour or more a day is uncontrolled and uncontrollable, and that anyone can invade it to do whatever damage and mischief the mind suggests."

In response to fear, people avoid one another and weaken controls. Sometimes they call the police. Patrol cars arrive, an occasional arrest occurs, but crime continues and disorder is not abated. Citizens complain to the police chief, but he explains that his department is low on personnel and that the courts do not punish petty or first-time offenders. To the residents the police who arrive in squad cars are either ineffective or uncaring; to the police the residents are animals who deserve each other. The citizens may soon stop calling the police because they cannot do anything.

Changes in Mobility and Policing

The process we call urban decay has occurred for centuries in every city. But what is happening today is different in at least two important respects. First, in the period before, say, World War II, city dwellers—because of money costs, transportation difficulties, familial and church connections—could rarely move away from neighborhood problems. When movement did occur, it tended to be along public transit routes. Now mobility has become exceptionally easy for all but the poorest or those who are blocked by racial prejudice. Earlier crime waves had a kind of built-in self-correcting mechanism: the determination of a neighborhood or community to reassert control over its turf. Areas in Chicago, New York, and Boston would experience crime and gang wars, and then normalcy would return as the families for whom no alternative residences were possible reclaimed their authority over the streets.

Second, the police in this earlier period assisted in that reassertion of authority by acting, sometimes violently, on behalf of the community. Young toughs were roughed up, people were arrested on suspicion or for vagrancy, and prostitutes and petty thieves were routed. Rights were something enjoyed by decent folk, and perhaps also by the serious professional criminal, who avoided violence and could afford a lawyer.

This pattern of policing was not an aberration or the result of occasional excess. From the earliest days of the nation, the police function was seen primarily as that of a night watchman: to maintain order against the chief threats to order—fire, wild animals, and disreputable behavior. Solving crimes was viewed not as a police responsibility but as a private one. In the March 1969 *Atlantic*, one of us (Wilson) wrote a brief account of how the police role had slowly changed from maintaining order to fighting crimes. The change began with the creation of private detectives (often ex-criminals), who worked on a contingency fee basis for individuals who had suffered losses. In time the detectives were absorbed into municipal police agencies and paid a regular salary; simultaneously the responsibility for prosecuting thieves was shifted from the aggrieved private citizen to the professional prosecutor. This process was not complete in most places until the twentieth century.

In the 1960s, when urban riots were a major problem, social scientists began to explore carefully the order maintenance function of the police and to suggest ways of improving it—not to make streets safer (its original function) but to reduce the incidence of mass violence. Order maintenance became to a degree coterminous with community relations. But as the crime wave that began in the early 1960s continued without abatement throughout the decade and into the 1970s, attention shifted to the role of the police as crime fighters. Studies of police behavior ceased by and large to be accounts of the order maintenance function and became instead efforts to propose and test ways whereby the police could solve more crimes, make more arrests, and gather better evidence. If these things could be done, social scientists assumed, citizens would be less fearful.

Order and Crime Prevention

A great deal was accomplished during this transition, as both police chiefs and outside experts emphasized the crime-fighting function in their plans, in the allocation of resources, and in deployment of personnel. The police may well have become better crime fighters as a result. And doubtless they remained aware of their responsibility for order. But the link between order maintenance and crime prevention, so obvious to earlier generations, was forgotten.

That link is similar to the process whereby one broken window becomes many. The citizen who fears the ill-smelling drunk, the rowdy teenager, or the importuning beggar is not merely expressing his distaste for unseemly behavior; he is also giving voice to a bit of folk wisdom that happens to be a correct generalization: namely, that serious street crime flourishes in areas in which disorderly behavior goes unchecked. The unchecked panhandler is in effect the first broken window. Muggers and robbers, whether opportunistic or professional, believe they reduce their chances of being caught or even identified if they operate on streets where potential victims are already intimidated by prevailing conditions. If the neighborhood cannot keep a bothersome panhandler from annoying passersby, the thief may reason, it is even less likely to call the police to identify a potential mugger or to interfere if the mugging actually takes place.

Some police administrators concede that this process occurs but argue that motorized patrol officers can deal with it as effectively as foot patrol officers. We are not so sure. In theory an officer in a squad car can observe as much as an officer on foot; in theory the former can talk to as many people as the latter. But the reality of police-citizen encounters is powerfully altered by the automobile. An officer on foot cannot separate himself from the street people; if he is approached, only his uniform and his personality can help him manage whatever is about to happen. And he can never be certain what that will be: a request for directions, a plea for help, an angry denunciation, a teasing remark, a confused babble, a threatening gesture.

In a car an officer is more likely to deal with street people by rolling down the window and looking at them. The door and the window exclude the approaching citizen; they are a barrier. Some officers take advantage of this barrier, perhaps unconsciously, by acting differently if in the car than they would on foot. We have seen this countless times. The police car pulls up to a corner where teenagers are gathered. The window is rolled down. The officer stares at the youths. They stare back. The officer says to one, "C'mere." He saunters over, conveying to his friends by his elaborately casual style the idea he is not intimidated by authority. "What's your name?" "Chuck." "Chuck who?" "Chuck Jones." "What'ya doing, Chuck?" "Nothin'." "Got a P.O. [parole officer]?" "Nah." "Sure?" "Yeah." "Stay out of trouble, Chuckie." Meanwhile, the other boys laugh and exchange comments among themselves, probably at the officer's expense. The officer stares harder. He cannot be certain what is being said, nor can he join in and, by displaying his own skill at street banter, prove that he cannot be put down. In the process the officer has learned almost nothing, and the boys have decided the officer is an alien force who can safely be disregarded, even mocked.

Our experience is that most citizens like to talk to a police officer. Such exchanges give them a sense of importance, provide them with the basis for gossip, and allow them to explain to the authorities what is worrying them (whereby they gain a modest but significant sense of having done something about the problem). You approach a person on foot more easily, and talk to him more readily, than you do a person in a car. Moreover you can more easily retain some anonymity if you draw an officer aside for a private chat. Suppose you want to pass on a tip about who is stealing handbags or who offered to sell you a stolen TV. In the inner city the culprit in all likelihood lives nearby. To walk up to a marked patrol car and lean in the window is to convey a visible signal that you are a fink.

The essence of the police role in maintaining order is to reinforce the informal control mechanisms of the community itself. The police cannot, without committing extraordinary resources, provide a substitute for that informal control. Conversely, to reinforce those natural forces the police must accommodate them. And therein lies the problem.

Whose Rules?

Should police activity on the street be shaped in important ways by the standards of the neighborhood rather than by the rules of the state? During the 1960s and 1970s, the shift of police from order maintenance to law enforcement has brought them increasingly under the influence of legal restrictions, provoked by media complaints and enforced by court decisions and departmental orders. As a consequence, the order maintenance functions of the police are now governed by rules developed to control police relations with suspected criminals. This is an entirely new development. For centuries the role of the police as watchmen was judged primarily not in terms of its complying with appropriate procedures but rather in terms of its attaining a desired objective. The objective was order, an inherently ambiguous term but a condition that people in a given community recognized when they saw it. The means were the same as those the community itself would employ, if its members were sufficiently determined, courageous, and authoritative. Detecting and apprehending criminals, by contrast, was a means to an end, not an end in itself; a judicial determination of guilt or innocence was the hoped-for result of the law enforcement mode. From the first, the police were expected to follow rules defining that process, although states differed in how stringent the rules should be. The criminal apprehension process was always understood to involve individual rights, the violation of which was unacceptable because it meant that the violating officer would be acting as a judge and jury—and that was not his job. Guilt or innocence was to be determined by universal standards under special procedures.

Ordinarily, no judge or jury ever sees the persons caught up in a dispute over the appropriate level of neighborhood order. That is true not only because most cases are handled informally on the street but also because no universal standards are available to settle arguments over disorder, and thus a judge may not be any wiser or more effective than a police officer. Until the early 1980s in many states, and even today in some places, the police make arrests on such charges as suspicious person or vagrancy or public drunkenness—charges with scarcely any legal meaning. These charges exist not because society wants judges to punish vagrants or drunks but because it wants an officer to have the legal tools to remove undesirable persons from a neighborhood when informal efforts to preserve order in the streets have failed.

Once we begin to think of all aspects of police work as involving the application of universal rules under special procedures, we inevitably ask what constitutes an undesirable person and why we should criminalize vagrancy or drunkenness. A strong and commendable desire to see that people are treated fairly makes us worry about allowing the police to rout persons who are undesirable by some vague or parochial standard. A growing and not-so-commendable utilitarianism leads us to doubt that any behavior that does not "hurt" another person should be made illegal. And thus many of us who watch over the police are reluctant to allow them to perform, in the only way they can, a function that every neighborhood desperately wants them to perform.

This wish to decriminalize disreputable behavior that "harms no one"—and thus remove the ultimate sanction the police can employ to maintain neighborhood order—is a mistake. Arresting a single drunk or a single vagrant who has harmed no identifiable person seems unjust, and in a sense it is. But failing to do anything about a score of drunks or a hundred vagrants may destroy an entire community. A particular rule that seems to make sense in the individual case makes no sense when it is made a universal rule and applied to all cases. It makes no sense because it fails to take into account the connection between one broken window left untended and a thousand broken windows. Of course agencies other than the police could attend to the problems posed by drunks or the mentally ill, but in most communities—especially where the deinstitutionalization movement has been strong—they do not.

The concern about equity is more serious. We might agree that certain behavior makes one person more undesirable than another, but how do we ensure that age or skin color or national origin or harmless mannerisms will not also become the basis for distinguishing the undesirable from the desirable? How do we ensure in short that the police do not become the agents of neighborhood bigotry?

We can offer no wholly satisfactory answer to this important question. We are not confident that there is a satisfactory answer except to hope that by their selection, training, and supervision, the police will be inculcated with a clear sense of the outer limit of their discretionary authority. That limit roughly is this: the police exist to help regulate behavior, not to maintain the racial or ethnic purity of a neighborhood.

Consider the case of the Robert Taylor Homes in Chicago, one of the largest public housing projects in the country. It is home for nearly 20,000 people, all black, and extends over ninety-two acres along South State Street. It was named after a distinguished black who had been chairman of the Chicago Housing Authority during the 1940s. Not long after it opened, in 1962, relations between project residents and the police deteriorated badly. The citizens felt that the police were insensitive or brutal; the police in turn complained of unprovoked attacks on them. Some Chicago officers tell of times when they were afraid to enter the Homes. Crime rates soared.

In the early 1980s the atmosphere has changed. Police-citizen relations have improved—apparently both sides learned something from the earlier experience. A boy stole a purse and ran off. Several young persons who saw the theft voluntarily passed along to the police information on the identity and residence of the thief, and they did this publicly, with friends and neighbors looking on. But problems persist, chief among them the presence of youth gangs that terrorize residents and recruit members in the project. The people expect the police to do something about this, and the police are determined to do just that.

But do what? Although the police can obviously make arrests whenever a gang member breaks the law, a gang can form, recruit, and congregate without breaking the law. And only a tiny fraction of gang-related crimes can be solved by an arrest; thus, if an arrest is the only recourse for the police, the residents' fears will go unassuaged. The police will soon feel helpless, and the residents will again believe that the police do nothing. What the police in fact do is to chase known gang

133

members out of the project. In the words of one officer, "We kick ass." Project residents both know and approve of this. The tacit police-citizen alliance in the project is reinforced by the police view that the cops and the gangs are the two rival sources of power in the area and that the gangs are not going to win.

None of this is easily reconciled with any conception of due process or fair treatment. Since both residents and gang members are black, race is not a factor. But it could be. Suppose a white project confronted a black gang or vice versa. We would be apprehensive about the police taking sides. But the substantive problem remains the same: how can the police strengthen the informal social control mechanisms of natural communities in order to minimize fear in public places? Law enforcement per se is no answer. A gang can weaken or destroy a community by standing about in a menacing fashion and speaking rudely to passersby without breaking the law.

The Individual or the Community?

We have difficulty thinking about such matters not simply because the ethical and legal issues are so complex but because we have become accustomed to thinking of the law in essentially individualistic terms. The law defines *my* rights, punishes *his* behavior, and is applied by *that* officer because of *this* harm. We assume in thinking this way that what is good for the individual will be good for the community, and what does not matter when it happens to one person will not matter if it happens to many. Ordinarily those are plausible assumptions. But in cases where behavior that is tolerable to one person is intolerable to many others, the reactions of the others—fear, withdrawal, flight—may ultimately make matters worse for everyone, including the individual who first professed indifference.

It may be their greater sensitivity to communal as opposed to individual needs that helps explain why the residents of small communities are more satisfied with their police than are the residents of similar neighborhoods in big cities. Elinor Ostrom and her coworkers at Indiana University compared the perception of police services in two poor, all-black Illinois towns—Phoenix and East Chicago Heights—with those of three comparable all-black neighborhoods in Chicago. The level of criminal victimization and the quality of police-community relations appeared to be about the same in the towns and the Chicago neighborhoods. But the citizens living in villages were much more likely than those living in the Chicago neighborhoods to say that they do not stay at home for fear of crime, to agree that the local police have "the right to take any action necessary" to deal with problems, and to agree that the police "look out for the needs of the average citizen." It is possible that the residents and the police of the small towns saw themselves as engaged in a collaborative effort to maintain a certain standard of communal life, whereas those of the big city felt themselves to be simply requesting and supplying particular services on an individual basis.

If this is true, how should a wise police chief deploy his meager forces? The first answer is that nobody knows for certain, and the most prudent course of action would be to try further variations on the Newark experiment, to see more precisely what works in what kinds of neighborhoods. The second answer is also a hedge—many aspects of order maintenance in neighborhoods can probably best be handled in ways that involve the police minimally, if at all. A busy, bustling shopping center and a quiet, well-tended suburb may need almost no visible police presence. In both cases the ratio of respectable to disreputable people is ordinarily so high as to make informal social control effective.

Even in areas that are in jeopardy from disorderly elements, citizen action without substantial police involvement may be sufficient. Meetings between teenagers who like to hang out on a particular corner and adults who want to use that corner might well lead to amicable agreement on a set of rules about how many people can be allowed to congregate, where, and when.

Where no understanding is possible—or possible, but not observed—citizen patrols may be a sufficient response. There are two traditions of communal involvement in maintaining order. One, that of the community watchmen, is as old as the first settlement of the New World. Until well into the nineteenth century, volunteer watchmen, not policemen, patrolled their communities to keep order. They did so by and large without taking the law into their own hands—without, that is, punishing persons or using force. Their presence deterred disorder or alerted the community to disorder that could not be deterred. There are hundreds of such efforts today in communities all across the nation. Perhaps the best known is that of the Guardian Angels, a group of unarmed young persons in distinctive berets and T-shirts who first came to public attention when they began patrolling the New York City subways but who claim now to have chapters in more than thirty American cities. Unfortunately, we have little information about the effect of these groups on crime. It is possible, however, that whatever their effect on crime, citizens find their presence reassuring and that they thus contribute to maintaining a sense of order and civility.

The second tradition is that of the vigilante. Rarely a feature of the settled communities of the East, it was primarily found in those frontier towns that grew up in advance of the reach of government. More than

350 vigilante groups are known to have existed; their distinctive feature was that their members did take the law into their own hands, by acting as judge, jury, and often executioner as well as policeman. Today the vigilante movement is conspicuous by its rarity, despite the great fear expressed by citizens that the older cities are becoming urban frontiers. But some community watchmen groups have skirted the line, and others may cross it in the future. An ambiguous case, reported in the *Wall Street Journal*, involved a citizens' patrol in the Silver Lake area of Belleville, New Jersey. A leader told the reporter, "We look for outsiders." If a few teenagers from outside the neighborhood enter it, "we ask them their business," he said. "If they say they're going down the street to see Mrs. Jones, fine, we let them pass. But then we follow them down the block to make sure they're really going to see Mrs. Jones."

Police as the Key

Although citizens can do a great deal, the police are plainly the key to order maintenance. For one thing, many communities, such as the Robert Taylor Homes, cannot do the job by themselves. For another, no citizen in a neighborhood, even an organized one, is likely to feel the sense of responsibility that wearing a badge confers. Psychologists have done many studies on why people fail to go to the aid of persons being attacked or seeking help, and they have learned that the cause is not apathy or selfishness but the absence of some plausible grounds for feeling that one must personally accept responsibility. Ironically, avoiding responsibility is easier when a lot of people are standing about. On streets and in public places, where order is so important, many people are likely to be around, a fact that reduces the chance of any one person's acting as the agent of the community. The police officer's uniform singles him out as a person who must accept responsibility if asked. In addition, officers, more easily than their fellow citizens, can be expected to distinguish between what is necessary to protect the safety of the street and what merely protects its ethnic purity.

But the police forces of America are losing, not gaining, members. Some cities have suffered substantial cuts in the number of officers available for duty. These cuts are not likely to be reversed in the near future. Therefore, each department must assign its existing officers with great care. Some neighborhoods are so demoralized and crime-ridden as to make foot patrol useless; the best the police can do with limited resources is respond to the enormous number of calls for service. Other neighborhoods are so stable and serene as to make foot patrol unnecessary. The key is to identify neighborhoods at the tipping point: where the public order is deteriorating but not unreclaimable, where the streets are used frequently but by apprehensive people, where a window is likely to be broken at any time and must quickly be fixed if all are not to be shattered.

Most police departments do not have ways of systematically identifying such areas and assigning officers to them. Officers are assigned on the basis of crime rates (meaning that marginally threatened areas are often stripped so that police can investigate crimes in areas where the situation is hopeless) or on the basis of calls for service (despite the fact that most citizens do not call the police when they are merely frightened or annoyed). To allocate patrol wisely, the department must look at the neighborhoods and decide, from firsthand evidence, where an additional officer will make the greatest difference in promoting a sense of safety.

One way to stretch limited police resources is being tried in some public housing projects. Tenant organizations hire off-duty police officers for patrol work in their buildings. The costs are not high (at least not per resident), the officer likes the additional income, and the residents feel safer. Such arrangements are probably more successful than hiring private watchmen, and the Newark experiment helps us understand why. A private security guard may deter crime or misconduct by his presence, and he may go to the aid of persons needing help, but he may well not intervene—that is, control or drive away—someone challenging community standards. Being a sworn officer—a real cop—seems to give one the confidence, the sense of duty, and the aura of authority necessary to perform this difficult task.

Patrol officers might be encouraged to go to and from duty stations on public transportation and, while on the bus or subway car, to enforce rules about smoking, drinking, disorderly conduct, and the like. The enforcement need involve nothing more than ejecting the offender (the offense after all is not one with which a booking officer or a judge wishes to be bothered). Perhaps the random but relentless maintenance of standards on buses would lead to conditions on buses that approximate the level of civility we now take for granted on airplanes.

But the most important requirement is to think that maintaining order in precarious situations is a vital job. The police know this is one of their functions, and they also believe correctly that it cannot be done to the exclusion of criminal investigation and responding to calls. We may have encouraged them to suppose, however, on the basis of our oft-repeated concerns about serious, violent crime, that they will be judged exclusively on their capacity as crime fighters. To the extent that this is the case, police administrators will continue to concentrate police personnel in the highest crime areas (though not necessarily in the areas most vulnerable to criminal invasion), emphasize their training in the law and criminal apprehension (and not their training in managing street life), and join too quickly in campaigns to decriminalize harmless behavior (although public drunkenness, street prostitution, and pornographic displays can destroy a community more quickly than any team of professional burglars).

Above all, we must return to our long-abandoned view that the police ought to protect communities as well as individuals. Our crime statistics and victimization surveys measure personal losses, but they do not measure communal losses. Just as physicians now recognize the importance of fostering health rather than simply treating illness, so the police—and the rest of us—ought to recognize the importance of maintaining, intact, communities without broken windows.

11

The Enduring Problem of Business Ethics

To some capitalism is morally neutral; to others it is morally corrupting; to a few it can in small measure improve human character by its tendency to soften crude manners and lengthen short time horizons. Albert Hirschman has brilliantly reviewed the high moral hopes of some men in the eighteenth century for interests as opposed to passions. With this dispute in mind I organized a course called "The Morality of Capitalism." Some of my colleagues looked at me as if I were teaching one on "Squaring the Circle" or "Building a Perpetual Motion Machine." Yet the intellectual founder of capitalism, Adam Smith, was first and foremost a moral philosopher, and throughout The Wealth of Nations *he pondered—rather bleakly in fact—the tendency of an efficient economic system to produce politically or morally undesirable behavior. There is no better way to understand the moral risks and opportunities in capitalism than to return to the words of its first expositor.*

The fundamental ethical question to be asked of any economic system is whether, taken as a whole and over the long term, it will encourage or discourage good conduct.[1] We can imagine a system that efficiently makes many people wealthy but in a way, or with such other consequences, that we would find repugnant. Critics of capitalism of course believe that Adam Smith created just such a system. John Ruskin felt that in *An Inquiry into the Nature and Causes of the Wealth of Nations* Smith had defended a system of organized greed, perpetuating the blasphemy that "thou shalt hate the Lord thy God, damn His laws, and covet thy neighbour's goods."[2] Stripped of the ecclesiastical language, that is the view of many critics today. One can detect echoes of this sentiment in many contemporary attacks on corporate ethics. It is not by accident, these critics say, that corporations do bad things; it is in the nature of corporations linked by market exchanges to do bad things as a matter of

139

course. To such critics, "business ethics" is an oxymoron, akin to "young Republican" or "military justice."

Many admirers of Smith think that he devised an argument for an economic system that has no inherent tendencies; it is neither moral nor immoral but amoral. Capitalism is marvelously efficient in organizing production and distribution but is indifferent to moral questions. Morality is the province of theology, politics, and the law; it is the task of the custodians of these other provinces to devise and enforce legal norms. Capitalists will always seek to minimize costs; if breaking the law is costly, law-breaking will be minimized as surely as is malingering. It would be absurd to think that business people have any special moral obligations beyond those dictated by self-interest. After all, did not Smith himself write at one point that "society may subsist among different men, as among different merchants, from a sense of its own utility, without any mutual love or affection; . . . it may still be upheld by a mercenary exchange of good offices according to an agreed valuation."[3]

The Wealth of Nations

The Wealth of Nations, published in 1776, was truly a revolutionary book, even more revolutionary than the American Declaration of Independence, which was written the same year. The best-known phrase from that book refers to the invisible hand. It bears repeating:

> Every individual . . . neither intends to promote the public interest, nor knows how much he is promoting it. . . . [B]y directing [his] industry in such a manner as its produce may be of the greatest value, he intends only his own gain, and he is in this, as in many other cases, led by an invisible hand to promote an end which was no part of his intention. Nor is it always the worse for society that it was no part of it. By pursuing his own interest he frequently promotes that of society more effectually than when he really intends to promote it. I have never known much good done by those who affected to trade for the public good. It is an affectation, indeed, not very common among merchants, and very few words need be employed in dissuading them from it.[4]

This is the phrase that defenders of capitalism cite to support their view that the economic system runs best without government intervention and that critics of capitalism quote to support their view that capitalism embodies only individual selfishness. Smith would surely have agreed with the defenders, but would he also have agreed with the critics?

The general view is that *The Wealth of Nations* is purely a work of economics. That is not quite true. Smith concludes his discussion of various economic systems in book 4 with the statement that the "system of natural liberty" will accelerate the progress of society toward "real wealth and greatness," but he adds that this system, which leaves every man free to pursue his own interest, must operate within "the laws of justice."[5] One of the duties of the sovereign is to administer those laws. A careless reader might think that the parts of book 5 in which Smith discusses that duty are concerned only with the administration of justice in the conventional sense, for example, the prevention of fraud and theft. That is indeed the tone of the book, but in places Smith touches on a more profound issue, namely, the relationship between political economy and human character.[6] The tendency of some readers to overlook these brief passages is probably reinforced by the dislike Smith expresses for the tendency of the common people to join austere religious sects, the morals of which have "frequently been rather disagreeably rigorous and unsocial."[7]

The defenders of Smith and of capitalism argue that the apparently amoral quality of *The Wealth of Nations* is no defect, for not only did he clearly set forth the essentials of a productive economy—prices set by voluntary market transactions so as to take full advantage of the division of labor—he did so to show how mankind could be lifted out of poverty. Capitalism may not depend on morality for its operations, but it leads to a profoundly moral outcome.

The first page of the introduction states the great puzzle that Smith set out to solve: among savage nations made up of hunters and fishermen, every man is employed, and the differences in wealth are not great, but most people are poor. In civilized nations, by contrast, many people do not work at all, there are great inequalities in wealth and income, but few people, provided they are industrious and frugal, live in poverty.[8] The magnificent accomplishment of *The Wealth of Nations* was to explain how mankind could be lifted out of poverty provided we were willing to accept a "system of natural liberty,"[9] one consequence of which would be inequality in wealth.

But if capitalism (which is our term—not Smith's) were to have this happy outcome, it would require that people participating in it possess certain traits that if not exactly moral in character, were closely related to morality. For the invisible hand to work, many people would have to save and invest, thereby postponing the pleasures of immediate consumption: "Capitals are increased by parsimony, and diminished by prodigality and misconduct."[10] This prodigality results, Smith argued, from "the passion for present enjoyment."[11] Here he seems to anticipate Max Weber's argument a century later that capitalism requires a long time horizon that is exemplified by the Protestant ethic.[12] But Smith, unlike Weber, says next to nothing about the sources of frugality; he seems to assume that it would naturally occur among enough people to compensate for the inevitable prodigality of others.[13] Perhaps to an eighteenth-century Scotsman, thriftiness and the propensity to save seemed natural, but they hardly seem inevitable to us today.

Even many defenders of capitalism have come away from its bible wondering whether the world it portrays could actually exist. Would people linked to one another solely by the process of commercial exchange be capable of producing a society sufficiently decent that it would be tolerable to its creators? If man is motivated chiefly or solely by a desire to "truck, barter, and exchange,"[14] and if he deals with his fellow man solely by appeals to his self-interest,[15] is it possible we will have anything but a kind of commercial war of all against all in which sharp dealing and a lust for immediate advantage take precedence over every other consideration? Although Smith certainly believed that capitalism produces a more just (though certainly not unblemished) outcome than any other economic system, and although there are hints here and there that he may have felt that capitalism required a certain virtue in the people, we can understand what he might have said about business ethics only if we first examine another book he wrote, this one an effort to explain how men acquire morality.

The Theory of Moral Sentiments

The Theory of Moral Sentiments was published seventeen years before The Wealth of Nations appeared. Whereas Wealth is about self-regarding behavior, Sentiments emphasizes other-regarding behavior. The central process in the former is exchange, the central one in the latter is sympathy. Again Smith announces his intention in the first sentences: no matter how selfish man may appear to be, "there are evidently some principles in his nature, which interest him in the fortune of others, and render their happiness necessary to him, though he derives nothing from it except the pleasure of seeing it."[16]

Smith explains that we acquire sympathy for the distress of others naturally, by imagining "what we ourselves should feel in the like situation."[17] Morality does not arise out of any innate moral sense or as a consequence of divine instruction but out of the process of growing up and living in the company of others. Of course we may merely pretend to feel sorrow for the grief of others or joy for the joy of others, all the while hoping to ingratiate ourselves with these people for our own advantage. This happens, but it is not the main story, because most of us feel sympathy for people (such as newborn infants) and animals (such as an injured cat) that do not reciprocate our feelings and cannot do anything for us.

These feelings of sympathy are not mere emotions but become guides to our own action. We feel sympathy for others when they suffer through no fault of their own; we take pleasure in the joys of others when that joy seems fully deserved. If a miser is miserable because he has not gained all the wealth he wishes to have, we have no sympathy for his misery. If an author is happy because of the applause he has received for writings that he has plagiarized, we do not share his happiness. All men desire praise, but by observing the emotions of others and evaluating the motives of those emotions, we come to distinguish between praise and praiseworthiness.[18]

As we judge others, so we notice that they judge us. We feel sympathy for others when their sorrow is unmerited; we come therefore to expect sympathy from others when we also suffer unjustly. If we withhold praise when it is not deserved, we expect others to withhold praise from us when it is not deserved.

Out of this social relation there arises conscience, which Smith calls the "impartial spectator."[19] The impartial spectator is a disinterested inner voice, "the great inmate of the breast,"[20] that judges our actions as we judge the actions of others. The impartial spectator is the lasting residue of our disinterested judgments of others, a kind of inner person who recalls—and regularly reminds us of—how we have judged the behavior of others. We do not always listen to that inner voice, but we do in our calmer moments, and if we have ignored that voice during our rages and frenzies, we usually feel guilty afterward as we reflect on how it has judged us.

Like Aristotle, Smith believed that man was by nature a social animal, not only meant to live in society but inconceivable apart from society. His great contribution was to explain how society teaches us morality. Though in the first instance that teaching may depend on our self-interest—for example, our desire to be praised and re-warded—in its full course that teaching does not rely for its lasting effect on personal advantage. The proof that morality, and not merely utility, truly lies at the root of our humanity can be found by looking at the most obvious features of human life. We marry, we have children, we care for those children despite the inconvenience and occasional ingratitude we experience. No rationally self-interested man would conclude that marriage was the most cost-effective way to obtain companionship or sexual favors; no rationally self-interested woman would think that the rare and dubious pleasures of conversing with a thirteen-year-old were worth the twelve years of nursing, cleaning, feeding, and controlling that must be invested in the production of such a person. Families and children are the result not of utility but of sentiment.

In short the Adam Smith who invented capitalism, described the useful effects of the invisible hand, and showed how the free pursuit of self-interest would lead to greater prosperity than any system of state-controlled exchanges was also the Adam Smith who, more deeply than anyone since, explored the sources and power of human sympathy and the relationship between sympathy and justice.

Some scholars find the contrast between the two books—one emphasizing sympathy, the other self-interest—so great as to constitute a contradiction. I will not enter into the debate over the so-called Adam Smith problem except indirectly. What I wish to explore instead is how Smith, given what he said about both economics and society, would have seen the ethical problems that business would face.

Ethical Problems of Capitalism

He saw five moral problems raised by capitalism. First, the affluence that it produces impoverishes the spirit of those who produce it. The division of labor means that those who do the labor are in an efficient economy "confined to a very few simple operations." Since the minds of most men are formed by their ordinary employment, the men who spend their whole lives doing one or two repetitive tasks will find their minds atrophying. These men will become "as stupid and ignorant as it is possible for a human creature to become."[21] Smith here anticipated the character portrayed by Charlie Chaplin in *Modern Times*—the man tending one bolt on one cog on one wheel for so long that in time he becomes a cog on the wheel. Society, unless it acts to prevent this, will pay a high price for the mechanization of the human spirit: man will become incapable "of conceiving any generous, noble, or tender sentiment, and consequently of forming any just judgment concerning many even of the ordinary duties of private life."[22] He will lack any conception of the public interest and be incapable of defending the nation in war.

Second, affluence creates cities, and these cities afford meeting places for merchants who wish to conspire together to fix prices and restrain competition. Rural folk, dispersed in distant places, cannot easily combine together,[23] but urban businessmen can readily do so.

> People of the same trade seldom meet together, even for merriment and diversion, but the conversation ends in a conspiracy against the public, or in some contrivance to raise prices. It is impossible indeed to prevent such meetings, by any law which either could be executed, or would be consistent with liberty and justice.[24]

Third, the privileges and the admiration enjoyed by the rich and famous weaken their commitment to virtue. "In the middling and inferior stations of life," Smith writes, "the road to virtue and that to fortune ... are, happily, in most cases, very nearly the same." The success of such people—what we would call the middle and the working classes—"depends upon the favour and good opinion of their neighbours and equals; and without a tolerably regular conduct these can very seldom be obtained."[25] But among the rich and famous the road to success and that to virtue often diverge. In these circles success often depends not on having a good reputation but on flattery and falsehood. Because these people are admired, they set fashion; people seeking to enter the ranks of the fashionable imitate their vices and follies; they "give themselves airs," and in so doing regulate their own behavior not by the reputation they may have among hardworking people but by their standing in the world of fashion and vanity.[26]

Fourth, government can cause vice. Merchants may profess to like competition, but secretly they abhor it and, whenever they have the chance, try to create monopolies and privileges for themselves and to impose restrictions and tariffs on their competitors.[27] Sometimes they succeed in restricting trade through their own efforts, but few privately organized cartels and monopolies can long endure; some firm, hoping for a quick profit, will undercut the agreement and undersell the monopolist. Yet government can give legal effect to private arrangements, and only government can tax or subsidize. The logic of Smith's argument is that politicians have the same desire to "truck, barter, and exchange" as do merchants and consumers. Their marketplace is politics, their currency is votes. And so they are powerfully tempted to trade their powers for the votes and favors of the merchants who seek protection. "The member of parliament who supports every proposal for strengthening this monopoly [that is, high tariffs on imported goods], is sure to acquire not only the reputation of understanding trade, but great popularity and influence with an order of men whose numbers and wealth render them of great importance."[28] Smith would not have been surprised to learn that a high-ranking American politician was thought by the leaders of Texas savings and loan institutions to be a wise and understanding fellow. Smith knew that government was necessary; without it property would be insecure, the nation defenseless, and essential public works lacking. Smith hoped for the best from government but expected the worst; how he would have resolved the issue we shall never know, for he did not live to write the promised book on government and jurisprudence.

Finally, some problems are associated with the rise of large commercial enterprises in which ownership and management are separate. Smith was familiar with and wrote at length about such joint stock companies as the East India Company, the Hudson's Bay Company, and the South Sea Company. They are not quite what we have in mind when we think of the modern large corporation. Moreover these companies enjoyed exclusive trading privileges in England's various colonies, and thus Smith's complaints about them—and they were lengthy and detailed—were for the most part criticism of the evils arising from monopolistic, not competitive practices.[29] These merchants had become in effect sovereigns in the lands where they traded, and bad sovereigns at that. They lacked "that sort of authority which naturally over-awes the people" and so instead relied on military force and despotic rule.[30]

In principle joint stock companies are good things. The directors of such firms profit only if the firm as a whole profits, and so the private interest of the directors is connected with the prosperity of the enterprise.[31] But in practice such companies can become large in ways that separate the interests of the directors from those of the shareholders. Smith clearly anticipates what we now call agency problems. When the capital of the South Sea Company came to exceed thirty-three million pounds, its directors became the managers of other people's money rather than of their own, and so "folly, negligence and profusion" prevailed.[32]

Agency problems continue to plague not only shareholders but managers as well. The latter problem arises in large measure from the size of the enterprise. Vast and complex enterprises isolate men from the judgment of their peers. In a corporation, cause and effect are often widely separated; he who gives the order often cannot observe how it is carried out, and he who receives the order often cannot know what exactly was intended. Thus the order giver is judged by those associates who know only what he intended and not what he achieved, while the order taker is judged by those who know only what was achieved but not what was intended. Under these circumstances the voice of conscience, of the impartial spectator, may be muted. The order giver reveals this when he sometimes says, "I don't care how you get it done, just get it done"; similarly the order taker reveals it when he says, "I can't help it, I'm just following orders."

Smith hinted at the kinds of problems caused by size and distance when he noted that clerks of the East India Company would often trade on their own account against the wishes of their masters. Separated by ten thousand miles from headquarters, the clerks were not likely to be content with their modest salaries when with a little energy they could amass much larger sums by private (and unauthorized) dealings.[33] A clerk, for example, might well have told an Indian peasant in his employ to plow up his rice fields and to replant them with poppies so that the clerk could make a huge profit out of manufacturing and selling opium.[34]

What would Adam Smith propose to cope with the several kinds of immorality that can arise from the successes of capitalism? The remedy he suggested for the alienating effects of routine work was public education. Schools can broaden minds that labor has narrowed. The remedy he suggested for business conspiracies was wise laws. The law may not be able to prevent all combinations in restraint of trade, but at least the law should not encourage them. What remedy he may have had in mind for the tendency of government to promote privilege is unclear, but almost surely it would have included a commitment to a government of limited powers.

For the licentiousness of the idle rich, Smith supplied no remedy. He thought it inevitable and up to a point desirable. Although he disdained the pursuit of frivolity and luxury, he knew that human wants were boundless and that their pursuit was the powerful engine that would drive the economy to even greater achievements, especially since the rich man consumes no more food than the poor.[35] Moreover, although he was skeptical of the admiration with which many people viewed the rich and famous, this admiration within bounds was a useful prod to ambition. Smith did not much care for the frivolous or extravagant members of the wealthy, but he thought their pursuits were largely harmless provided only that serious people did not try to ape them.[36]

We can only guess how he might have dealt with the problems arising out of the size and impersonality of the corporation. The tone and spirit of *The Theory of Moral Sentiments* implies that he might have stressed the importance of giving a louder voice to the impartial spectator so that executives at the top would feel obliged to come into contact with, and allow themselves to be judged by, those people at the bottom who must carry out their orders. The leader of a great enterprise must see the whole enterprise as his community, much as the captain must see the well-being of his ship as entirely his responsibility. The conscience of both executive and captain must be shaped by how their actions are judged by all who are affected by them. Leaders must amplify the voice within so that others may hear what they hear from the impartial spectator. They must, in modern parlance, set the right tone at the top.

Adam Smith provides us with a far richer and deeper assessment of the ethical aspects of capitalism than can be found in the writings of most present-day critics. Unlike them, he begins by defining virtue: it is the capacity for entering imaginatively into the feelings of others and allowing their sympathy to guide our own actions. A moral man is one whose sense of duty is shaped by conscience, that is, by that impartial spectator within our breast who evaluates our own action as others would evaluate it. The dictates of that spectator must of necessity approximate the Golden Rule, for we cannot be expected to be judged praiseworthy by others if we treat others differently from how we expect to be treated by them. Although Smith sometimes seems to deny this, taken as a whole the qualities of character he admires in men as citizens are exactly those that are necessary to make capitalism work: frugality, prudence, a reasonable concern for the opinions of others, and a distant time horizon.

The apparently amoral tone of *The Wealth of Nations* is more apparent than real, for at various places he discusses at least five moral problems that can result from the success of capitalism. He does not explicitly link the arguments of *The Theory of Moral Sentiments* with the problems identified in *The Wealth of Nations*, but the linkages can plausibly be guessed.

As an economic order, capitalism in Smith's judgment was more just than the mercantilist alternative because it would produce greater prosperity for a greater number of people, albeit at the cost of greater inequality of wealth. Whether this economic gain would in the long run outweigh its moral hazards, especially its tendency to impoverish the human spirit as a result of drudgery, urban life, and the impersonality of large-scale enterprises, is unclear. Karl Marx believed that Smith had foreseen the ultimate failure of capitalism, and some non-Marxist supporters of Smith agree. We can take some comfort in the realization that society has ways of adapting to these hazards—not only have we invested heavily in education, as Smith had urged, we (that is, we in the United States) have been careful to build walls that, however imperfectly, restrict the ability of merchants and politicians to engage in mutually advantageous conspiracies and to provide mechanisms for protecting the essential rights of the various stakeholders in large enterprises.

But we have not found a way of moderating the tendencies toward frivolity and licentiousness among the affluent or those who wish to ape the affluent. Insofar as frivolity was the only problem, Smith was tolerant, as we should be. But licentiousness was and is another matter. In Smith's time, when a few courtiers and idlers dissipated their wealth on fashion, the problem did not seem great. But when segments of a vast and growing upper-middle class celebrate the pleasures of self-indulgence in drugs, vulgarity, and personal gratification, the tone at the top—not only of the firm but, worse, of society—is threatened in a way that would have appalled Smith.

12

Character and Ecstasy: Against the Legalization of Drugs

The clearest test of our willingness to assign a character-forming role to government comes when we must answer the question, Shall the possession and distribution of certain drugs be legal or illegal? I am not one of those who think that there is an easy answer to that question. I believe that society has the right and obligation to protect people from their worst instincts—up to a point. The use of heroin and crack cocaine properly falls within the ambit of contraband whose use should be discouraged by, among other things, criminal sanctions. When I gave a seminar at RAND on this topic, a friend there asked whether the cost of enforcing those sanctions might ever be so high that the moral gain from their use—that is, the avoidance of debased and degraded lives—would no longer be worth the candle. I can imagine such a state of affairs, but were I in it, I cannot imagine what I would say, or what difference it would make: if the costs of prohibition had become so astronomical, it could only mean that we were no longer living in an ordered society that induced in its members an aversion to ecstasy at any cost and a commitment to personal dignity even at some cost.

In 1972 President Richard Nixon appointed me chairman of the National Advisory Council for Drug Abuse Prevention. Created by Congress, the council was charged with providing guidance on how best to coordinate the national war on drugs. (Yes, we called it a war then too.) In those days the drug we were chiefly concerned with was heroin. When I took office, heroin use had been increasing dramatically. Everybody was worried that this increase would continue. Such phrases as "heroin epidemic" were commonplace.

That same year the eminent economist Milton Friedman published as essay in *Newsweek* in which he called for legalizing heroin. His argument was on two grounds: as a matter of ethics the government has no right to tell people not to use heroin (or to drink or to commit suicide); as a matter of economics the prohibition of drug use imposes costs on society that far exceed the benefits. Others, such as the psychoanalyst Thomas Szasz, made the same argument.

We did not take Friedman's advice. (Government commissions rarely do.) I do not recall that we even discussed legalizing heroin, although we did discuss (but did not take action on) legalizing a drug, cocaine, that many people then argued was benign. Our marching orders were to figure out how to win the war on heroin, not to run up the white flag of surrender.

That was 1972. In 1990 we have the same number of heroin addicts that we had then: half a million, give or take a few thousand. Having that many heroin addicts is no trivial matter; these people deserve our attention. But not having had an increase in that number for more than fifteen years is also something that deserves our attention. What happened to the heroin epidemic that many people once thought would overwhelm us?

The facts are clear: a more of less stable pool of heroin addicts has been getting older, with relatively few new recruits. In 1976 the average age of heroin users who appeared in hospital emergency rooms was about twenty-seven; ten years later it was thirty-two. More than two-thirds of all heroin users appearing in emergency rooms are now over the age of thirty. Back in the early 1970s, when heroin got onto the national political agenda, the typical heroin addict was much younger, often a teenager. Household surveys show the same thing: the rate of opiate use (which includes heroin) has been flat for the better part of two decades. More fine-grained studies of inner-city neighborhoods confirm this. John Boyle and Ann Brunswick found that the percentage of young blacks in Harlem who used heroin fell from 8 percent in 1970–1971 to about 3 percent in 1975–1976.

Why did heroin lose its appeal for young people? When the young blacks in Harlem were asked why they stopped, more than half mentioned "trouble with the law" or "high cost" (and high cost is of course directly the result of law enforcement). Two-thirds said that heroin hurt their health; nearly all said they had had a bad experience with it. We need not rely, however, simply on what they said. In New York City in 1973–1975, the street price of heroin rose dramatically, and its purity sharply declined, probably as a result of the heroin shortage caused by the success of the Turkish government in reducing the supply of opium base and of the French government in closing down heroin-processing laboratories located in and around Marseilles. These were short-lived gains for, just as Friedman predicted, alternative sources of supply—mostly in Mexico—quickly emerged. But the three-year heroin shortage interrupted the easy recruitment of new users.

Health and related problems were no doubt part of the reason for the reduced flow of recruits. Over the preceding years, Harlem youth had watched as more and more heroin users died of overdoses, were poisoned by adulterated doses, or acquired hepatitis from dirty needles. The word got around: heroin can kill you. By 1974 new hepatitis cases and drug overdose deaths had dropped to a fraction of what they had been in 1970.

Alas, treatment did not seem to explain much of the cessation in drug use. Treatment programs can and do help heroin addicts, but treatment did not explain the drop in the number of new users (who by definition had never been in treatment) or even much of the reduction in the number of experienced users.

No one knows how much of the decline to attribute to personal observation as opposed to high prices or reduced supply. But other evidence suggests strongly that price and supply played a large role. In 1972 the national advisory council was especially worried by the prospect that U.S. servicemen returning to this country from Vietnam would bring their heroin habits with them. Fortunately a brilliant study by Lee Robins of Washington University in St. Louis put that fear to rest. She measured drug use of Vietnam veterans shortly after they had returned home. Although many had used heroin regularly while in Southeast Asia, most gave up the habit when back in the United States. The reason: here heroin was less available, and sanctions on its use were more pronounced. Of course if a veteran had been willing to pay enough—which might have meant traveling to another city and would certainly have meant making an illegal contact with a disreputable dealer in a threatening neighborhood in order to acquire a (possibly) dangerous dose—he could have sustained his drug habit. Most veterans were unwilling to pay this price, and so their drug use declined or disappeared.

Reliving the Past

Suppose we had taken Friedman's advice in 1972. What would have happened? We cannot be entirely certain, but at a minimum we would have placed the young heroin addicts (and, above all, the prospective addicts) in a different position from the one in which they actually found themselves. Heroin would have been legal. Its price would have been reduced by 95 percent (minus whatever we chose to recover in taxes). Now that it could have been sold by the same people who make aspirin, its quality would have been assured: no poisons, no adulterants. Sterile hypodermic needles would have been readily available at the neighborhood drugstore, probably at the same counter where the heroin was sold. No need to travel to big cities or unfamiliar neighborhoods—heroin could have been purchased anywhere, perhaps by mail order.

There would no longer have been any financial or medical reason to avoid heroin use. Anybody could have afforded it. We might have tried to prevent children from buying it, but as we have learned from our efforts to prevent minors from buying alcohol and tobacco, young people have a way of penetrating markets theoretically reserved for adults. Returning Vietnam veterans would have discovered that Omaha and Raleigh had been converted into the pharmaceutical equivalent of Saigon.

Under these circumstances can we doubt for a moment that heroin use would have grown exponentially? Or that a vastly larger supply of new users would have been recruited? Professor Friedman is a Nobel Prize–winning economist whose understanding of market forces is profound. What did he think would happen to consumption under his legalized regime? Here are his words: "Legalizing drugs might increase the number of addicts, but it is not clear that it would. Forbidden fruit is attractive, particularly to the young."

Really? I suppose that we should expect no increase in Porsche sales if we cut the price by 95 percent, no increase in whiskey sales if we cut the price by a comparable amount—because young people only want fast cars and strong liquor when they are forbidden. Perhaps Friedman's uncharacteristic lapse from the obvious implications of price theory can be explained by a misunderstanding of how drug users are recruited. In his 1972 essay he said that "drug addicts are deliberately made by pushers, who give likely prospects their first few doses free." If drugs were legal, it would not pay anybody to produce addicts because everybody would buy from the cheapest source. But as every drug expert knows, pushers do not produce addicts. Friends or acquaintances do. In fact pushers are usually reluctant to deal with nonusers because a nonuser could be an undercover cop. Drug use spreads in the same way any fad or fashion spreads: somebody who is already a user urges friends to try or simply shows already eager friends how to do it.

But we need not rely on speculation, however plausible, that lowered prices and more abundant supplies would have increased heroin usage. Great Britain once followed such a policy and with almost exactly those results. Until the mid-1960s British physicians were allowed to prescribe heroin to certain classes of addicts. (Possessing these drugs without a doctor's prescription remained a criminal offense.) For many years this policy worked well enough because the addict patients were typically middle-class people who had become dependent on opiate painkillers while undergoing hospital treatment. There was no drug culture. The British system worked for many years, not because it prevented drug abuse but because there was no problem of drug abuse that would test the system.

All that changed in the 1960s. A few unscrupulous doctors began passing out heroin in wholesale amounts. One doctor prescribed almost 600,000 heroin tablets—that is, more than thirteen pounds—in just one year. A youthful drug culture emerged with a demand for drugs far different from that of the older addicts. As a result, the British government required doctors to refer users to government-run clinics to receive their heroin.

But the shift to clinics did not curtail the growth in heroin use. Throughout the 1960s the number of addicts increased—John Kaplan of Stanford estimated by fivefold—in part as a result of the diversion of heroin from clinic patients to new users on the streets. An addict would bargain with the clinic doctor over how big a dose he would receive. The patient wanted as much as he could get, the doctor wanted to give as little as was needed. The patient had an advantage in this conflict because the doctor could not be certain how much was really needed. Many patients would use some of their maintenance dose and sell the remaining part to friends, thereby recruiting new addicts. As the clinics learned of this, they began to shift their treatment away from heroin and toward methadone, an addictive drug that, when taken orally, does not produce a high but will block the withdrawal pains associated with heroin abstinence.

Whether what happened in England in the 1960s was a mini-epidemic or an epidemic depends on whether one looks at numbers or at rates of change. Compared with the United States, the numbers were small. In 1960, 68 heroin addicts were known to the British government; by 1968, 2,000 were in treatment, and many more refused treatment. (They would refuse in part because they did not want to get methadone at a clinic if they could get heroin on the street.) Richard Hartnoll estimates that the actual number of addicts in England is five times the number officially registered. At a minimum the number of British addicts increased by thirtyfold in ten years; the actual increase may have been much larger.

In the early 1980s the numbers began to rise again, and this time nobody doubted that a real epidemic was at hand. The increase was estimated to be 40 percent a year. By 1982 there were thought to be 20,000 heroin users in London alone. Geoffrey Pearson reports that many cities—Glasgow, Liverpool, Manchester, and Sheffield among them—were now experiencing a drug problem that once had been largely confined to London. The problem again was supply. The country was being flooded with cheap, high-quality heroin, first from Iran and then from Southeast Asia.

The United States began the 1960s with a much larger number of heroin addicts and probably a bigger at-risk population than was the case in Great Britain. Although it would be foolhardy to suppose that the British system, if installed here, would have worked the same way or with the same results, it would be equally foolhardy to suppose that a combination of heroin available from leaky clinics and from street dealers who faced only minimal law enforcement risks would not have produced a much greater increase in heroin use than we actually experienced. My guess is that if we had allowed either doctors or clinics to prescribe heroin, we would have had far worse results than were produced in Britain, if for no other reason than the vastly larger number of addicts with which we began. We would have had to find some way to police thousands (not scores) of physicians and hundreds (not dozens) of clinics. If the British civil service found it difficult to keep heroin in the hands of addicts and out of the hands of recruits when it was dealing with a few hundred people, how well would the American civil service have accomplished the same tasks when dealing with tens of thousands of people?

Back to the Future

In 1990 cocaine, especially in its potent form, crack, is the focus of attention. In 1990 as in 1972 the government is trying to reduce its use. In 1990 as then some people are advocating legalization. Is there any more reason to yield to those arguments in 1990 than there was almost two decades earlier?[1]

I think not. If we had yielded in 1972, we almost certainly would have had today a permanent population of several million, not several hundred thousand, heroin addicts. If we yield in 1990, we will have a far more serious problem with cocaine.

Crack is worse than heroin by almost any measure. Heroin produces a pleasant drowsiness and, if hygienically administered, has only the physical side effects of constipation and sexual impotence. Regular heroin use incapacitates many users, especially poor ones, for any productive work or social responsibility. They will sit nodding on a street corner, helpless but at least harmless. By contrast, regular cocaine use leaves the user neither helpless nor harmless. When smoked (as with crack) or injected, cocaine produces instant, intense, and short-lived euphoria. The experience generates a powerful desire to repeat it. If the drug is readily available, repeat use will occur. Those people who progress to bingeing on cocaine become devoted to the drug and its effects to the exclusion of almost all other considerations: job, family, children, sleep, food, even sex. Dr. Frank Gawin at Yale and Dr. Everett Ellinwood at Duke report that a substantial percentage of all high-dose,

154

binge users become uninhibited, impulsive, hypersexual, compulsive, irritable, and hyperactive. Their moods vacillate dramatically, leading at times to violence and homicide.

Women are much more likely to use crack than heroin, and if they are pregnant, the effects on their babies are tragic. Douglas Besharov, who has followed the effects of drugs on infants for over twenty years, writes that nothing he learned about heroin prepared him for the devastation of cocaine. Cocaine harms the fetus and can lead to physical deformities or neurological damage. Some crack babies have for all practical purposes suffered a disabling stroke while still in the womb. The long-term consequences of this brain damage are lowered cognitive ability and the onset of mood disorders. Besharov estimates that about 30,000 to 50,000 such babies are born every year, about 7,000 in New York City alone. There may be ways to treat such infants, but from everything we know, the treatment will be long, difficult, and expensive. Worse, the mothers who are most likely to produce crack babies are precisely the ones who, because of poverty or temperament, are least able and willing to obtain such treatment. In fact anecdotal evidence suggests that crack mothers are likely to abuse their infants.

The notion that abusing drugs such as cocaine is a victimless crime is not only absurd but dangerous. Even ignoring the fetal drug syndrome, crack-dependent people, like heroin addicts, are individuals who regularly victimize their children by neglect, their spouses by improvidence, their employers by lethargy, and their coworkers by carelessness. Society is not and could never be a collection of autonomous individuals. We all have a stake in ensuring that each of us displays a minimal level of dignity, responsibility, and empathy. We cannot of course coerce people into goodness, but we can and should insist that some standards must be met if society itself—on which the existence of the human personality depends—is to persist. Drawing the line that defines those standards is difficult and contentious, but if crack and heroin use does not fall below it, what does?

The advocates of legalization will respond by suggesting that my picture is overdrawn. Ethan Nadelmann of Princeton argues that the risk of legalization is less than most people suppose. More than twenty million Americans between the ages of eighteen and twenty-five have tried cocaine (according to a government survey), but only a quarter-million use it daily. From this Nadelmann concludes that at most 3 percent of all young people who try cocaine develop a problem with it. The implication is clear: make the drug legal, and we have to worry about only 3 percent of our youth.

The implication rests on a logical fallacy and a factual error. The fallacy is this: the percentage of occasional cocaine users who become binge users when the drug is illegal (and thus expensive and hard to find) tells us nothing about the percentage who will become dependent when the drug is legal (and thus cheap and abundant). Drs. Gawin and Ellinwood report, in common with several other researchers, that controlled or occasional use of cocaine changes to compulsive and frequent use "when access to the drug increases" or when the user switches from snorting to smoking. More cocaine more potently administered alters, perhaps sharply, the proportion of "controlled" users who become heavy users.

The factual error is this: the federal survey Nadelmann quotes was done in 1985, before crack had become common. Thus, the probability of becoming dependent on cocaine was derived from the responses of users who snorted the drug. The speed and potency of cocaine's action increase dramatically when it is smoked. We do not yet know how greatly the advent of crack increases the risk of dependency, but all the clinical evidence suggests that the increase is likely to be large.

It is possible that some people will not become heavy users even when the drug is readily available in its most potent form. So far there are no scientific grounds for predicting who will and who will not become dependent. Neither socioeconomic background nor personality traits differentiate between casual and intensive users. Thus the only way to settle the question of who is correct about the effect of easy availability on drug use, Nadelmann or Gawin and Ellinwood, is to try it and see. But that social experiment is so risky as to be no experiment at all, for if cocaine is legalized and if the rate of its abusive use increases dramatically, there is no way to put the genie back in the bottle, and it is not a kindly genie.

Have We Lost?

Many people who agree that there are risks in legalizing cocaine or heroin still favor it because they think we have lost the war on drugs. "Nothing we have done has worked," and the current federal policy is just "more of the same." Whatever the costs of greater drug use, surely they would be less than the costs of our present, failed efforts.

That is exactly what I was told in 1972—and heroin is not quite so bad a drug as cocaine. We did not surrender, and we did not lose. We did not win either. What the nation accomplished then was what most efforts to save people from themselves accomplish: the problem was contained and the number of victims minimized, all at a considerable cost in law enforcement and increased crime. Was the cost worth it? I think so, but others may disagree. What are the lives of would-be addicts worth? I recall some people saying to me then, "Let them kill themselves." I was appalled. Happily, such views did not prevail.

Have we lost today? Not at all. High-rate cocaine use is not commonplace. A National Institute of Drug Abuse (NIDA) survey reported that less than 5 percent of high school seniors used cocaine within the past thirty days. Of course, this survey missed young people who dropped out of school and miscounted those who lied on the questionnaire, but even if we inflate the NIDA estimate by some plausible percentage, it is still not much above 5 percent. Medical examiners reported in 1987 that about 1,500 died from cocaine use; hospital emergency rooms reported about 30,000 admissions related to cocaine abuse.

These are not small numbers, but neither are they evidence of a nationwide plague that threatens to engulf us all. Moreover cities vary greatly in the proportion of people who are involved with cocaine. To get city-level data, we need to turn to drug tests carried out on arrested persons, who obviously are more likely to be drug users than the average citizen. The National Institute of Justice, through its Drug Use Forecasting Project, collects urinalysis data on arrestees in twenty-two cities. As we have already seen, opiate (chiefly heroin) use has been flat or declining in most of these cities over the last decade. Cocaine use has gone up sharply but with great variation among cities. New York, Philadelphia, and Washington, D.C., all report that two-thirds or more of their arrestees tested positive for cocaine, but in Portland, San Antonio, and Indianapolis the percentage was one-third or less.

In some neighborhoods matters have reached crisis proportions. Gangs control the streets, shootings terrorize residents, and drug dealing occurs in plain view. The police seem barely able to contain matters. But in these neighborhoods—unlike at Palo Alto cocktail parties—the people are not calling for legalization, they are calling for help. And often not much help has come. Many cities are willing to do almost anything about the drug problem except spend more money on it. The federal government cannot change that; only local voters and politicians can. It is not clear that they will.

It took about ten years to contain heroin. As of 1990, we have had experience with crack for only about three or four years. Each year we spend perhaps $11 billion on law enforcement (and some of that goes to deal with marijuana) and perhaps $2 billion on treatment: large sums but not sums that should lead anyone to say, "We just can't afford this anymore."

The illegality of drugs increases crime, partly because some users turn to crime to pay for their habits, partly because some users are stimulated by certain drugs (such as crack or PCP) to act more violently or ruthlessly than they otherwise would, and partly because criminal organizations seeking to control drug supplies use force to manage their markets. These also are serious costs, but no one knows how much they would be reduced if drugs were legalized. Addicts would no longer steal to pay black-market prices for drugs, a real gain. But some, perhaps a great deal, of that gain would be offset by the great increase in the number of addicts. These people, nodding on heroin or living in the delusion-ridden high of cocaine, would hardly be ideal employees. Many would steal simply to support themselves, since snatch-and-grab, opportunistic crime can be managed even by people unable to hold a regular job or plan an elaborate crime. Those British addicts who get their supplies from government clinics are not models of law-abiding decency. Most are in crime, and although their per capita rate of criminality may be lower thanks to the cheapness of their drugs, the total volume of crime they produce may be quite large. Of course society could decide to support all unemployable addicts on welfare, but then gains from lowered rates of crime would have to be offset by large increases in welfare budgets.

Proponents of legalization claim that the costs of having more addicts around would be largely if not entirely offset by having more money available with which to treat and care for them. The money would come from taxes levied on the sale of heroin and cocaine.

To obtain this fiscal dividend, however, legalization's supporters must first solve an economic dilemma. If they want to raise a lot of money to pay for welfare and treatment, the tax rate on the drugs will have to be quite high. Even if they themselves do not want a high rate, the politicians' love of sin taxes would probably guarantee that it would be high. But the higher the tax, the higher the price of the drug, and the higher the price, the greater the likelihood that addicts will turn to crime to find the money for it and that criminal organizations will be formed to sell tax-free drugs at below-market rates. If we managed to keep taxes (and thus prices) low, we would get that much less money to pay for welfare and treatment, and more people could afford to become addicts. There may be an optimal tax rate for drugs that maximizes revenue while minimizing crime, bootlegging, and the recruitment of new addicts, but our experience with alcohol does not suggest that we know how to find it.

Benefits of Illegality

The advocates of legalization find nothing to be said in favor of the current system except, possibly, that it keeps the number of addicts smaller than it would otherwise be. In fact the benefits are more substantial than that.

First, treatment: all the talk about providing treatment on demand implies a demand for treatment. That is not quite right. Some drug-dependent people genuinely want treatment and will remain in it if offered; they should receive it. But far more want only short-term help after a bad crash; once stabilized and bathed, they are back on the street again, hustling. And even many of the addicts who enroll in a program and honestly want help drop out after a short while when they discover that help takes time and commitment. Drug-dependent people have short time horizons and a weak capacity for commitment. These two groups—those looking for a quick fix and those unable to stick with a long-term fix—are not easily helped. Even if we increase the number of treatment slots—as we should—we would have to do something to make treatment more effective.

One thing that can often make it more effective is compulsion. Douglas Anglin of UCLA, in common with many other researchers, has found that the longer one stays in a treatment program, the better the chances of a reduction in drug dependency. But he, again like most other researchers, has found that dropout rates are high. He has also found, however, that patients who enter treatment under legal compulsion stay in the program longer than those not subject to such pressure. His research on the California civil commitment program, for example, found that heroin users involved with its required drug-testing program had over the long term a lower rate of heroin use than similar addicts who were free of such constraints. If compulsion is a useful component of treatment for many addicts, it is not clear how compulsion could be achieved in a society in which purchasing, possessing, and using the drug were legal. It could be managed, I suppose, but I would not want to have to answer the challenge from the American Civil Liberties Union that it is wrong to compel a person to undergo treatment for consuming a legal commodity.

Next, education: we are now investing substantially in drug-education programs in the schools. Although we do not yet know for certain what will work, there are some promising leads. But I wonder how credible such programs would be if they were aimed at dissuading children from doing something perfectly legal. We could, of course, treat drug education like smoking education: inhaling crack and inhaling tobacco are both legal, but you should not do it because it is bad for you. That tobacco is bad for you is easily shown; the surgeon general has seen to that. But what do we say about crack? It is pleasurable, but devoting yourself to so much pleasure is not a good idea (though perfectly legal)? Unlike tobacco, cocaine will not give you cancer or emphysema, but it will lead you to neglect your duties to family, job, and neighborhood? Everybody is doing cocaine, but you should not?

Again it might be possible under a legalized regime to have effective drug-prevention programs, but their effectiveness would depend heavily on first having decided that cocaine use, like tobacco use, is purely a matter of practical consequences; no fundamental moral significance

159

attaches to either. But if we believe—as I do—that dependency on certain mind-altering drugs is a moral issue and that their illegality rests in part on their immorality, then legalizing them undercuts, if it does not eliminate altogether, the moral message.

That message is at the root of the distinction we now make between nicotine and cocaine. Both are highly addictive; both have harmful physical effects. But we treat the two drugs differently, not simply because nicotine is so widely used as to be beyond the reach of effective prohibition but because its use does not destroy the user's essential humanity. Tobacco shortens one's life; cocaine debases it. Nicotine alters one's habits; cocaine alters one's soul. The heavy use of crack, unlike the heavy use of tobacco, corrodes those natural sentiments of sympathy and duty that constitute our human nature and make possible our social life. To say, as does Nadelmann, that distinguishing morally between tobacco and cocaine is "little more than a transient prejudice" is close to saying that morality itself is but a prejudice.

The Alcohol Problem

Now we have arrived where many arguments about legalizing drugs begin: is there any reason to treat heroin and cocaine differently from the way we treat alcohol?

There is no easy answer to that question because, as with so many human problems, one cannot decide simply on the basis either of moral principles or of individual consequences; one has to temper any policy by a common-sense judgment of what is possible. Alcohol, like heroin, cocaine, PCP, and marijuana, is a drug—that is, a mood-altering substance—and consumed to excess, it certainly has harmful consequences: auto accidents, barroom fights, bedroom shootings. It is also, for some people, addictive. We cannot confidently compare the addictive powers of these drugs, but the best evidence suggests that crack and heroin are much more addictive than alcohol.

Many people, Nadelmann included, argue that since the health and financial costs of alcohol abuse are so much higher than those of cocaine or heroin abuse, it is hypocritical folly to devote our efforts to preventing cocaine or drug use. But as Mark Kleiman of Harvard has pointed out, this comparison is quite misleading. What Nadelmann is doing is showing that a legalized drug (alcohol) produces greater social harm than illegal ones (cocaine and heroin). But of course. Suppose that in the 1920s we had made heroin and cocaine legal and alcohol illegal. Can anyone doubt that Nadelmann would now be writing that it is folly to continue our ban on alcohol because cocaine and heroin are so much more harmful?

160

And let there be no doubt about it—widespread heroin and cocaine use are associated with all manner of ills. Thomas Bewley found that the mortality rate of British heroin addicts in 1968 was twenty-eight times as high as the death rate of the same age group of nonaddicts. Even though in England at the time an addict could obtain free or low-cost heroin and clean needles from British clinics. Perform the following mental experiment: suppose we legalized heroin and cocaine in this country. In what proportion of auto fatalities would the state police report that the driver was nodding off on heroin or recklessly driving on a coke high? In what proportion of spouse assault and child abuse cases would the local police report that crack was involved? In what proportion of industrial accidents would safety investigators report that the forklift or drill-press operator was in a drug-induced stupor or frenzy? We do not know exactly what the proportion would be, but anyone who asserts that it would not be much higher than it is now would have to believe that these drugs have little appeal except when they are illegal. And that is nonsense.

An advocate of legalization might concede that social harm— perhaps harm equivalent to that already produced by alcohol—would follow from making cocaine and heroin generally available. But at least, he might add, we would have the problem out in the open, where it could be treated as a matter of public health. That is well and good if we knew how to treat—that is, cure—heroin and cocaine abuse. But we do not know how to do it for all the people who would need such help. We are having only limited success in coping with chronic alcoholics. Addictive behavior is immensely difficult to change, and the best methods for changing it—living in drug-free therapeutic communities, becoming faithful members of Alcoholics Anonymous or Narcotics Anonymous— require great personal commitment, a quality that is, alas, in short supply among the persons—young people, disadvantaged people—who are often most at risk for addiction.

Suppose that today we had not fifteen million alcohol abusers but half a million. Suppose that we already knew what we have learned from our long experience with the widespread use of alcohol. Would we make whiskey legal? I do not know, but I suspect there would be a lively debate. The surgeon general would remind us of the risks alcohol poses to pregnant woman. The National Highway Traffic Safety Administration would point to the likelihood of more highway fatalities caused by drunk drivers. The Food and Drug Administration might find that there is a nontrivial increase in cancer associated with alcohol consumption. At the same time the police would report great difficulty in keeping illegal whiskey out of our cities, officers being corrupted by bootleggers, and alcohol addicts often resorting to crime to feed their habit. Libertarians for their part would argue that every citizen has a right to drink anything he wishes and that drinking is in any event a victimless crime.

However the debate might turn out, the central fact would be that the problem was still at that point a small one. The government cannot legislate away the addictive tendencies in all of us nor can it remove completely even the most dangerous addictive substances. But it can cope with harms when the harms are still manageable.

Science and Addiction

One advantage of containing a problem while it is still containable is that it buys time for science to learn more about it and perhaps to discover a cure. Almost unnoticed in the current debate over legalizing drugs is that basic science has made rapid strides in identifying the underlying neurological processes involved in some forms of addiction. Stimulants such as cocaine and amphetamines alter the way certain brain cells communicate with one another. That alteration is complex and not entirely understood, but in simplified form it involves modifying the way in which a neurotransmitter called dopamine sends signals from one cell to another.

When dopamine crosses the synapse between two cells, it is in effect carrying a message from the first cell to activate the second one. In certain parts of the brain that message is experienced as pleasure. After the message is delivered, the dopamine returns to the first cell. Cocaine apparently blocks this return, or reuptake, so that the excited cell and others nearby continue to send pleasure messages. When the exaggerated high produced by cocaine-influenced dopamine finally ends, the brain cells may (in ways that are still a matter of dispute) suffer from an extreme lack of dopamine, thereby making the individual unable to experience any pleasure at all. This would explain why cocaine users often feel so depressed after enjoying the drug. Stimulants may also affect the way in which other neurotransmitters, such as serotonin and noradrenaline, operate.

Whatever the exact mechanism may be, once it is identified it becomes possible to use drugs to block either the effect of cocaine or its tendency to produce dependency. There have already been experiments using desipramine, imipramine, bromocriptine, carbamazepine, and other chemicals. There are some promising results.

Tragically we spend little on such research, and the agencies funding it have not occupied influential or visible posts in the federal bureaucracy. If there is one aspect of the war-on-drugs metaphor that I dislike, it is its tendency to focus attention almost exclusively on the troops in the trenches, whether engaged in enforcement or treatment, and away from the research and development efforts back on the home front, where the war may ultimately be decided.

The prospects of scientists in controlling addiction will be strongly influenced by the size and character of the problem they face. If the problem is a few hundred thousand chronic, high-dose users of an illegal product, the chances of making a difference at a reasonable cost will be much greater than if the problem is a few million chronic users of legal substances. Once a drug is legal, not only will its use increase, but many of those who then use it will prefer the drug to the treatment: they will want the pleasure, whatever the cost to themselves or their families, and they will resist—probably successfully—any effort to wean them away from experiencing the high that comes from inhaling a legal substance.

If I Am Wrong

No one can know what our society would be like if we changed the law to make access to cocaine, heroin, and PCP easier. I believe, for reasons given, that the result would be a sharp increase in use, a more widespread degradation of the human personality, and a greater rate of accidents and violence.

I may be wrong. If I am, then we will needlessly have incurred heavy costs in law enforcement and some forms of criminality. But if I am right, and the legalizers prevail anyway, then we will have consigned millions of people, hundreds of thousands of infants, and hundreds of neighborhoods to a life of oblivion and disease. To the lives and families destroyed by alcohol, we will have added countless more destroyed by cocaine, heroin, PCP, and whatever else a basement scientist can invent.

Human character is formed by society; indeed human character is inconceivable without society, and good character is less likely in a bad society. Will we, in the name of an abstract doctrine of radical individualism, and with the false comfort of suspect predictions, decide to take the chance that somehow individual decency can survive amid a more general level of degradation?

I think not. The American people are too wise for that, whatever the academic essayists and cocktail party pundits may say. But if Americans today are less wise than I suppose, then Americans at some future time will look back on us now and wonder, what kind of people were they that they could have done such a thing?

13

Learning More about Character— How Do Children Grow Up?

There is a great deal to character formation that I do not understand, and that I think no one understands. In particular no one understands the persistence in this country of a large urban underclass. Everybody has ideas as to what should be done about it, but with few exceptions they are only educated guesses. In 1982 I became part of a study group organized by the MacArthur Foundation to advise on what, if anything, it should do about crime. We finally decided that the only serious advice we could give was that we desperately needed to know why some people acquired a decent character and others did not. To support that view, David Farrington, Lloyd Ohlin, and I wrote a book explaining what we did not know and how we thought we could learn it. The volume appeared in 1986 under the title Understanding and Controlling Crime *(New York: Springer-Verlag). It became the basis for a major new research effort, the Program in Human Development and Criminal Behavior, now being directed at the Harvard School of Public Health by Dr. Felton Earls and Professor Albert Reiss. What follows is chapter 1, written by me, which supplies an overview of the book and its argument for a long-term study of how children grow up in urban America.*

Policy makers who wish to put in place new programs to reduce crime, or to expand the scope of effectiveness of programs already in place, will quickly discover that the knowledge necessary to do this responsibly does not exist except in fragmentary and unsatisfactory form. Whether we wish to prevent delinquency or to rehabilitate offenders, whether we seek to strengthen families or to improve schools, whether we believe that juvenile courts should get tougher or provide better services, we will be forced to admit, if we are honest, that we only have scattered clues and glimmers of hope (and sometimes not even that) on which to base our actions.

This knowledge gap is the largest single impediment to strengthening our society's capacity to cope more effectively with crime. This is the central factual conclusion of the Justice Program Study Group, and it is on the basis of this conclusion that we have chosen to recommend a new research strategy that combines the virtues of longitudinal and experimental methods. In this chapter we provide an overview of our conclusions and outline a new research strategy.

There is nothing new in saying that we do not know enough to mount a well-conceived set of new programs, and there is something a bit lame in calling for more research. In the early 1960s, when crime rates in the United States began their dramatic increase, we knew even less about how to cope with the problem than we do today. Many people were comfortably optimistic about the efficacy of rehabilitation programs; it took a decade or more of research and writing for the realization to sink in that this optimism was misplaced. Others were certain that hiring more police officers and having them engage more frequently in random preventive patrol would cut down on street crime. Again a decade passed before this certainty was shattered by studies suggesting that feasible changes in levels of preventive patrol would have few or no demonstrable effects on crime rates. Still others believed that the causes of crime could easily be addressed by programs that provided job training, more schooling, and reduced racial segregation. Job training and job creation programs flourished; the proportion of young persons staying in school increased; the more obvious forms of racial segregation were overcome. Billions of dollars were spent. Crime continued to rise.

We do not conclude from the history of the 1960s and 1970s that efforts at crime prevention and criminal rehabilitation are wrong or always doomed to failure, that the police can do nothing about crime, or that efforts to attack the causes of crime are a waste of time. We do conclude that broad-brush, inadequately designed, poorly tested programs are not likely to make much of a difference. We have learned a great deal about what does not work, or does not work as easily as we once thought. And we have identified those methods of research and experimentation that are best suited for shedding new light on the development of individual differences in criminality and on the strategic opportunities for intervention in that process of development.

When we call for more research then, it is not because we have learned nothing in the past. On the contrary, as we shall suggest, the best and most useful programs in effect today are based squarely on the best past research. Nor is the call for more research indicative of any desire on our part to postpone action or to underplay the gravity of the problem of crime in contemporary America. Rather we suggest that the time is ripe for taking a new set of measured steps toward the prevention or reduction of crime and that these new steps can build on efforts already underway. But these steps require a careful specification of the precise points and methods of intervention if we are to avoid wasted resources and dashed hopes.

What Do We Know?

We know a great deal about who commits crimes. We know that the typical high-rate offender is a young male who began his aggressive or larcenous activities at an early age, well before the typical boy gets into serious trouble. We know that he comes from a troubled, discordant, low-income family in which one or both parents are likely to have criminal records themselves. We know that the boy has had trouble in school—he created problems for his teachers and does not do well in his studies. On leaving school, often by dropping out, he works at regular jobs only intermittently. Most employers regard him as a poor risk. He experiments with a variety of drugs—alcohol, marijuana, speed, heroin—and becomes a frequent user of whatever drug is most readily available, often switching back and forth among different ones. By the time he is in his late teens, he has had many contacts with the police, but these contacts usually follow no distinctive pattern because the boy has not specialized in any particular kind of crime. He steals cars and purses, burgles homes and robs stores, fights easily when provoked, and may attack viciously even when not provoked. While young, he commits many of his crimes in the company of other young men, although whether this is because they have influenced him to do so or he has simply sought out the company of like-minded friends is not clear. After several arrests the young man, now in his early twenties, will probably spend a substantial amount of time in jail or prison. The chances are good that not long after he is released from an institution, he will commit more crimes. He runs a high risk of having his life cut short by violent means—the victim of a murder or a fatal car accident.

With these facts in mind, it is not hard to specify a plausible crime control strategy:

- Identify these high-risk youngsters at an early age and provide services, counseling, and assistance to their families.
- Help them become better students.
- Provide assistance and training in finding jobs.
- Improve the quality of life in their neighborhoods.

167

- Reduce the availability of dangerous drugs, and provide treatment programs for those persons who abuse such drugs as are available.

But if they commit a serious crime:

- Arrest and prosecute them promptly.
- Send them to a correctional program that is suited to their temperament and personal history.
- While in that program, help them maintain contact with those decent friends and family members whom the offenders cherish.
- On release from that program, help them find a job and give them financial and other forms of assistance so that they can try to make a go of it back in society.
- If they return to crime after their release, send them to an even more secure correctional institution for an even longer time.

Not only is such a strategy plausible, but many elements of it are being practiced almost everywhere, and all elements of it are practiced in some places. But what is plausible might not always be feasible, and what is feasible might not always be valuable. How can families be assisted? Which forms of assistance make a difference and which are wasted efforts? How do you help a rebellious, unmotivated, low-achieving student? What can be done to place a young man with a poor school record and disorderly habits in a worthwhile job? Indeed how in many inner-city neighborhoods do you find a job for even a competent, well-motivated young man? Which aspects of neighborhood life are worth improving, and how do you do it? Does it make a difference who the boy's friends are, and if it does, how can you change those associations? If the youngster likes to drink or take drugs, how do you talk him out of it, especially if all his friends are doing the same thing? If he is arrested early in his criminal career, will this deter him from future crimes or so stigmatize him that he is driven to seek out criminal friends and criminal opportunities? If he is sentenced to some correctional program, which one will be best suited for him, and how do we know it will work?

On the basis of past research, scholars and practitioners have been able to describe the typical criminal career with some accuracy. The path-breaking studies of criminal careers by, among others, William McCord and Joan McCord, Sheldon Glueck and Eleanor Glueck, Donald West and David Farrington, and Marvin Wolfgang and colleagues[1] have taught us to be especially concerned with the small proportion of boys who become very-high-rate offenders. On the basis of this teaching, police officers have formed special units to detect and to apprehend high-rate offenders, prosecutors have reorganized their staffs so as to expedite the investigation and prosecution of high-rate and dangerous offenders, judges have been supplied with methods to help them distinguish between low-rate and high-rate offenders, and parole boards have devised prediction scales to help them discriminate between low-rate and high-rate offenders when the boards are deciding whom to release on parole. We believe these research-based changes in criminal justice practice have been useful, though none is free from criticism. In this and other ways research has helped society improve its response to crime.

But a great deal remains to be done. If we wish, for example, to improve the policy of selectively seeking out high-rate offenders for arrest, prosecution, and incarceration, we need to know much more about who such persons are and how they can be identified. Even then, of course, there will remain some ethical and legal questions about the fairness of a selective policy. But more important, the research that has been so helpful in focusing attention on the high-rate offender has taught us little, if anything, about how we might prevent a boy from becoming a high-rate offender in the first place. If we could reduce the probability that any given boy who commits one or two offenses will go on to commit ten or twelve, we will have spared society countless victimizations. To do this, we need to learn more about how to prevent the onset of a serious delinquent career and how best to handle the would-be offender in the school system and the active offender in the criminal justice system. We think these things can be learned—not enough perhaps to make dramatic reductions in crime but enough to improve significantly our present policies. At present we cannot recommend ways to make these improvements because we are at the limits of what can reasonably be inferred from available evidence.

What Do We Need to Know?

Let us review what we know about the correlates of criminality to assess which of these are in fact causes of crime and of course which might be changed by planned interventions.

The Family. Almost no one denies that high-rate offenders are likely to come from homes that are cold, discordant, and inconsistent with respect to management of discipline. There is also evidence that such offenders are more likely to come from large, low-income families than from small, higher-income ones. Moreover some people believe that single-parent homes and abusive parents produce a disproportionate number of offenders, but the evidence on that is not clear.

Let us assume that what has happened in a family does in fact cause, and is not simply an accidental correlate of, delinquency. (As we shall see in a moment, that assumption is not always warranted.) At least three

169

different hypotheses could explain how this causal connection might occur:

1. Economic adversity causes family stress that in turn causes parental discord and (possibly) child abuse. Discord prevents the effective socialization of the child, and abuse teaches him that violence is an approved or useful way of getting what he wants.

2. The parents' temperament (poorly controlled hostility, little regard for the feelings of others, excessive drinking) leads to discord between mother and father, poor or inconsistent child-rearing practices, and unsuccessful employment experiences. The child is inadequately socialized; the marriage founders.

3. The child's temperament (alternately passive and fussy, possibly hyperkinetic, hard to manage) leads to stress in the family, discord between the parents, and the frantic resort to inappropriate child-rearing methods. The child becomes delinquent, and the parents seem unable to prevent it. They blame each other for this failure, which intensifies their quarrels and increases the risk of the marriage dissolving.

Several of these causal patterns may operate simultaneously. But let us assume for purposes of discussion that one pattern explains the child's becoming predisposed toward delinquency. Which pattern it is will determine what policies we might wish to endorse, and these policies are likely to differ greatly according to that pattern. Studies that measure the correlation between family circumstances and delinquency cannot uncover the causal pattern; all such studies will simply reaffirm that there is some connection among family adversity, parental discord, weak child-rearing practices, individual temperaments, and early delinquency.

If the first hypothesis is correct, for example, then policies designed to relieve the economic burden on poor families would become important. We might wish to propose the adoption of more comprehensive and effective job training and job placement programs or some form of a guaranteed annual income (or negative income tax) or major changes in the amount of and eligibility for welfare and other public assistance programs. This would have to be done carefully. If the benefits are too great, work incentives would be weakened, and mothers might find it profitable to remain unmarried and unemployed. But if the benefits are too small, economic adversity would not be reduced sufficiently to prevent acute family stress. Nonetheless we know where to start.

If the second hypothesis is correct, changing economic circumstances of the family would have little or no effect on how the child was reared. In this case economic adversity is not the cause of family stress (although it may contribute to it). Rather it is the temperament of the mother of father (or perhaps both) that leads to impulsiveness, constant bickering, unpredictable eruptions of hostility or moodiness, and drug or alcohol abuse; these behaviors lead to both failure in the job market and failure as parents. Psychologists believe that temperament is to some degree inherited; estimates of heritability ordinarily range around 0.25 or 0.30.[2] And alcoholism has a strong genetic component.[3] Measures to raise the incomes of such families might succeed, but the behavior of these families would remain much as before. We could instead explore policies that would improve the competence of these parents by teaching them how they might better achieve their own goals by managing their children more effectively, supplementing this with intensive efforts to treat alcoholism or drug abuse. If we cannot design programs that effectively intervene in existing families, we might wish to explore ways of enlarging and improving the provision of foster care for children in at-risk families. The family (or juvenile) court might play a more aggressive role in the early identification of such families. Such programs are not easily conceived or implemented, but if put in place, they would address the key factor in the etiology of delinquency.

Now suppose the third hypothesis is correct—that the child himself is in a sense causing his own delinquency because he is presenting to otherwise capable and caring parents an especially difficult socialization problem. There is evidence, for example, that low-birth-weight children are inordinately at risk for child abuse because, it seems, such children are relatively passive (they do not reward parents with cooing and smiling), they have difficult temperaments, and are likely to be below normal in intelligence.[4] Or the child may be born with minimal brain damage, possibly owing to parental or perinatal stress (such as alcohol or drug abuse by the mother or oxygen deprivation during birth).[5] Or the child may have had a normal birth but be hyperkinetic, so that he is difficult to control. Improving the competence of the parents might make some difference in how the child is raised, but routine competence may be insufficient. Indeed family discord may arise because the parents wrongly blame each other (or themselves) for their apparent failures. Should this causal pattern exist, we would want to explore ways of reducing the incidence of prenatal and perinatal stress (by, for example, improving prenatal care, dissuading pregnant women from using alcohol or drugs, and altering diets) and ways of managing hyperkinetic children (by appropriate drug and other therapies).

None of these policies is at all fanciful, although each is difficult and requires careful testing. Increasing family income is politically but not technically difficult; improving parental competence has been successful in some experimental projects;[6] we are learning more all the time about ways of managing difficult children. Some readers may feel that the problem of crime is sufficiently serious, that the prudent course is to try everything at once, but that is unrealistic. If all were tried simultaneously and the combination produced a good result, we would not know which program was making the difference. Then, if for fiscal or political reasons programs had to be cut, we would not know which could be safely cut. Moreover, each program would be controversial because of cost or incentive effects, because of the degree of intrusiveness into family life, or because medical methods for altering behavior make people worry about the potential for manipulation and the risk of harmful side effects. It would be far better to discover what causal pattern is in fact operating before designing any large-scale effort to alter it. With existing knowledge we cannot make that judgment.

Schooling. There is little doubt that high-rate delinquents tend to do poorly in school. There is great doubt as to why this should be so. As a result, we cannot be certain what kinds of school programs, if any, would make a lasting difference for a large number of children who seem predisposed to delinquency. Again there are several alternative hypotheses:

1. Children with mild behavioral problems become labeled as troublemakers in school. As a result, teachers come to have lowered expectations for them, the stigmatized children associate with other troublemakers, and breaking the rules comes to be more satisfying than conforming to adult standards.

2. Children with below-normal levels of intelligence or other learning disabilities find school work frustrating or boring. They become restless and take satisfaction in activities—fighting, truancy, rowdiness, sports— for which their cognitive defects do not disqualify them.

3. Predelinquent children are aggressive and antisocial before they come to school. School may provide them with greater opportunities for mischief and acquaint them with some like-minded friends, but school does not cause their delinquency.

As with family processes, so with school processes: the causal pattern and hence the appropriate remedial strategy are unclear. If youngsters become delinquent because they are labeled troublemakers, then changing teacher expectations and behavior should reduce delinquency. If frustration born of learning difficulties leads to delinquency, then devising better ways to teach and stronger rewards for mastering classroom assignments should reduce the frustration and thus the delinquency. If children have already become overly aggressive and undisciplined before entering school, then schools or preschool programs will have to be created and managed that will if possible counteract these predispositions.

Some experimental evidence suggests that certain preschool programs may succeed in reducing later delinquency and that schools with a certain ethos and balance of academic talents may reduce delinquency during the school years. These glimmers of hope are worth pursuing, but many questions remain unanswered. We cannot be confident that the reduction is real because (with respect to preschool programs) it has so far been measured only in one or two experimental projects that involve a small number of pupils. Such projects may appear to succeed because the experimenters are able to attract the most talented and dedicated teachers; whether the same treatment would work if applied by less gifted teachers to large numbers of pupils is not clear.

Even if the delinquency reduction effect of preschool education is real, no one yet knows what it is about the program that produces this effect or for what kinds of children the program is best suited. Does preschool education work because it removes the child from adverse family conditions, or does it work because it supplements and strengthens the well-intentioned efforts of parents to cope with a difficult child? Would preschool education be harmful for children who are thereby removed from a good family, or would such education help all children whatever their family life? Is the key element of the program the cognitive preparation of the child for group activities? Does the program reduce the rate at which any enrolled child will later commit offenses or only the rate at which certain kinds of children (say, those who would otherwise become low-rate offenders) commit future delinquencies?

Many of the same questions can be asked about research showing the desirable effects of attending schools with a certain organizational ethos or character. Is the reduction in delinquency and school misconduct limited to the school-age years or does it persist after school? Is there a reduction in the serious delinquencies of high-rate offenders or only in the kinds of minor offenses and truancies that are displayed by a large proportion of all school children? Can a desirable school ethos be created by plan so that children randomly assigned to such a school will show markedly better behavior than similar children assigned to a conventional school?

We seem closer to identifying ways of improving schools than we are to finding methods of improving families, but we are far from knowing how to mount large-scale efforts through the schools and whether, if mounted, they would have a minor or major effect on later criminality. There have been countless school-based programs tried in the past; the results of most have been dashed hopes. To improve the chances of success, we have to know more precisely what the causal connections are, if any, between schooling and later conduct. We are not much closer to answering that question today than we were in the 1950s.

Drug Abuse. High-rate offenders typically are involved with drugs or alcohol abuse. Studies at RAND[7] and elsewhere suggest that regular drug abuse is one of the characteristics of the most dangerous offenders. Offenders, for example, may commit six times as many nondrug crimes when they are using heroin on a daily basis as they would during periods when they are off the drug.[8]

Almost everything we know about persons who are physiologically or psychologically addicted to drugs comes from studying those who are deeply into their addictive behavior and happen to have been arrested or to have volunteered for a treatment program. Such persons are likely to be a quite unrepresentative sample of all those who have experimented with drugs. Because of this, we cannot be confident we know the characteristics of persons who are high-rate users as opposed to casual experimenters or chippers. There is a sharp disagreement among experts about the effects on high-rate users of a law-enforcement crackdown on drug trafficking. Some argue that such policies reduce the availability of drugs and thus reduce their use; others argue that these policies merely drive up the price of the drugs and thus induce users to commit more crimes to pay for their habits; still others suggest that crackdowns have no discernible effect at all on the supplies available to regular users.

To answer either question requires that we learn more about the individual characteristics of novices and desisters. Efforts to infer what factors predispose some persons to drug use have had to rely for the most part on studies of persons already known to be users, and much of that research has been limited to gathering readily available social and demographic data (age, ethnicity, family circumstances) plus, occasionally, psychological profiles. But quite possibly some physiological or biological factors put some young persons at greater risk for drug abuse than others, just as we already know that there is to some extent a genetic basis for the tendency to abuse alcohol. Systematically investigating these and other possibilities is essential if we are to do anything more to prevent drug abuse than mount broad-gauge, ill-focused, and usually untested educational programs designed to persuade young persons to avoid drugs.

Employment. Since high rates of criminality occur disproportionately among people who have low incomes and spotty employment records, it is only natural to assume that poverty and unemployment cause crime. They may, but the case for that connection has not been firmly established; and there exist other possible explanations for this observed connection, for example:

1. People turn to crime because they are unable to find jobs.
2. Certain intellectual and temperamental characteristics (for example, low verbal aptitude, impulsiveness, little regard for others) may cause some people both to turn to crime and to be unattractive to prospective employers.
3. People who find crime rewarding (for example, drug dealers) may reject available jobs and thus be counted as unemployed.
4. Youngsters raised in neighborhoods where affluent criminals have become role models may not value the benefits of legitimate work.
5. People raised in neighborhoods suffering from chronic shortages of jobs may assume without individually exploring the market that jobs are not available and hence that training for jobs is pointless.

Although some studies have shown a correlation between crime on the one hand and unemployment, economic recessions, and lowered labor force participation on the other, these correlations are in many cases not strong. Other studies find no such correlation. And where significant correlations do exist, they tell us little about which of the causal mechanisms listed above, or others that we might imagine, are actually operating. The inconclusive nature of these studies may well result from their relying, with few exceptions, on aggregate data, that is, on the crime and unemployment rates for entire cities, counties, or states. What is needed are more studies measuring the effects of individual experiences in the labor market on individual tendencies to commit crime.

Efforts to reduce criminality by experimental interventions designed to supply job training, to find employment, and even to subsidize ex-offenders looking for employment have so far produced only a few encouraging results. But these programs have generally been directed at adult offenders, ex-convicts, or delinquent school dropouts who are age eighteen or older. It may be impossible to intervene successfully this late in the criminal or delinquent career; perhaps starting such programs much sooner, before crime itself has become rewarding, would make a greater difference. Or it may be that the temperamental and cognitive problems of persons who become high-rate offenders cannot be changed significantly by employment and job training programs. Or it may be that such programs will work but only if the participants are removed from those neighborhoods that make hustling more attractive than work.

In short, a serious investigation of the connection between crime and work may have to start much earlier in the lives of young men than is commonly supposed. In particular, we may need to know more about the earliest work experiences of youngsters and the relationship between schooling and work. The transition from school to work is poorly understood, especially for those young people who drop out of school early. In studying that connection we should not begin with the assumption that dropping out of school is always a bad idea. Some persons may benefit from leaving school before graduating, provided they can thereby enter into the discipline of the workplace.[9] We know too little about the differences among people that affect how entry into the work force is (or is not) accomplished.

Juvenile Court. The debate over the role of the juvenile court is a familiar one. Those who think crime can best be reduced by making the penalties for its commission greater want to see the court take seriously the first nontrivial infraction of a youngster by imposing on him some significant penalty (incarceration, mandatory community service, victim restitution) early in the delinquent career in hope that this first short, sharp shock of punishment will deter future and greater misdeeds. If the youngster should persist in criminality, the penalties should be steadily increased, if necessary by transferring him to the jurisdiction of adult court where long sentences can be handed out. Juvenile records should automatically be made available to adult court authorities when the youngster reaches the age of transition. Some studies suggest that this strategy may work.[10]

Those people who think crime can best be prevented by providing services rather than punishment and by avoiding the stigmatizing effects of early punishment recommend a different strategy. Unless the offense is serious, the child should be diverted from the criminal justice system and into counseling and helping agencies: foster homes, halfway houses, and the like. Juvenile proceedings and records should be confidential, and the juvenile record should not automatically follow the child into adulthood. Early punishment does not deter, it merely labels the recipient in a way that is destructive to his self-esteem and exposes him to a greater likelihood of hostile police surveillance. Many delinquents are the product of child abuse, and the juvenile court should work to undo the harmful effects of these early experiences. Transferring the juvenile to adult court rarely makes sense. There are studies that seem to support this line of reasoning.[11]

The debate is as old as the juvenile court itself. We are under no illusion that research will settle it since at stake are not merely facts but also deeply held convictions about the right relationship between the child and society. But the facts are not irrelevant. And they are much in dispute. Precisely because juvenile records are relatively inaccessible in many jurisdictions, few studies have followed a group of young persons as they have moved from their first experience with the juvenile authorities to their last and on into the adult system. Because the juvenile system often does not produce statistics equivalent to those produced about adult offenders (even the number of juveniles handled by the court is rarely broken down by type of offense), there are not even many correlational studies of how juvenile courts process young offenders and with what effect.

As a result we cannot say with confidence that, other things being equal, a delinquent who is punished after his first offense is more or less likely to commit another crime than one who is treated. We only have fragmentary evidence as to the effect—in sentence length and later criminality—of transferring juveniles to adult court. We cannot be certain that adult offenders are sentenced differently when their full juvenile records are known than when they are not.

Moreover, we do not know the consequences of having decriminalized the so-called status offenses (that is, behaviors that if engaged in by an adult would not be regarded as criminal). Liberals and conservatives alike in recent years have pressed the states to eliminate such categories as "person in need of supervision" from the offenses dealt with by juvenile courts. But there is some reason to worry about this. First, many persons in need of supervision often turn out to be the same persons who are committing delinquent acts. Second, if the juvenile court does not attend, however imperfectly, to the needs of persons needing supervision (runaways, truants, and the like), who will? We recall the enthusiasm that in the 1960s greeted plans to deinstitutionalize mental patients and the dismay that set in during the 1980s, when it became evident that the deinstitutionalized patients now made up a large share of the homeless, uncared for by anyone save occasionally a sheriff who found space for them in the local jail.

Adult Courts and Corrections. The issues swirling about the adult criminal justice system are no less obscure. The debate over the purpose of that system—deterrence, incapacitation, rehabilitation, retribution—is a familiar one. Like the debate over the juvenile court, facts alone will not resolve it. But facts will narrow the zone of disagreement by shedding light on the consequences of policy alternatives.

We know more about adult crime than about juvenile crime and more about adult corrections than juvenile corrections. We have better data for adult than for juvenile offenders on recidivism, the extent of drug and alcohol abuse, and the past employment record. In fact much of what we know about the nature of criminality has been learned by tracing backward the careers of arrested adult offenders. But these retrospective studies are subject to substantial errors in the accuracy of the offenders' memories and their willingness to be candid. Moreover retrospective studies do not illuminate the causal sequences by which one circumstance (say, trouble in school) did or did not lead to another (say, trouble in finding a job). And good retrospective studies are few in number. As a result, even for the workings of the adult criminal justice system, much of what we know, for example, about deterrence, comes from cross-sectional or correlational studies that leave the issue of causality rather clouded.

Does imprisonment deter the person imprisoned, or are prisons schools of crime that increase the number and enhance the success of subsequent efforts at crime? We have some aggregate studies that shed light on this issue (our best guess is that, on the average, imprisonment makes the offender neither better nor worse) but few that permit us to be confident about our conclusions. And such studies as do exist tell us only what the effect of imprisonment is on the average—none tells us with much precision what the effects may be on different kinds of inmates, and hardly any tell us whether nonimprisonment sanctions (fines, community service, restitution) deter offenders, and if so, what kinds of sanctions, how, and under what circumstances.

The criminal justice system has always been selective about whom it imprisoned. The current debate over selective incapacitation is new only in being a debate; the practice is as old as the first trial. For all practical purposes the issue is not whether the system will be selective (by trying to focus on the most dangerous or the highest-rate offenders) but whether it can be significantly more accurate than chance in identifying those offenders and can do so at an acceptable cost in money and fairness. As we stated at the outset of this chapter, important and sophisticated attempts have been made (by researchers at RAND, among others) to specify the characteristics of high-rate offenders so that they can be identified as early in their careers, and as early in the criminal justice system, as possible. But these studies are retrospective inquiries into the self-reported criminal careers of incarcerated inmates. Not only are they subject to the previously mentioned errors in recall and honesty, but they are likely to be biased by examining only those offenders who happen to be in prison. If one wished to change sentencing policies to make more efficient use of scarce prison space by giving prison terms to high-rate offenders, the key issue is what will happen to the crime rate if these decision rules are applied to convicted offenders who are not now in prison and whose individual offense rates are unknown.

Much the same argument can be made about the current state of our knowledge of rehabilitative techniques. There is no reason to be optimistic as yet about our ability to reduce recidivism rates by plan and for large numbers of offenders. But neither is there reason to believe that no program can ever be effective for anyone. Some experts have argued that the disappointing results of rehabilitative programs arise from failing to see that the desirable effects on some persons are counterbalanced by the undesirable effects on others, giving an average result of no effect. If different programs are designed for different kinds of offenders, better results, at least in some cases, would be obtained. We do not know whether this conjecture is well founded or not, but we see no reason why it should be dismissed out of hand.

Individual Differences. At least one central theme runs throughout this discussion of what we need to know to improve our ability to prevent crime: the importance of knowing more about individual differences among offenders and nonoffenders. The great bulk of policy-relevant research groups offenders together into broad categories, often differentiated (if at all) only by such obvious characteristics as sex, age, race, and official record. But if we wish to reduce the probability of low-rate offenders becoming high-rate offenders, we must develop greater insight into far more subtle differences among individuals and their circumstances. If families differ in the extent to which they produce delinquents, it is not because such families differ in the age or race of the parents; rather it is because they differ in the extent to which they form strong bonds of affection with their children, manage effectively the daily routine of socialization and guidance, and cope satisfactorily with both the cognitive and temperamental characteristics of their offspring and the economic and social aspects of their environment. Similarly, if schools differ in their ability to induce reasonable levels of obedience in their pupils, it is not because the schools differ in the age of their buildings or the size of their libraries, but because they differ in the mix of talents among their students and the habits and styles of their teachers.

How Can We Find Out?

Because the design of almost any new crime reduction policy requires us to choose among equally plausible but competing theories about how individuals respond to the circumstances in which they find themselves, the policy maker's first task is to recognize the need for a research strategy that will guide and test that design. This is especially true if our goal is primary prevention, that is, reducing the chances of a given child becoming delinquent in the first place. Uncovering the subtle interaction between individual characteristics and social circumstances requires policy-related research of a sort and on a scale that has not been attempted before.

Some people are ready to acknowledge that we have gaps in our knowledge but argue that they can be filled from the lessons of practical experience. This is misleading. Practical experience is itself a form of research; it is an effort to learn by observation. The key question is

179

whether those observations are accurate or inaccurate, systematic or casual, verified or not. Practical experience is an important guide to action, but it is only a guide. To become the basis for a general rule, it must be systematically tested. There are three ways to do this, which we illustrate by considering how we might answer the following question: What is the relationship between the behavior of parents and the later delinquency of their children?

Cross-Sectional Research. The first method is to compare the families of delinquent children with those of not-so-delinquent ones. Social scientists call this cross-sectional research because it involves examining the similarities and differences among a cross section of families studied at one point in time. It is akin to taking a snapshot. A snapshot can tell us many things: whether families with delinquent children are bigger or smaller, poorer or richer, more punitive or less punitive than families without such offspring. But it cannot tell us whether the size, the wealth, or the disciplinary practices of the families caused the higher rate of delinquency. In an attempt to deal with this problem, social scientists will try to hold constant every feature of the families but one to see if, after controlling for these other factors, this one factor by itself is associated with delinquency. The process is akin to sorting the snapshots, so that in one pile there are only, for example, snapshots of big, poor families, and then looking through these pictures to see if the families with harsh disciplinary practices are also the ones with more delinquent children. This sorting helps narrow down the possibilities by showing whether disciplinary practices are related to delinquency independent of family size and poverty. But this method cannot settle the question of causality. Suppose that harsh discipline occurs disproportionately among families with delinquent children. There remain three possibilities: the disciplinary practices have caused the delinquency, the existence in the family of delinquent children has caused the parents to increase the severity of their discipline, or there is some unknown third factor (perhaps a predisposition to violence) that has caused the parents to be harsh and the children to be delinquents.

Longitudinal Research. The second method is to follow the development of one or more families over time. Social scientists call this longitudinal research. It is akin to taking not a snapshot but a motion picture. A motion picture helps settle the question of causality because it can tell us which factors came earlier and which later in the development of the children. If children begin misbehaving and then the parents adopt tough disciplinary practices, the latter cannot have caused the former. Even longitudinal research cannot conclusively settle the question of causality.

Some unobserved changes may occur that affect the child's development in ways that lead the observer to suppose erroneously that child misbehavior caused the severe parental discipline (or vice versa). The parents, for example, may have experienced some serious stress (perhaps a major illness) that caused the change in disciplinary practices, but that, unnoticed by the observer, was ignored in the causal analysis. (An analogy: Doctors who have done longitudinal research on the effects of vigorous exercise on the risk of heart disease sometimes conclude that people who exercise a lot are less likely than those who are sedentary to have a heart attack. But this finding might ignore the fact that persons who exercise a lot are different from those who do not in many other ways and that these other differences may actually explain the lowered risk of heart disease.) Although it is not perfect, the motion-picture method is always superior to the snapshot method in at least ruling out factors that could not have caused criminality.

Of course, getting this motion picture is no easy matter. One way is to start following some families from the moment they have children. Because it is forward-looking, this is called prospective longitudinal research. It has the great advantage that the families are picked without knowing in advance which will have delinquent children and which will not so the results cannot be biased by the scientist's prior knowledge of the presence of delinquency. But it also has a disadvantage: since most families will not raise high-rate offenders, a lot of the research will be wasted effort—the scientist will never see anything but trivial examples of misconduct. To solve this problem, the investigator can pick families known to have delinquent children and then ask the parents and their offspring to recall their past experiences. This is a retrospective longitudinal study. But as we noted, such a method introduces whatever biases (and they are likely to be great) that may be caused by poor memories and deliberate misrepresentation as well as the bias caused by not knowing how normal (that is, noncriminal) families behave. For these reasons most scholars agree that a prospective study is superior to a retrospective one.

Experimental Research. The third method is to intervene deliberately in the lives of children and their families in a way that will permit the investigator to determine what effect, if any, the intervention has. This is called experimental research. A true experiment should randomly assign (say, by a flip of a coin) the families to either treatment or no treatment. (Those in the former group are the experimentals, those in the latter, the controls.) By random assignment one can ensure that the two groups differ only in the presence or absence of treatment. Hence it is

181

possible to demonstrate the effect, if any, of a treatment independent of all other factors.

Some investigators have tried to conduct quasi experiments by matching (in age, sex, race, or whatever) people in a treatment program with people not in it. This can produce quite misleading results because there is always the possibility that despite the matching the two groups will differ in some important but unnoticed way. Indeed, given the subtlety of the factors that produce crime, it is almost certain that these differences will exist. Suppose a doctor treating abused children by providing them with psychotherapy wishes to find out if the treatment works. That doctor creates a quasi experiment by finding an equal number of similarly abused children who are not treated and looks at how the treated children turn out compared to the untreated ones. This is better than no experiment at all, but the results can be biased. We already know that the treated children volunteered for treatment or were referred for treatment by a social worker. Those who volunteer are likely to be quite different, psychologically and perhaps sociologically, from those who do not volunteer; similarly children whom social workers know about and want to help may well be quite different from those the workers do not know or are not motivated to help.

A true experiment should have other features as well. There should be a long-term follow-up. Many treatments work for a while simply because many people respond to anything special that is done for them but do not have any lasting effects. There is no hard-and-fast rule, but in general follow-ups of less than eighteen to twenty-four months are probably too brief. There should be several measures of the desired outcome, not just one. Most measures of crime (for example, arrest records, conviction records, self-reported crimes) are erroneous to some degree. Using just one outcome measure may deceive the investigator into thinking that nothing has changed when in fact something has or into believing that there has been a change when in fact there has not. A treatment, for example, may reduce the rate at which persons are arrested, but if the treatment only made the subjects more skillful in avoiding arrest, the true criminality of the subjects may not have lessened at all. And the evaluation of the experiment should be carried out by someone other than the therapist. A person committed professionally and emotionally to making some treatment work is likely to describe as successes outcomes that an impartial observer would describe as failures and to find evidence where none really exists that would justify continuing the program.

Previous Studies. Not many prospective longitudinal studies or intervention experiments have been done. Of the eleven major longitudinal studies meeting certain minimal standards that have been carried out in the United States, scarcely any track closely all the likely causal factors. Most have gathered no data on the medical and physiological condition of the infant or on the mother's prenatal and perinatal experiences. Most have not attempted to assess the temperament of the child or its parents with standard psychological tests. Few have used both arrests and self-reports as measures of criminality. Of those that have measured the child-rearing practices of the families, most have relied on occasional retrospective interviews with the parents rather than on direct observation or frequent and contemporaneous interviews. Most discuss the child's school performance, but only occasionally is there an effort to specify how early in the school years any difficulties emerged or the extent to which those difficulties are linked to learning disabilities. Almost every longitudinal study has followed only one group of children for a number of years rather than several groups at various ages for a number of years. The authors of such studies cannot know whether the development of criminal behavior in their subjects follows a pattern that occurs generally or a pattern that is unique to a group growing up in a certain period. (For example, children growing up in the 1950s, when drug abuse was relatively rare, may develop criminal careers in ways quite different from those growing up in the 1960s, when drug abuse was widespread.) Finally, the existing longitudinal studies offer little insight into the impact, if any, of efforts to change the subjects, such as special school or job training programs.

Given the difficulty in finding opportunities to assign persons randomly to treatment or control groups and to follow up such persons over a long period, it is surprising how many criminological experiments have actually been conducted. In general they test a treatment for only a short period. None shows the impact of a treatment on an entire criminal career. Only a minority of them show that the treatment had any desirable effects, and those tend to be prevention experiments.[12] Few successes have been reported for programs aimed at rehabilitating serious offenders, although there is some evidence that certain kinds of offenders—that is, those that have been rather unsuccessful at crime and are young and reasonably intelligent—may benefit from some programs. Even where encouraging results can be found, they are limited to one or two relatively small experiments that have yet to be duplicated in other settings and that are vulnerable to methodological criticisms. But the occasional success story provides a glimmer of hope that is worth exploring and suggests where in the development of a criminal career may be found the best opportunity for a helpful intervention.

A New Strategy

The best way to create useful new knowledge about the prevention of crime is to mount one or more major projects that combine the strengths of longitudinal and experimental designs. Although we are strongly convinced of the importance of the longitudinal experimental method, the details we give later in this report are meant only to illustrate what the combination of these designs might be like rather than to specify a rigid, unchangeable method. Such a design should have the following main features.

Multiple Cohorts. Rather than pick one group of subjects born in the same year (a cohort) and follow them from birth to age twenty or later, we recommend picking several cohorts born in different years and following each for about six years. There might be, for example, four cohorts followed from birth to age six, six to twelve, twelve to eighteen, and eighteen to twenty-four. This shortens the time until research results are obtained and enables the investigators to distinguish between the effects of aging (for example, becoming a teenager) and the effects of an historical period (for example, growing up in the 1990s as opposed to the 1980s). Each cohort could have about 1,000 subjects.

Urban Sample. Although criminal careers can begin anywhere, crime rates are generally much higher in large cities. Moreover, choosing a cohort from a single metropolitan area permits one set of investigators located in that city to oversee all the subjects and to study the social and institutional context in which crime occurs. The metropolitan area selected should be relatively stable to minimize losses resulting from people moving out of the city. Within the area the subjects picked should be males representative of the entire population in race and ethnicity, although it may be desirable to oversample some groups that would have too few members in the cohort if it were picked wholly at random. The exact method of selecting subjects we leave to further inquiry. There is a case to be made for including females as well as males, but if the cohort is no larger than 1,000 and half are female, the number of subjects who are likely to become high-rate offenders will be drastically reduced. (Of 500 males, only 6 to 12 percent—30 to 60 persons—are likely to become serious repeat criminals; if the sample has 1,000 males, then the number of repeaters rises to between 60 and 120.) Of course, the same number of repeaters (or more) could be found if the cohort of males and females totaled 2,000 subjects or if the subjects were not chosen at random but by oversampling groups known to be especially at risk for criminality. In addition to cohorts chosen from the general population, we suggest that two cohorts be selected from persons, aged fifteen to twenty-one, who have been arrested, and from those, aged eighteen to twenty-four, who are just beginning their first prison sentences. We also suggest that, if possible, the project should be repeated in more than one metropolitan area.

Multiple Measures of Misconduct. Data about crime should include arrest reports, self-reports, and (to the extent possible) the reports of peers, parents, and teachers. But crime and delinquency should not be the only measures of misconduct; the investigators should also gather information about disciplinary problems in the home and school, truancy, traffic violations, sexual promiscuity, alcohol and drug abuse, and employment problems.

Comprehensive Individual Data. We cannot stress too much the importance of gathering information bearing on all the major causal factors that might be implicated in criminality. Every investigator will be alert to the significance of family processes, school experiences, and peer group influences. But important as these social circumstances may be, they operate on individuals who enter this world with certain temperamental characteristics, predispositions, abilities, and weaknesses that are the product of inheritance, prenatal experiences, perinatal trauma, events during the first few months of life, or some combination of all these conditions.[13] We do not argue that these factors cause crime, only that (as every parent knows) they shape the interaction between infant and caregiver and that these interactions in turn shape the personality of the child. Nor do we argue that the personality of the one-year-old becomes the personality of the twelve-year-old; people change, although there is some impressive evidence that aggression among males is one of the more stable personality factors. Failing to gather individual data, including medical and psychological factors, has the effect of ruling out these factors as contributory causes and prevents the development of programs designed to combat whatever causal power they may have.

Experimental Treatments. A fraction of each cohort should if possible be randomly assigned to a treatment program, and the effect of the program should be carefully evaluated. The treatments should be selected from among those for which preliminary evidence (from existing experiments) suggests a reasonable possibility of success. Examples of possible programs follow.

Younger cohorts. Preschool education programs and parent training programs might be used for a portion of the cohort to test the effect of these programs on young persons whose life histories will already be known in considerable detail. One of the difficulties in assessing the significance of such treatments (which the proposed study will overcome) is that so little is known about the behavior of the subjects before they enter the program. The evaluators may underestimate the effect of the program (because the participants change in ways not evident in the standard outcome measures) or may fail to distinguish between the kinds of participants for whom the program is helpful and the kinds for whom it may be harmful.

Older cohorts. Older children and teenagers might be experimentally involved in programs designed to alter peer group relationships, to improve school performance, and to develop resistance to alcohol and drug abuse.

Arrested cohorts. Persons who have been arrested might be randomly diverted from court or exposed to some degree of punishment appropriate to their offense, or randomly assigned to juvenile or adult court.

Imprisoned cohorts. The effect on imprisoned persons of different release patterns (early release on parole, release on work furlough) or different conditions of release (with or without financial assistance or job placement) has been tested already but not with the detailed information about the inmates' life histories that this project envisions. With this rich body of information, it should be possible to disentangle positive, negative, and neutral influences so that we would know for what kinds of inmates particular programs have desirable or undesirable effects.

Organizing for Research

No project of the size and complexity we are proposing has ever been attempted in criminological or criminal justice research. Because it is unprecedented, it is especially risky. But it is not unacceptably risky. Even if many of the experiments cannot be carried out because of organizational, financial, or legal problems, we will still have gathered an extraordinarily valuable body of information about the natural history of criminal and noncriminal careers. Moreover, analogous projects have been undertaken in other fields. It is not uncommon, for example, for large cohorts of subjects to be followed carefully for many years in medical research and for special treatments (for example, reducing blood cholesterol levels) to be given to some members of the cohort.

We have relatively little to say about the organizational structure or structures within which this project should be undertaken. The Justice

Program Study Group commissioned a number of papers from scholars around the United States who proposed various methods for designing and executing longitudinal and experimental research and held a conference at which these papers were discussed. It is clear that further work needs to be done before the final design and structure can be settled. We are not certain whether one entity (for example, a university-based research group) should design and manage the research as a single project or whether several allied research groups should collaborate in designing the research with data gathering left to a specialized organization. We are not certain of the right mix of governmental and private funds with which to support this venture. (We estimate that it may cost $1 million per year for several years, but the cost may be higher if the size of the cohorts or the number of experiments is increased.)

Moreover, we do not wish to undercut other research strategies. A great deal has been learned using cross-sectional methods. By taking these snapshots and analyzing their contents, we have learned about the role of alcohol and heroin in certain kinds of crime, the extent to which victims sometimes precipitate attacks on themselves, the degree to which juvenile crime occurs in groups, the association between school failure and delinquency, and the psychological differences among types of offenders. Through retrospective longitudinal studies we have learned about the kinds of persons who become high-rate as opposed to low-rate offenders and the association between criminality and intelligence, family discord, and unemployment. Indeed, it is possible to grasp the potential benefits of a prospective longitudinal study that includes experimental interventions only by drawing on what we already have learned from different research methods.

Progress in medicine came from research and experimentation. Some of that research was catch as catch can—trying a new drug or treatment to see if it helped arrest the course of a serious ailment. In time, methods for testing more accurately the effects of new drugs were developed so that today checking the efficacy and safety of new products has become routine. But it gradually became clear to physicians that if serious diseases were to be prevented rather than simply treated, scientists would have to study sick people to see how they got that way (retrospective longitudinal research) and healthy people to see what caused some to become ill (prospective longitudinal research). Groups of persons—cohorts—were followed for years to learn about the effects on health of heavy smoking, high levels of cholesterol, and exposure to various environmental hazards. The lesson of these complex, long-term projects was the discovery that society may be underinvesting in preventing illness and overinvesting in treating illness, given the relative gains from prevention and treatment.

Research today on how best to deal with crime is no further along than was research in the nineteenth century on how best to deal with illness. We have learned some clues about how to treat some problems, and we have a good idea about what the very sick patient (that is, the high-rate offender) looks like and what his circumstances have been. But we have only the most rudimentary ideas about the developmental sequence of criminality and thus we have only a few tantalizing clues as to where in that sequence we might intervene with good effect.

It may be that there is no way we can intervene on any large scale. The causes of crime may be buried so deeply in the human psyche, intimate family processes, and profound cultural norms that we cannot learn how to make meaningful changes, or if we do learn, we would find the necessary methods to be abhorrent. We may have to content ourselves with dealing with symptoms rather than causes and doing so on the basis of the rather crude instruments now at our disposal, such as police officers, target hardening, prisons, fines, and drug treatment programs.

We do not know whether to be optimistic or pessimistic. We do know that we have not tried hard to find out. There have been hundreds of important studies of the effects of smoking on health; there have been but a handful on what many people would regard as a far graver public health problem: criminality. We believe that we can do better and that we should. We are aware that many readers would prefer to reject our recommendations in favor of quick action to implement plausible schemes that seem to have immediate payoffs. We do not wish to dissuade them from doing whatever seems constructive in the short run. But we do urge them to set aside some time, effort, and money to prepare better for the long term. We are also aware that some readers, noting that crime rates have been flat or declining in the early 1980s, will conclude that the crisis is over and that major new studies of criminal careers are unnecessary. We remind them that our society was caught completely unprepared for the extraordinary increase in crime during the 1960s and 1970s, that many people may have suffered needlessly as a result, that crime rates will go up again, and that we are not much better prepared for the next crime wave than we were for the last.

Finally, we wish to stress that although our principal charge has been to make recommendations regarding crime, our strategy, if it is of any value at all, will have benefits that go well beyond any crime reduction potential. People who frequently commit crimes are not normal in all other aspects of their lives. For the high-rate offender, crime is usually but one manifestation of a life that is generally disorderly and pathological. The high-rate offender tends also to be the failing student, the drunken driver, the unreliable employee, and the abusive or neglectful parent. An inquiry into the causes of criminality is at the same time an inquiry into the causes of general defects in character and behavior; lessons learned about how to prevent crime will almost surely be lessons learned about how to produce better citizens. Scholars in many fields in addition to criminology will find the data of a major longitudinal experimental study of great value in understanding how to help people who constitute not just a large fraction of the workload of practitioners in criminal justice but also of those in education, social work, mental health, and manpower development. We hope that agencies interested in such matters will lend their support to this venture. If it succeeds for one, it is likely to succeed for all.

14

The Moral Sense

After completing the original edition of On Character, *I set about trying to think systematically about how people come to have moral dispositions and whether these vary so greatly across cultures that they add up to nothing of general significance. The result was my book,* The Moral Sense, *published in 1993. In it I surveyed what scholars had learned about the tendency of people in a variety of cultures to attach importance to fairness, self-control, duty, and sympathy and drew attention to the fact, obvious to any parent but for long less obvious to scholars who wrote about parenting, that children from a very early age express—and are eager to express—those sentiments. Modern social science has recovered, perhaps without quite intending to, an older understanding of human nature common to thinkers as otherwise different as Aristotle, David Hume, and Adam Smith. My first statement of this argument took the form of my presidential address to the American Political Science Association in September 1992.*

The central problem for social science is to explain social order. How do people manage to live together? One can discern two ways of answering that question. The first view is normative and communal: people learn from their culture customs that provide an internal compass guiding them to act in ways that minimize conflict and ensure comity. The second view is rationalistic and individualistic: order is created by explicit and implicit agreements entered into by self-seeking individuals to avert the worst consequences of their predatory instincts. In the first view, order is natural and prior to any social contract or government institution; in the second, order is contrived and dependent on agreements and sanctions. Rules are obeyed in the first case because they have moral force, in the second because they convey personal advantage. In the first view, compliance is automatic and general; in the second, it is strategic and uncertain.[1]

The normative view has been under heavy attack for several decades for at least three reasons: it seems to imply a complacent functionalism; it appears to minimize or deny the value of conflict; and it lacks the theoretical power found in the assumption that people always seek their own interests. I believe that one can grant, up to a point, all of those objections and still be left dissatisfied with the alternative, namely, that social order is contrived, based on calculation, and dependent on individual assent.

I wish to reestablish a version of the normative view. My argument is that while conflict within societies is ubiquitous and diversity among them obvious, people everywhere have a natural moral sense that is not entirely the product of utility or convention. By *moral sense* I mean a directly felt impression of some standards by which we ought to judge voluntary action. The standards are usually general and imprecise. Hence, when I say that people have a moral sense, I do not wish to be understood as saying that they have an intuitive knowledge of moral rules. Moral rules are often disputed and usually in conflict; but the process by which people resolve those disputes or settle those conflicts leads them back to sentiments that seem to them to have a worth that is intuitively obvious. Those sentiments constitute the fundamental glue of society, a glue with adhesive power that is imperfect but sufficient to explain social order to some degree. The philosophers of the Scottish Enlightenment, in particular Francis Hutcheson writing in 1742, David Hume in 1740, and Adam Smith in 1759, explored with care and subtlety the reasons why certain sentiments commend themselves to us as worthy. I am under no illusion that I can improve on what they accomplished; but I hope to show, by drawing on the social and biological sciences, that their fundamental claims are consistent with much of what we have learned since the mid-eighteenth century.

One can infer the existence of a moral sense from behaviors that cannot easily be explained by even enlightened self-interest. There is less crime than one would expect from the probability of detection and punishment.[2] Even in the poorest neighborhoods, a complete breakdown of law and order does not lead most people to engage in looting. There are more obligations honored than one can explain knowing only that it is often useful to honor them. For example, we sometimes keep promises when it is not in our interest to do so, we often vote in elections even though we cannot affect the outcomes, we make charitable donations to organizations that confer no recognition on us, and some of us help people in distress even when no one is watching to applaud our good deed.

It will be objected that voting, donating, and helping are far from common actions and thus that little of moral significance can be inferred from their occasional performance. I do not fully accept that objection, but I recognize its force. Let me turn, then, to behavior that is well nigh universal, that cannot be explained by individual calculations of utility or by negotiated social contracts, and that has obvious moral implications in any plausible meaning of the word *moral*: child care.

The Child as Recipient and Source of the Moral Sense

People bring children into this world and nurture them through long years of dependency. They do that with no hope of immediate gain and every expectation of sleepless nights, financial burdens, and daily vexations. David Hume, in his attempt to base morality upon sentiments, was led ineluctably to the parent-child relationship as the founding sentiment. Justice, he argued, was an artifice, a set of rules useful because they make people secure in their property and enable them to transmit it in an orderly fashion. But why do people care about the transmission of property? Because of "the natural affection, which they bear their children." That natural affection implies an obligation; people everywhere praise those who care for their children and despise those who do not.[3] Note how easily Hume inferred an "is" statement from an "ought" statement scarcely eight pages beyond the famous passage in which he suggested that this cannot be done.

Two objections may be made to that view. Scholars bent on finding self-serving explanations for behavior will argue that parents produce offspring because the latter are useful as unpaid laborers and future breadwinners. While that no doubt occurs and may explain why some parents feel a duty to their children, it cannot explain why children should feel any obligation to their parents. The youngsters are free riders who benefit from nurturance whether they later support those who nurtured them or not. Yet children feel and act upon obligations to their parents despite the fact that such actions are unprofitable.

Scholars resolute to explain all behavior as culturally determined and thus morally relativistic will argue that child care is by no means universal. Many writers have asserted that a sense of childhood is a recent invention, preceded, at least in Europe, by centuries of neglect, abuse, death, and abandonment.[4] If mothers still kill their own babies and if parents have only recently stopped sending them to foundling homes, the love of children must be a recently acquired and thus socially learned disposition. In the words of Lloyd de Mause, the history of childhood is a "nightmare from which we have only recently begun to awaken."[5] The further back in time we go, the more likely the child was to be killed, abandoned, beaten, terrorized, and sexually abused. Edward Shorter gathered data on the use of wet nurses and foundling homes in the eighteenth century that, to him, bespoke a "traditional lack of maternal love."[6] A sense of childhood—and the love of children—is seen as a modern invention, ascribed variously to religion, capitalism, and the Enlightenment.

It is odd that such a view should have had so large an impact, since we already knew from studies of contemporary primitive societies, such as the San of the Kalahari Desert, that children are not only loved but indulged without benefit of modern science, enlightened teaching, or capitalist requirements.[7] It is even odder that conclusions about people's feelings about children were inferred from data about how children were treated, since the treatment of children might well have been shaped as much by circumstances as by attitudes.[8] For example, wet-nursing was used by women who, because of their employment in agriculture, could not breast-feed their own infants and for whom no other safe source of food was available.[9] In any event, wet-nursing was far less common than Shorter would have us believe. Perhaps 10 percent of all Parisian women, beyond that small percentage who were physiologically unable to nurse, put their children out to wet nurses.[10] There is no evidence to support the assumption that wet nurses or foundling homes were used because most or even many parents were indifferent to their children.

Such direct evidence as we have about the feelings of European parents and children toward one another is inconsistent with the view that a caring family is a recent invention. The painstaking research of Linda Pollock in over four hundred diaries and autobiographies, including many written by children, suggests quite strongly that British and American parents and children from the sixteenth to the nineteenth centuries felt toward each other much what we feel today: mutual attachment and great affection.[11]

But surely the existence of infanticide throughout history confirms the purely conventional nature of family attachments. How could a natural sentiment—affection for a child—ever coexist with the deliberate killing of that child? It is a profoundly important question and one that cannot be entirely resolved on the basis of the available historical and anthropological evidence. In his brief but chilling history of infanticide, William L. Langer noted that it has existed everywhere since time immemorial as an accepted procedure for disposing of deformed infants and limiting the size of the population during periods of extreme privation.[12] Jews had always condemned the practice;[13] but only with the advent of Christianity did there begin, in Europe at least, the widespread condemnation of the practice on moral grounds, and only with the spread of Christianity did the secular authorities make it a crime.[14] In hopes of providing an incentive that would reinforce the sanctions of the criminal law, many states created foundling homes in which mothers could leave their unwanted infants. Those hopes were realized beyond the capacity of the system to accommodate them. In 1833, 164,319 babies were left in French foundling homes. At about the same time, one such home in Saint Petersburg had 25,000 infants on its rolls, with 5,000 being admitted yearly.[15] The crowding was so great, and regulation so lax, that conveying a baby to a foundling home was often tantamount to sentencing it to death from neglect.

While that grisly history confirms how often infants were killed or abandoned, it is not very clear about the sentiments and motives of those who killed or abandoned infants. Langer suggests that the motive for infanticide reflected extreme circumstances, typically a child who was either deformed or beyond the capacity of its poor parents to feed. To that must be added the threat of social stigma, moral obloquy, or penal sanction faced by unwed mothers. But those are only suggestions, not conclusions based on a close study of parental feelings. For the history of infanticide to shed light on the existence of a moral sense, it is essential to know how the parents, and especially the mothers, felt about what they did. What proportion disposed of the baby without remorse as a matter of convenience, and what proportion did so in anguish and out of necessity? Langer attributed the decline in infanticide in the late nineteenth and early twentieth centuries to the advent of modern contraception coupled with more stringent state regulation. That is a troubling hypothesis, for it implies that convenience dictated whether the baby would be killed or not. It neglects entirely what may have been the more important causes of the decline: a rise in the standard of living sufficient to enable poor parents to support several children, a change in the attitude toward unwed mothers great enough to make it thinkable to keep an illegitimate child, and an improvement in medical care adequate to ensure the ultimate good health of sickly infants.

The only way to assess the moral significance of infanticide is either to examine the feelings of the parents directly or to consider what happens when the conditions giving rise to it change. As with child neglect more generally, it is a mistake to infer sentiments from actions. In the modern world, infanticide still occurs; but there are no reliable data on how often.[16] The closest thing we have to systematic data is a survey of 112 preindustrial societies from which the authors concluded that infanticide was "common" in about a third of them.[17] The word *common* was not defined, nor does anyone have any idea how many times infanticide actually occurs in any society.

So far as one can tell, infanticide occurs today under essentially the same conditions as in the past but less frequently: there is so little food that the child cannot be fed (especially a problem with twins), or the child is born so deformed or sickly that its chances of survival are slight.[18] Infanticide may also occur when the child's paternity (hence legitimacy) is in dispute. Of the 112 instances in which a cultural justification for infanticide could be found in the anthropological literature, all but 15 involved food shortages, deformity, or uncertain paternity.[19] Less common are instances of female infanticide to minimize the number of girls for whom dowries must be provided.[20] No sentiment is sovereign; each must compete with others. A mother's affection for one infant must

195

compete with her affection for another and with her own desire to survive. In a poor area of Brazil, mothers cope with that competition by not naming the baby until its survival seems assured.[21]

That a mother's affection for her infant is not sovereign, however, does not mean that her affection is not natural. Suppose for a moment that mother-child attachments were purely a matter of convention such that infanticide was governed by personal advantage or cultural practice. Under those circumstances, one would expect to find some societies— perhaps many—in which babies were killed even though food was plentiful, paternity certain, and the child healthy. After all, even healthy, easy-to-support children can be, for many years, a great nuisance. We would also expect to find some societies in which children were killed in the second or third year of life, rather than immediately after birth, especially since (as every parent knows) a two-year-old child is often a greater burden than a newborn infant.

But, in fact, all of the predictions that follow from a purely relativist view of human nature are, so far as one can tell, false. When economic stresses end, infanticide becomes far less common and is almost always made a criminal act. Healthy babies of certain paternity are rarely destroyed. Infanticide almost never occurs after the first year of life; indeed, infanticide rarely occurs except during the first few hours of life.[22] That is so since infanticide must be committed before bonding takes place. If the baby does not die almost immediately, the mother's distress is very great, at least in the few instances in which scholars have been on the scene to record the events.[23]

Sociability and the Emergence of the Moral Sense

The view that there is not a natural moral sense sufficient to account, to any significant degree, for social order began, I believe, when philosophers argued that the human mind was a tabula rasa. If everything, including morality, had to be learned, then anything could be learned. Cultural relativism was the inevitable result of viewing human nature as wholly passive and completely malleable.

Modern science has destroyed that view. It is now clear that nature has prepared the child to be an active participant in his social development and disposed him to see and judge the world in moral terms. In the words of certain anthropologists, the child is an "intuitive moralist."[24]

Newborn infants engage in social activity before they are taught it. They root, suck, and express distress at the sound of other babies' crying. They prefer human sounds to other sounds, female sounds to male ones, and maternal sounds to other female sounds.[25] Such prosocial behavior is not learned. Infants born blind will smile though they have never seen a smile; infants born both deaf and blind will laugh during play, though they have never heard laughter, and frown when angry, though they have never seen a frown.[26] The newborn infant can tell its mother's voice from that of another. It will imitate several facial and hand gestures within two weeks of birth and some gestures within thirty-two hours of birth.[27] Most, if not all, of the universal human facial expressions—those expressing happiness, sadness, surprise, interest, disgust, anger, and fear—can be observed in the newborn child.[28] Within two weeks, infants will reach for a presented object[29] and will cry at the sound of another baby's crying[30] but not at the recorded sound of their own crying.[31] Within six months, babies can tell the difference between the face of a friendly and an unfriendly adult.[32] Within two years, children will share toys, offer help, and console others who are in distress.[33]

The mother responds to those prosocial behaviors with nurturance, affection, and communication. She smiles at the child's smile and laughs at its laughter, picks it up when it cries, feeds it when it is hungry, and plays with it when it is bored. Some people believe that if you reward behavior, it will be repeated. One might infer from that general truth the particular claim that if you pick up a crying baby, it will always cry, and that if you play with a fussy baby, it will always fuss. Not so. The natural sociability of the child inclines it to acquire greater autonomy and confidence, not greater dependence and manipulativeness, when its desire for attachment is met with an equivalent response from its parent.

That is the great paradox of attachment. Bonded children will grow up to be, not dependent, but independent, at least within such latitude as the culture allows. Human infants become attached to humans who make eye contact, whether or not they supply food. Bonding, once it has occurred, will so persist despite punishment that abused children will remain attached to abusive parents. It is clear from those facts that bonding is driven by powerful biological forces and is not simply the result of a utility-maximizing organism's engaging in whatever behaviors bring it immediate rewards.

The child has within it, so to speak, a template that makes some kinds of learning quite easy and others very difficult. For example, a child can be conditioned to fear rats and spiders but not to fear opera glasses.[34] He is preprogrammed, if you will, to discriminate between things that are relevant to his life (because they can hurt) and things that are not,[35] much as he is preprogrammed to learn language at a certain time and in a certain way.[36]

That natural sociability shapes the child's relationships with its parents, siblings, and peers. In all those encounters, the child is not a passive organism repeating whatever acts are rewarded; nor is it a blank slate on which the world can write any message. The child is an active partner not only in shaping, but in judging, its experiences, as is evident when we consider the emergence of two of the moral sentiments, sympathy and fairness.

Sympathy

Children are by nature sociable; in the family they learn to extend sociability into generosity. That extension requires the instruction and example of parents, other kin, and older playmates; but the original impulse requires no instruction. The innate sociability of children makes them sensitive to the moods and actions of others. At first they try to control those moods and actions simply for their own pleasure; later they grasp that what pleases them may not please others, and so they act on the basis of some knowledge of the feelings of others. Children learn without much instruction that their own happiness is in some ways affected by the happiness of others; with some instruction, they learn that the happiness of others can be improved by modest sacrifices in their own well-being. Their own experiences and the teachings of others produce habits of action that routinely take into account the feelings of others. All that occurs early in life, before the children have understood sermons, mastered moral precepts, or read cautionary tales.

No infant needs to learn to assert its own needs; it cries when it is hungry or in distress. Until recently, however, many psychologists assumed that it had to learn everything else. Its capacity for sympathy was, in that view, an acquired characteristic. No doubt how a child is raised will affect the extent to which it is empathic or altruistic, but we now know that the infant brings to its own rearing a keen sensitivity to the distress of others. As early as ten months of age, toddlers react visibly to signs of distress in others and often become agitated; when they are one-and-a-half years old, they seek to do something to alleviate the other's distress; and by the time they are two years old they verbally sympathize, offer toys, make suggestions, and look for help.[37] Although those youngsters are no doubt expressing some learned reactions to distress, they seem prepared to learn those things. It is obvious that infants are biologically inclined to seek help and attention; it may also be that they are biologically inclined to offer help and give attention.[38]

That innate sensitivity to the feelings of others—a sensitivity that, to be sure, varies among individuals—is so powerful that it makes us grasp not only the feelings of friends and family members but also those of some strangers, many fictional characters, and even animals. We wince when the motion picture hero is threatened and exult when he is triumphant; we are disturbed by the sight of a wounded dog and pleased by the sight of someone else's baby.

It is sometimes argued that we display those feelings because it is expected of us or because we hope to curry favor with others or make ourselves seem worthy of reciprocal benevolence. That is certainly part of the story, but it is not the whole story. In a remarkable series of experiments, Bibb Latané and J. M. Darley showed that those explanations were probably wrong.[39] They staged a number of "emergencies" in stores, offices, and laundromats that ranged from medical problems and fire alarms to thefts and disorderly conduct. In every case, a lone bystander was more likely to help the "victim" than was a group of bystanders.

That finding casts great doubt on the notion that altruism among strangers is merely a form of reciprocity by which helpers get credit for good deeds that can later be cashed in for other rewards, such as status. If altruism were really a self-interested investment in the future, then people should more frequently help victims when others can witness the good deed. But they do so less frequently. There is a social inhibition against helping that probably derives from the fact that in a group, the sense of personal responsibility is diffused. It is as if each person in a group says to himself or herself, "Maybe somebody else will do it." When we are alone, we feel more keenly a sense of responsibility; we must answer not to the public but to the voice within.

Benevolence is often motivated by a desire for fame, status, or favors; but if that were all there was to it, our language would not be rich in words designed to distinguish selfish from selfless actions, kind from unkind persons, and heroism from bravado. If we really believed that altruism was merely reciprocity, we would purge our language of all such distinctions, and then the only difference between Tiny Tim and Scrooge would be age.

Fairness

Perhaps the first moral judgment uttered by the child is, "That's not fair!" At first such a claim may be largely self-interested, a way of making persuasive the real claim, "I want!" But at a very early age, the claim of fairness begins to take on the quality of a disinterested standard. It does so because fair play—taking turns, sharing toys, following rules—is a necessary condition for the child to satisfy its natural sociability. Judy Dunn, who closely observed children between the ages of eighteen and thirty-six months, found that about half spontaneously offered to share things and noted instances, familiar to every parent, of even younger babies' offering a toy, pacifier, or piece of food to another person.[40] Those offerings reflect a desire on the part of the toddler to win approval, initiate play, or maintain contact. Around the world, children offer food as a way of establishing friendly relations even before they are able to talk.[41] The tendency to share increases with age and is accompanied by a rapid growth in the sense of what rules ought to govern play and contact.

Jean Piaget formulated his theory of the development of moral judgment by watching children play marbles. What struck him most forcibly is that the complex and subtle rules of that game are not taught by adults to children; they are taught by children to each other.[42] Out of ordinary play and interaction there emerges a fairly clear sense of rules and justifications: "principles of possession, positive justice, [and] excuses on grounds of incapacity or lack of intention."[43] Those rules are not specific to particular situations but are understood generally, so that they can be applied differently in different contexts without sacrificing the principle underlying the rule.

Children, from infancy on, court other people. They differ in the skill and enthusiasm with which they do that and the clarity and consistency of the rules that they infer from that courtship, but the process is not driven by self-interest narrowly conceived. A child, especially a two-year-old, is learning that it has a self that is different from the self of others; but it is also beginning to learn that its self requires the presence of others to achieve happiness. In the language of economists, children learn that utilities are interdependent—that one's happiness depends to some degree on the happiness of others—long before they can say "interdependent." Children learn that they ought to obey certain rules because it pleases others at the same time that they learn that breaking rules can be fun (up to a point) because it teases others.

By the time they are in elementary school, the idea of fairness has acquired a fairly definite meaning: people should have equal shares. But once the equality principle is grasped, exceptions to it become apparent. For example, it does not seem right that a lazy boy should be paid as much as an energetic one when working on the same task. By the time they have left elementary school, children will go to great lengths to discuss and weigh competing principles (merit, age, need) for allocating things in a fair way. Most striking about that process, notes Ann Cale Kruger, is that they discuss those matters almost entirely without reference to adult authority figures or adult rules, regardless of whether they are being interviewed by adults or secretly overheard.[44] Far from expressing an internalized set of adult rules or looking furtively over their shoulders for any sign of adult power, older children discuss, in sophisticated detail, principles of justice that have evolved from their own interactions. Their affiliation with others in natural social groupings is the continuing source of their moral judgments.

A vast body of research on adult behavior provides compelling evidence for the importance of fairness as a guide to how we behave. In those studies (and here as well), fairness is defined much as Aristotle defined distributive justice: "What is just ... is what is proportionate"[45]—that is, things should be divided among people in proportion to their worth or merit. In modern equity theory, a division of something between two people is fair if the ratio between the first person's worth (effort, skill, or deeds) and gains (earnings, benefits, or rewards) is the same as the ratio between the second person's worth and gains.

In a famous set of studies in the 1960s, various experimenters hired men to conduct interviews and paid them on a piece-rate basis. During the hiring, the "employer" (an experimenter) made clear to some men that he thought them unqualified (implying that they would be overpaid for the work to be done) while saying to others that they were fully qualified (implying that they would be equitably paid). The men were then sent out to work. Those who were made to feel unqualified (and hence overpaid) produced fewer but better interviews than did the men who were given to believe that they were being fairly paid. When some employees were made to feel that they were underpaid—that their skills were worth more than they would earn—they produced far more interviews (but of lower quality) than did employees who believed they were fairly paid.[46]

That is not what one would expect if people were only interested in maximizing their income. Both the "overpaid" and the "equitably" paid workers earned the same amount per interview completed. If getting the most money was all that mattered, both groups would try to complete as many interviews as possible, and the earnings of each group (the employees were randomly assigned) would be identical. What their employer thought of them would be irrelevant. The fact that the "overpaid" workers did less work (thereby sacrificing earnings) but did work of higher quality (thus sacrificing effort) can be explained in terms of their concern for equity.

There are many circumstances in which the self-interest of a person is not at all engaged, yet that person experiences—and often acts upon—strong feelings of fair play. Most of us are outraged at members of Congress who bounce checks although the cost to us is close to zero. We are upset if, while waiting in a line to buy tickets to attend the theater, someone cuts in line ahead of us even though the addition of one person to the line almost certainly will not affect our chances of entering the theater and only trivially affects our choice of seats. But we believe that we have been treated unfairly because, by arriving earlier than the intruder, we have established a stronger claim (however tiny the difference) and thus are entitled to a greater reward (however small the increment). On the other hand, if the intruder can show that in fact he was there all night waiting for a seat and only stepped away momentarily to get a cup of coffee, we shall probably acknowledge his right to reclaim his place and shall even (though less cheerfully) acknowledge the rights of his five companions—all in the same position and all with the same prior claims.

Evolution and the Moral Sentiments

The natural sociability of mankind gives rise to sentiments of sympathy, fairness, and reciprocity in every culture that we can imagine. Although custom will shape the reach of those sentiments by determining who is worthy of sympathy and what constitutes equality of worth or effort, the sentiments themselves emerge spontaneously. They do so because they are essential to human reproduction, family life, and small-group cohesion. Those sentiments, in short, confer reproductive fitness. Ordinarily, parents who are innately disposed to care for their children produce more surviving children than do people lacking that disposition and so come to constitute an ever larger fraction of the gene pool.

Even John Stuart Mill readily admitted that man is naturally social, but then, unaccountably (and quite unlike Hume and Smith), argued that "the moral feelings are not innate but acquired," which implies that the "social feelings of mankind" and the "deeply rooted" sense that "there should be a natural harmony between his feelings and aims and those of his fellow creatures" have no moral content.[47] That was, as Charles Darwin was to remark eight years later, "extremely improbable": if the moral sentiments had no innate basis—had not been selected for by evolution—it is quite unlikely that so many of us would acquire them.[48]

The moral sentiments can lead to altruistic behavior, as when one individual risks his life that another might survive. Biologists have devised two theories to explain why altruism might spread in a population, rather than be extinguished by the greater rate of survival of wholly self-interested individuals. The first is the notion of inclusive fitness,[49] which holds that evolution will select for creatures that run risks for the benefit of others with whom they share genes and in proportion to the degree of that sharing. Flippantly but not inaccurately, J. B. S. Haldane[50] put it this way: I will risk death to save my child from a raging river if the odds are at least two to one that I will succeed (because she shares roughly half my genes); but I will jump in the river to save my cousin only if the odds favoring success are seven in eight (because she has only one-eighth of my genes). Trying to save my grandmother makes no sense at all because, being past child-bearing age, she can pass on none of my genes to the next generation.

That calculus may explain why, on the average, we strive harder to save our own children than somebody else's, and it is certainly consistent with the fact that children are more likely to be abused by their stepparents than by their natural parents;[51] but it cannot explain why we should ever run any risk at all of saving our grandmother, our adopted child, or our dog. Yet many people will jump into the river for grandmothers, adopted children, and even dogs.

Studies of adoptive families provide no evidence that parents of adopted children are any less loving, solicitous, or protective than are the parents of biological children. Mothers who have both an adopted and a biological child report no difference in their feelings toward them.[52] If anything, adoptive parents are more protective and less controlling than biological ones,[53] a puzzling finding if one believes that investment in child care is driven by a desire to reproduce one's genes. Adopted children report that they were loved as if they were natural children.[54]

People in primitive, as well as advanced, societies form strong attachments to animals.[55] There are, of course, great variations in the extent to which animals are cherished; but beneath those variations there is a deeper constancy: in virtually every society and in virtually every historical period, people have been attracted to certain kinds of animals in ways that are hard to distinguish from the way in which we treat infants—difficult to explain in terms of economic necessity (the desire for food or help) and impossible to explain in terms of reproductive fitness.[56]

One can attempt to solve those puzzles of affectional behavior directed toward nonkin and nonhumans while remaining within a narrow interpretation of the evolutionary perspective by advancing the notion of reciprocal altruism: we engage in altruistic acts, such as helping nonrelatives, caring for adopted children, or being affectionate toward pets, to impress others with our dependability and hence to increase our opportunities to have profitable exchanges with those others.[57] There is a great deal of truth in that; having a reputation for doing one's duty, living up to promises, and helping others will enhance one's own opportunities. Moral behavior is far more likely when utility conspires with duty, and the strongest moral codes are invariably those that are supported by considerations of both advantage and obligation.[58]

But sometimes, sentiment alone, unsupported by utility, motivates our actions, as when someone makes an anonymous benefaction or a lone bystander helps an endangered person. While anonymous giving may be relatively rare, it is generally the case that a lone bystander is more likely to go to the aid of a threatened person than a bystander who is part of a group—the opposite of what one would predict if reputation enhancement were the motive for altruistic actions.[59]

Evolutionary biology provides a powerful insight into human behavior at the level of the species, but it fares less well at the level of daily conduct. That deficiency arises in part because evolutionary biologists ordinarily do not specify the psychological mechanism by which a trait that has been selected for governs behavior in particular cases.[60] The strict and exclusive altruism of social insects is different from the more inclusive altruism of humans.

Sympathy for persons who are not offspring and creatures that are not human is a characteristic of almost all humans. Indeed, we regard as inhuman anyone who acts as if he had no feeling for others, and we criticize as insincere people who merely feign such fellow feeling. If sympathy is widespread, it must have been adaptive; but what was selected for was not a simple desire for reproductive success: it was a generalized trait that both encouraged reproductive fitness and stimulated sympathetic behavior.

That trait, I suggest, is affiliative behavior. Evolution has selected for the attachment response: if infants and parents were not predisposed to develop strong attachments for one another, it would be impossible to provide for the postpartum development of the human central nervous system. A predisposition to attachment is necessary if a child is to be sustained for that long period of dependency and nurturance during which the human brain becomes fully developed.

But it is a mistake to suppose that the psychological predisposition for which evolution has selected will be as precise in its effect on human behavior as the social instinct is among ants. Our large brain almost guarantees that the effect of attachment will be complex and diffuse if for no other reason than that the human brain makes possible not only complex actions but also our imagining such actions. The predisposition to attachment is a pervasive but somewhat general drive that imperfectly discriminates between parents and parent substitutes; is evoked by adoptive, as well as natural, infants; extends to creatures that have just a few of the characteristics of the human infant; and embraces not only family but also kin and many nonkin.

One of the cues (in evolutionary jargon, "releasers") that stimulates such an affectional response in adults is "cuteness"—by which I mean that set of traits by which we judge an organism to be delightfully attractive. We respond to certain features of people and animals in ways that suggest that we share a roughly common definition of cuteness: eyes large relative to the skull, chubby cheeks and a rounded chin, awkward movements, a cuddly epidermis, small size, and a distinctive smell.[61] Nonparents, as well as parents, respond to those cues; and the response extends beyond the human infant to other creatures with those infantile traits. I suggest that social scientists and moral philosophers have paid too little attention to the concept of "cute." People use the word all the time; philosophers and scientists almost never use it. Its frequent use suggests that it may refer to an important mechanism by which our moral sentiments are extended beyond ourselves and our immediate families.

There are other concepts, just as important and just as poorly understood, such as being a "fan," a "loyalist," or a "sentimentalist." Each suggests that our affiliative impulse is so strong that it can be evoked almost by remote control. We identify with people whom we do not know and who do not know us and with people who are entirely fictional. When we are in the audience of a play or motion picture, we are moved by the plight of imaginary people; when we watch an athletic spectacle or a military parade, we are moved by the exploits—and sometimes the mere sight—of people who are unaware of our existence. There is little in behavioral psychology or evolutionary biology that explains those emotions and their tendency to evoke in us moral sentiments.

The Moral Sense, Social Order, and Moral Choice

Our moral sense, however weak or imperfect, helps explain social order because that sense grows out of, and reflects, the fact that we are social beings, dependent upon one another, and because we are able to avail ourselves of the essential help of others, at least in the intimate precincts of life, only on the basis of understandings that arise spontaneously from, and necessarily govern, human relationships: the need to show some concern for the well-being of others, treat others with minimal fairness, and honor obligations. That natural sociability and the patterns of sympathy and reciprocity on which it rests are the basis, in my view, of Aristotle's argument for natural law: man is by nature social, and social groupings aim at some good.

The natural disposition to sociability can be put in the form of a thought experiment. Imagine people stripped of every shred of their social experiences and set loose in some Arcadian paradise and free to invent "culture." What would emerge? If they are young boys, the answer may be something akin to William Golding's *Lord of the Flies*,[62] though my guess is that a close study of abandoned children in war-torn nations would disprove even that hypothesis. But if they are men and women, what emerges would almost surely be something with strange customs, odd dress, and unfamiliar gods but invariably with familiar systems of infant care, familial obligation, kinship distinctions, and tribal loyalties.

The results of such a thought experiment taken together with the findings of modern science cast doubt, in my mind, on the philosophical value of imagining a man who is presocial, driven by a single motive, or unaware of the main and necessary features of social life. John Rawls may ask us to imagine ourselves in an "original position" behind a "veil of ignorance";[63] but no human being is ever in such a position and, to the extent he is human, cannot possibly be ignorant. Locke may ask us to believe that experience is the sole source of ideas;[64] but if we accept that, we shall have difficulty explaining why all children learn a language at roughly the same time and without having the rules of that language explained to them. Hobbes may ask us to believe that man is driven by the fear of violent death;[65] but were that our overriding concern, we would not give birth to children or lavish so much care on them. Why expend so much effort on something so perishable, whose birth threatens the mother's life, and whose protection increases our vulnerability to the predation of others? Rousseau may imagine an equally implausible alternative, man born with no inclination to civil society; but no such man can exist and, if he did exist, could not learn goodness by reading *Robinson Crusoe*.[66]

A proper understanding of our natural disposition to sociability not only helps explain social order, it provides the grounding for our judgments about that order. We cannot imagine praising a man who laughs while torturing an innocent baby;[67] we cannot defend a principle that says that every man is entitled to be the judge in his own case. We are not limited to condemning Auschwitz contingently and ironically; we can condemn it absolutely and confidently.[68]

Moral philosophy, like social science, must begin with a statement about human nature. We may disagree about what is natural; but we cannot escape the fact that we have a nature, that is, a set of traits and predispositions that limits what we may do and suggests guides to what we must do. That nature is mixed: we fear violent death but sometimes deliberately risk it; we want to improve our own happiness but sometimes work for the happiness of others; we value our individuality but are tormented by the prospect of being alone. It is a nature that cannot be described by any single disposition, be it maximizing our utility or enhancing our reproductive fitness. Efforts to found a moral philosophy on some single trait (the desire for happiness or the fear of punishment) or political philosophy on some single good (avoiding death or securing property) will inevitably produce judgments about what is right that at some critical juncture are at odds with the sober second thoughts of people who deliberate about what constitutes praiseworthy conduct and who decide, out of that deliberation, to honor the hero who risked violent death or to sympathize with the mother who sacrificed one child to save another.

As Ian Shapiro has noted, much contemporary political theory is "locked into a series of antinaturalist assumptions about human nature"; for example, original positions, veils of ignorance, the priority of rights.[69] Any reasonable theory must have a "view of human nature and human interests and an argument about the injunction for action this entails given a plausibly defended account of the pertinent causal structure of the social world."[70]

Aristotle gave such an account, but his views became unfashionable among those who sought to base moral or political philosophy on a single principle (for example, utility, liberty, or self-preservation), who worried about Aristotle's teleology, or who believed in the priority of the right over the good. But if one acknowledges that there is no single moral principle but several partially consistent ones and that neither happiness nor virtue can be prescribed by rule, one is better prepared for a more complete understanding of man's moral capacities, an understanding stated by Aristotle in phrases that in most respects precisely anticipate the findings of modern science. Although Aristotle's account is often dismissed as teleological (much as those of later scientists were dismissed as functionalist), his view does not involve any "mysterious nonempirical entities"[71] or any suspiciously conservative functionalism.

There is certainly nothing mysterious or nonempirical about Aristotle's assertion that men and women unite out of a "natural striving to leave behind another that is like oneself" because a "parent would seem to have a natural friendship for a child, and a child for a parent" or that "the household is the partnership constituted by nature for [the needs of] daily life."[72] Those are as close to self-evident propositions as one could utter. Only slightly less obvious, but still scarcely mysterious, are the arguments that "in the household first we have the sources and springs of friendship, of political organization, and of justice" and that "there is in everyone by nature an impulse toward this sort of partnership [that is, toward the city]."[73]

Those natural moral sentiments are an incomplete and partial guide to action. They are incomplete in that they cannot resolve a choice we must make between two loved persons or between the desire to favor a loved one and the obligation to honor a commitment. They are partial in that those sentiments extend chiefly to family and kin and leave nonkin at risk for being thought nonhuman. Resolving conflicts and extending our sentiments across the high but necessary walls of tribe, village, and racial grouping—an extension made more desirable by the interdependence of cosmopolitan living—require moral reasoning to take up the incomplete task of moral development.

Those deficiencies can lead the unwary philosopher to suppose that if a sentiment does not settle everything, it cannot settle anything or to infer that if people make different choices, they must do so on the basis of different sentiments. The first error leads to logical positivism; the second, to cultural relativism; and the two together, to modern nihilism or, at best, to "liberal irony." A proper understanding of human nature can rarely provide us with rules for action, but it can supply what

Aristotle intended: a grasp of what is good in human life and a rough ranking of those goods.[74]

Antinaturalist assumptions have impeded the search for explanations for social order, as well as efforts to justify different systems of order. Normative theories have stressed that order is the product of cultural learning without pausing to ask what it is we are naturally disposed to learn. Utilitarian theories have confidently responded by saying that we are disposed to learn whatever advances our interests without pausing to ask what constitutes our interests. And despite their differences in approach, they have both supported an environmental determinism and cultural relativism that has certain dangers. If man is infinitely malleable, he is as much at risk from the various despotisms of this world as he would be if he were entirely shaped by some biochemical process. Anthropologist Robin Fox has put the matter well: "If, indeed, everything is learned, then surely men can be taught to live in any kind of society. Man is at the mercy of all the tyrants who think they know what is best for him. And how can he plead that they are being inhuman if he doesn't know what being human is in the first place?"[75] Despots are quite prepared to use whatever technology will enable them to dominate mankind; if science tells them that biology is nothing and environment everything, then they will put aside their eugenic surgery and selective breeding programs and take up instead the weapons of propaganda, mass advertising, and educational indoctrination. The Nazis left nothing to chance; they used all methods.

Recent Russian history should have put to rest the view that everything is learned and man is infinitely malleable. After seventy-five years of cruel tyranny during which every effort was made to destroy civil society to create the New Soviet Man, we learn that people kept civil society alive, if not well. The elemental building blocks of that society were not isolated individuals easily trained to embrace any doctrine or to adopt any habits; they were families, friends, and intimate groupings in which sentiments of sympathy, reciprocity, and fairness survived and struggled to shape behavior.

Mankind's moral sense is not a strong beacon light, radiating outward to illuminate in sharp outline all that it touches. It is, rather, a small candle flame, casting vague and multiple shadows, flickering and sputtering in the strong winds of power and passion, greed and ideology. But brought close to the heart and cupped in one's hands, moral sense dispels the darkness and warms the soul.

Notes

CHAPTER 1: THINKING ABOUT CHARACTER

1. *Federalist* No. 55.
2. George Will, *Statecraft as Soulcraft* (New York: Simon and Schuster, 1983), p. 156.
3. Alexis de Tocqueville, *Democracy in America*, vol. 2, ed. Phillips Bradley (New York: Knopf, 1971), p. 122.
4. These two dispositions do not exhaust the subject. Aristotle's *Ethics* supplies a fuller list. Omitted here are duty, courage, and fairness, among others. I shall return to these matters.
5. The impulsivity and self-centeredness of high-rate offenders are revealed by a variety of psychological measures. On the Minnesota Multiphasic Personality Inventory (MMPI), offenders have elevated scores on scales measuring psychopathy (defined as a deficient attachment to others) and hypomania (defined as unproductive hyperactivity). On the California Psychological Inventory, offenders score low on the socialization scale (defined as an overvaluation of immediate goals, a lack of concern for the rights of others, an unwillingness to accept responsibility, and an inability to form deep attachments to others). On the Porteus Maze test, offenders earn high Q scores, meaning they frequently violate the maze-tracing rules in ways that suggest an impulsive desire to cut corners. Rorschach ink-blot tests suggest that delinquents are more likely than other boys of the same age and class to be impulsive, hostile, and resentful and to have difficulty in making contact with others. Teacher and parent interviews depict delinquent youth as impulsive, egocentric, aggressive, and suspicious. These studies are summarized and the sources given in James Q. Wilson and Richard J. Herrnstein, *Crime and Human Nature* (New York: Simon and Schuster, 1985), chap. 7.

CHAPTER 3: INCIVILITY AND CRIME

1. Ted Robert Gurr, "Contemporary Crime in Historical Perspective," *Annals* 434 (1977): 114–36; Ted Robert Gurr, "On the History of Violent Crime in Europe and America," in Egon Bittner and Sheldon L. Messinger, eds., *Criminology Review Yearbook*, vol. 2 (Beverly Hills, Calif.: Sage Publications, 1980); and Ted Robert Gurr, "Historical Trends in Violent Crime: A Critical Review of the Evidence," in Norval Morris and Michael Tonry, eds., *Crime and Justice*, vol. 3 (Chicago: University of Chicago Press, 1981).

2. Roger Lane, *Violent Death in the City: Suicide, Accident, and Murder in Nineteenth-Century Philadelphia* (Cambridge: Harvard University Press, 1979); Roger Lane, "Urban Police and Crime in Nineteenth-Century America," in Norval Morris and Michael Tonry, eds., *Crime and Justice*, vol. 2 (Chicago: University of Chicago Press, 1980); R. E. Johnson, *A Shopkeeper's Millennium: Society and Revivals in Rochester, New York, 1815–1837* (New York: Hill and Wang, 1978); J. F. Richardson, *The New York Police, Colonial Times to 1901* (New York: Oxford University Press, 1970); Gurr, "Historical Trends"; J. D. Hewitt and D. W. Hoover, "Local Modernization and Crime: The Effects of Modernization on Crime in Middletown, 1845–1910," *Law and Human Behavior* 6 (1982): 313–25; Eric H. Monkkonen, "A Disorderly People? Urban Order in the Nineteenth and Twentieth Centuries," *Journal of American History* 68 (1981): 536–59; and L. McDonald, "Theory and Evidence of Rising Crime in the Nineteenth Century," *British Journal of Sociology* 33 (1982): 404–24.

3. Lane, *Violent Death.*

4. M. J. Hindelang, M. R. Gottfredson, and T. J. Flanagan, *Sourcebook of Criminal Justice Statistics, 1980* (Washington, D.C.: Bureau of Justice Statistics, 1981), p. 290.

5. F. H. McClintock and N. H. Avison, *Crime in England and Wales* (London: Heinemann, 1968), p. 59.

6. Dane Archer and Rosemary Gartner, "Homicide in 110 Nations: The Development of the Comparative Crime Data File," in Bittner and Messinger, eds., *Criminology Review Yearbook*; Gurr, "On the History of Violent Crime"; and Christie Davies, "Crime, Bureaucracy, and Equality," *Policy Review* 23 (1983): 89–105.

7. A. D. Viccia, "World Crime Trends," *International Journal of Offender Therapy* 24 (1980): 270–77.

8. Charles F. Wellford, "Crime and the Dimensions of Nations," *International Journal of Criminology and Penology* 2 (1974): 1–10; and P. Wolf, "Crime and Development: An International Analysis of Crime Rates," *Scandinavian Studies in Criminology* 3 (1971): 107–20.

9. Lane, *Violent Death*, pp. 60, 71, 153.

10. P. C. Sagi and C. F. Wellford, "Age Composition and Patterns of Change in Criminal Statistics," *Journal of Criminal Law, Criminology, and Police Science* 59 (1968): 29–36; Jan M. Chaiken and Marcia R. Chaiken, "Crime Rates and the Active Criminal," in James Q. Wilson, ed., *Crime and Public Policy* (San Francisco: Institute for Contemporary Studies, 1983); Theodore N. Ferdinand, "Demographic Shifts and Criminality," *American Journal of Sociology* 73 (1970): 84–99; and James A. Fox, *Forecasting Crime Data* (Lexington, Mass.: D.C. Heath/Lexington Books, 1978).

11. Marvin Wolfgang and Paul E. Tracy, "The 1945 and 1958 Birth Cohorts: A Comparison of the Prevalence, Incidence, and Severity of Delinquent Behavior," paper presented to the Conference on Public Danger, Dangerous Offenders, and the Criminal Justice System, Kennedy School of Government, Harvard University, 1982.

12. Dane Archer and Rosemary Gartner, *Violence and Crime in Cross-National Perspective* (New Haven: Yale University Press, 1984), p. 143.
13. Roger Lane, *Roots of Violence in Black Philadelphia, 1860–1900* (Cambridge: Harvard University Press, 1986), pp. 7–14.
14. Archer and Gartner, "Homicide"; and Archer and Gartner, *Violence and Crime.*
15. V. A. C. Gatrell and T. B. Hadden, "Criminal Statistics and Their Interpretation," in E. A. Wrigley, ed., *Nineteenth-Century Society* (Cambridge: Cambridge University Press, 1972); and D. S. Thomas, *Social Aspects of the Business Cycle* (London: George Routledge and Sons, 1925).
16. Kenneth I. Wolpin, "An Economic Analysis of Crime and Punishment in England and Wales, 1894–1967," *Journal of Political Economy* 86 (1978): 815–40.
17. P. J. Cook and G. A. Zarkin, "Crime and the Business Cycle," *Journal of Legal Studies* 14 (1985): 115–28; and James Q. Wilson and P. J. Cook, "Unemployment and Crime: What Is the Connection?" *Public Interest* 79 (1985): 3–8.
18. James Q. Wilson, *Thinking About Crime*, rev. ed. (New York: Basic Books, 1983); and James Q. Wilson and Richard J. Herrnstein, *Crime and Human Nature* (New York: Simon and Schuster, 1985), pp. 416–21, 430–37.
19. Gurr, "Historical Trends"; and Norbert Elias, *The Civilizing Process: The History of Manners* (New York: Urizen, 1939; reprint, 1978).
20. Monkkonen, "A Disorderly People?"
21. Martin J. Wiener, *English Culture and the Decline of the Industrial Spirit, 1850–1980* (Cambridge: Cambridge University Press, 1981), pp. ix, 5–6.
22. Quoted in ibid., p. 13.
23. N. H. Clark, *Deliver Us from Evil: An Interpretation of American Prohibition* (New York: Norton, 1976).
24. Johnson, *A Shopkeepers' Millennium.*
25. W. J. Rorabaugh, *The Alcoholic Republic* (New York: Oxford University Press, 1979).
26. Aristotle, *Nichomachean Ethics* 2.1.i.
27. Wilson and Herrnstein, *Crime and Human Nature*, chap. 8; and Jerome Kagan, *The Nature of the Child* (New York: Basic Books, 1984).
28. Thomas W. Laqueur, *Religion and Respectability: Sunday Schools and Working Class Culture, 1780–1850* (New Haven: Yale University Press, 1976).
29. Gertrude Himmelfarb, *On Liberty and Liberalism: The Case of John Stuart Mill* (New York: Alfred A. Knopf, 1974), p. 298.
30. Lane, *Roots of Violence*, p. 16.
31. C. B. Stendler, "Sixty Years of Child Training Practices," *Journal of Pediatrics* 36 (1950): 122–34; and Martha Wolfenstein, "Fun Morality: An Analysis of Recent American Child-training Literature," in Margaret Mead and Martha Wolfenstein, eds., *Childhood in Contemporary Cultures* (Chicago: University of Chicago Press, 1955).
32. Duane F. Alwin, "From Obedience to Autonomy," *Public Opinion Quarterly* 52 (1988): 33–52.

33. Marvin Wolfgang, Robert F. Figlio, and Thorsten Sellin, *Delinquency in a Birth Cohort* (Chicago: University of Chicago Press, 1972); and David P. Farrington, Lloyd E. Ohlin, and James Q. Wilson, *Understanding and Controlling Crime* (New York: Springer-Verlag, 1986), pp. 40–41.

34. Joseph Adelson, "Drug Use and Adolescence," paper, Department of Psychology, University of Michigan, 1989.

35. David F. Musto, *The American Disease: Origins of Narcotic Control* (New Haven: Yale University Press, 1973).

36. Richard J. Herrnstein, "The Individual Offender," *Today's Delinquent* 7 (1988): 5–37.

37. Lane, *Roots of Violence*, p. 134.

38. Ibid., pp. 140–43.

39. William E. B. DuBois, *The Philadelphia Negro* (Philadelphia: University of Pennsylvania, 1899); Lane, *Roots of Violence*, pp. 148, 155.

40. Lawrence W. Levine, *Black Culture and Black Consciousness: Afro-American Folk Thought from Slavery to Freedom* (New York: Oxford University Press, 1977); Lane, *Roots of Violence*, p. 146; and Charles E. Silberman, *Criminal Violence, Criminal Justice* (New York: Random House, 1978).

41. Lane, *Roots of Violence*, p. 4.

42. Glenn C. Loury, "The Moral Quandary of the Black Community," *Public Interest* 79 (1985): 9–22.

43. At least in Western culture, S. E. Finer of Oxford University, in a paper delivered at a conference on liberal democratic societies, notes that the legal systems of China and Japan did not become as individualistic as those of the West. One might expand on this to suggest that modern Japan seems to have embraced the rationalistic and scientific components of the Enlightenment without having adopted its individualistic emphasis. Reason is served, but reason in the service of collectivities—families, neighborhoods, firms, the nation—not of individuals. See S. E. Finer, "Problems of the Liberal Democratic State: An Historical Overview."

CHAPTER 4: CHARACTER AND BIOLOGY

1. There have been careful comparisons made of dozens of identical twins raised apart with respect to personality; there have not been many comparisons made of criminal identical twins reared apart because (happily) high-rate criminality is relatively rare and twins raised apart are even rarer. But it is hard to imagine that if the two members of a monozygotic twin pair have very similar personalities, one could commit many crimes and the other not. But because the possibility cannot be ruled out, adoption studies are important. See also James Q. Wilson and Richard J. Herrnstein, *Crime and Human Nature* (New York: Simon and Schuster, 1985), chap. 3.

2. Sarnoff A. Mednick, W. F. Gabrielli, Jr., and B. Hutchings, "Genetic Influences in Criminal Convictions: Evidence from an Adoption Cohort," *Science* 224 (1984): 891–94; David C. Rowe, "Biometrical Genetic Models of Self-Reported Delinquent Behavior: A Twin Study," *Behavior Genetics* 13

(1983): 473–89; and David C. Rowe and D. Wayne Osgood, "Heredity and Sociological Theories of Delinquency: A Reconsideration," *American Sociological Review* 49 (1984): 526–40.

3. Felton Earls, "Sex Differences in Psychiatric Disorders: Origins and Developmental Influences," *Psychiatric Development* 1 (1987): 1–23; J. Garai and A. Scheinfeld, "Sex Differences in Mental and Behavioral Traits," *Genetic Psychology Monographs* 77 (1968): 169–299; R. F. Eme, "Sex Differences in Childhood Psychopathology: A Review," *Psychological Bulletin* 86 (1979): 574–95; and E. E. Maccoby and C. N. Jacklin, "Psychological Sex Differences," in Michael Rutter, ed., *Scientific Foundations of Developmental Psychiatry* (London: William Heinemann, 1980).

4. Travis Hirschi and Michael Gottfredson, "Age and the Explanation of Crime," *American Journal of Sociology* 89 (1983): 552–84.

5. This interaction is itself partly biological. That is to say, the hormones that determine whether a fetus is male or female do not stop acting at the moment of birth, nor is that action insensitive to social factors. Marian Diamond has shown that not only is the brain structure of laboratory animals affected by sex hormones, but the effect is influenced by environmental conditions. The influence of hormones on the brain structure of a rat living in an enriched environment will be different from the influence of those hormones on a rat living in an impoverished environment. See Marian Cleeves Diamond, *Enriching Heredity: The Impact of the Environment on the Anatomy of the Brain* (New York: Free Press, 1988), esp. pp. 94–95, 126, 157. It is quite possible that a similar interaction occurs in human infants such that babies who are neglected, isolated, or abused may behave differently not simply from what they have learned but from an alteration that has been induced in their biochemistry.

6. Earls, "Sex Differences."

7. Dan Olweus et al., "Testosterone, Aggression, Physical, and Personality Dimensions in Normal Adolescent Males," *Psychosomatic Medicine* 42 (1980): 253–69.

8. L. E. Kreuz and R. M. Rose, "Assessment of Aggressive Behavior and Plasma Testosterone in a Young Criminal Population," *Psychosomatic Medicine* 34 (1972): 321–32; J. Ehrekrantz, E. Bliss, and M. Sheard, "Plasma Testosterone: Correlation with Aggressive Behavior and Social Dominance in Man," *Psychosomatic Medicine* 36 (1974): 469–75; and R. T. Rada, R. Kellner, and W. W. Winslow, "Plasma Testosterone and Aggressive Behavior," *Psychomatics* 17 (1976): 138–42.

9. Kreuz and Rose, "Assessment of Aggressive Behavior."

10. J. Richard Udry, "Biosocial Models of Adolescent Problem Behaviors," paper, University of North Carolina Population Center, 1988.

11. Linmarie Sikich and Richard D. Todd, "Are the Neurodevelopment Effects of Gonadal Hormones Related to Sex Differences in Psychiatric Illness?" paper, Department of Psychiatry, Washington University School of Medicine, 1988.

12. Earls, "Sex Differences."

13. Lars Knorring, Lars Oreland, and Bengt Winblad, "Personality Traits Related to Monamine Oxidase Activity in Platelets," *Psychiatry Research* 12 (1984): 11–26; Robert Coursey, Monte S. Buchsbaum, and Dennis L. Murphy, "Two-Year Follow-up of Subjects and Their Families Defined as at Risk for Psychopathology on the Basis of Platelet MAO Activities," *Neuropsychobiology* 8 (1982): 51–56; and Robert Coursey, Monte S. Buchsbaum, and Dennis L. Murphy, "Psychological Characteristics of Subjects Identified by Platelet MAO Activity and Evoked Potentials as Biologically at Risk for Psychopathology," *Journal of Abnormal Psychology* 2 (1980): 151–64.

14. Neurotransmitters are also implicated in impulsivity and aggression, although the mechanisms are not well understood. Humans with low levels of serotonin, for example, are more likely to be impulsive and aggressive and to be vulnerable to an early onset of alcoholism. It is not clear, however, whether abnormal levels of serotonin cause behavioral problems or whether these behaviors lead to changes in serotonin levels. See D. H. Fishbein, D. Lozovsky, and J. H. Jaffe, "Impulsivity, Aggression, and Neuroendocrine Responses to Sertonergic Stimulation in Substance Abusers," *Biological Psychiatry* 15 (1989): 1049–66; M. Linnoila et al., "Low Cerebrospinal Fluid 5-Hydroxyindolacetic Acid Concentration Differentiates Impulsive from Nonimpulsive Violent Behavior," *Life Sciences* 33 (1983): 2609–14; and Michael T. McGuire, "Biochemical Screening to Predict Behavior," *University of Southern California Law Review* 65 (1991): 565–78.

15. Naomi Breslau, Nancy Klein, and Lida Allen, "Very Low Birthweight: Behavioral Sequelae at Nine Years of Age," *Journal of the American Academy of Child and Adolescent Psychiatry* 27 (1988): 605–12.

16. H. L. Needleman et al., "Deficits in Psychologic and Classroom Performance of Children with Elevated Dentine Lead Levels," *New England Journal of Medicine* 300 (1979): 689–95; R. W. Thatcher and M. L. Lester, "Nutrition, Environmental Toxins and Computerized EEG," *Journal of Learning Disabilities* 18 (1985): 287–97; J. D. Oliver, "Lead and Hyperactivity," *American Journal of Psychiatry* 133 (1976): 10–18; and Deborah W. Denno, *Biology and Violence* (Cambridge: Cambridge University Press, 1990), pp. 84–86, 106–7.

17. David P. Farrington, "Age and Crime," in Michael Tonry and Norval Morris, eds., *Crime and Justice*, vol. 7 (Chicago: University of Chicago Press, 1986), pp. 189–250; and Rolf Loeber, "The Stability of Antisocial and Delinquent Child Behavior," *Child Development* 53 (1982): 1431–46.

18. John Bowlby, *Attachment and Loss* (New York: Basic Books, 1969); M. D. S. Ainsworth, M. C. Blehar, E. Waters, and S. Wall, *Patterns of Attachment: A Psychological Study of the Strange Situation* (Hillsdale, N.J.: Erlbaum, 1978); and L. Alan Sroufe, "Attachment Classification from the Perspective of Infant-Caregiver Relationships and Infant Temperament," *Child Development* 56 (1985): 1–14.

19. Jerome Kagan, *The Nature of the Child* (Cambridge: Harvard University Press, 1984); Jay Belsky and Michael Rovine, "Temperament and Attachment Security in Strange Situations: An Empirical Rapprochement," *Child Development* 58 (1987): 787–95; and Carroll E. Izard, Maurice Haynes, Gail

Chisholm, and Katherine Baak, "Emotional Determinants of Infant-Mother Attachment," paper, Department of Psychology, University of Delaware, 1988.

20. Lawrence J. Schweinhart, "Can Preschool Programs Help Prevent Delinquency?" in James Q. Wilson and Glenn C. Loury, eds., *Families, Schools, and Delinquency Prevention*, vol. 3 of *From Children to Citizens* (New York: Springer-Verlag, 1987).

21. James S. Coleman, Thomas Hoffer, and Sally Kilgore, *High School Achievement* (New York: Basic Books, 1982).

22. John E. Chubb and Terry M. Moe, *Politics, Markets, and Schools* (Washington, D.C.: Brookings Institution, 1990).

CHAPTER 11: THE ENDURING PROBLEM OF BUSINESS ETHICS

1. See, for example, Edwin M. Epstein, "The Corporate Social Policy Process: Beyond Business Ethics, Corporate Social Responsibility, and Corporate Social Responsiveness," *California Management Review* 29 (Spring 1987): 99–114; and William C. Frederick, "Toward CSR$_3$: Why Ethical Analysis Is Indispensable and Unavoidable in Corporate Affairs," *California Management Review* 28 (Winter 1986): 126. I have benefited from the comments of Professor Peter Minowitz on an earlier draft of this chapter.

2. John Ruskin, *Fors Clavigera: Letters to the Workmen and Labourers of Great Britain* (1876), as quoted in Gertrude Himmelfarb, *The Idea of Poverty* (New York: Alfred Knopf, 1984), p. 42. A good collection of nineteenth-century critics of Smith is Elisabeth Jay and Richard Jay, *Critics of Capitalism: Victorian Reactions to "Political Economy"* (Cambridge: Cambridge University Press, 1986).

3. Adam Smith, *The Theory of Moral Sentiments*, ed. D. D. Raphael and A. L. Macfie (Oxford: Clarendon Press, 1976), part 2, sec. ii, chap. 3, par. 2. Hereinafter cited as TMS, followed by part, section, chapter, and paragraph numbers corresponding to the definitive Glasgow edition published by Oxford.

4. Adam Smith, *An Inquiry into the Nature and Causes of the Wealth of Nations*, ed. R. H. Campbell, A. S. Skinner, and W. B. Todd (Oxford: Clarendon Press, 1976), bk. 4, chap. 2, par. 9. Hereinafter cited as WN, followed by book, chapter, section (if any), and paragraph numbers corresponding to the definitive Glasgow edition published by Oxford.

5. WN 4.9.51.

6. WN 5.1.b.5, 5.1.f.30, 6.1.f.30, 50–51, 60–61.

7. WN 5.1.g.12.

8. WN, intro. 4; see also Istvan Hont and Michael Ignatieff, "Needs and Justice in the *Wealth of Nations*, An Introductory Essay," in Hont and Ignatieff, eds., *Wealth and Virtue: The Shaping of Political Economy in the Scottish Enlightenment* (Cambridge: Cambridge University Press, 1983), p. 1.

9. WN 4.9.51.

10. WN 2.3.14.

11. WN 2.3.28.
12. Max Weber, *The Protestant Ethic and the Spirit of Capitalism,* trans. Talcott Parsons (New York: Charles Scribner's Sons, 1930).
13. WN 2.3.27–28.
14. WN 1.2.1.
15. WN 1.2.2.
16. TMS 1.1.1.1.
17. TMS 1.1.1.2.
18. TMS 3.1.2, 2.1.
19. TMS 1.1.5.8, 2.2.1–4, 3.3.1.
20. TMS 3.3.1.
21. WN 5.1.f.50.
22. Ibid.
23. WN 1.10.c.23.
24. WN 1.10.c.27.
25. TMS 1.3.3.5.
26. TMS 1.3.3.6–8.
27. WN 4.2.43.
28. Ibid.
29. WN 4.7.c.103, 108; 5.1.e.26.
30. WN 4.7.c.104.
31. WN 5.1.e.11.
32. WN 5.1.e.22, 18.
33. WN 4.7.c.105.
34. WN 4.7.c.101.
35. WN 1.11.c.
36. WN 5.1.g.10.

CHAPTER 12: CHARACTER AND ECSTASY

1. I do not here take up the question of marijuana. For a variety of reasons—its widespread use and its lesser tendency to addict—it presents a different problem from cocaine or heroin. For a penetrating analysis, see Mark Kleiman, *Marijuana: Costs of Abuse, Costs of Control* (New York: Greenwood, 1989).

CHAPTER 13: LEARNING MORE ABOUT CHARACTER

1. William McCord, Joan McCord, and I. K. Zola, *Origins of Crime* (New York: Columbia University Press, 1959); Sheldon Glueck and Eleanor Glueck, *Unraveling Juvenile Delinquency* (Cambridge: Harvard University Press, 1950); Donald West and David Farrington, *The Delinquent Way of Life* (London: Heinemann, 1977); and Marvin Wolfgang, Robert Figlio, and Thorsten Sellin, *Delinquency in a Birth Cohort* (Chicago: University of Chicago Press, 1972).

2. R. B. Cattell, *The Inheritance of Personality and Ability* (New York: Academic Press, 1982).

3. M. Bohman, "Some Genetic Aspects of Alcoholism and Criminality," *Archives of General Psychiatry* 35 (1978): 269–76; and C. R. Cloninger, M. Bohman, and S. Sigvardsson, "Inheritance of Alcohol Abuse," *Archives of General Psychiatry* 38 (1981): 861–68.

4. Jay Belsky, "Child Maltreatment: An Ecological Integration," *American Psychologist* 35 (1980): 320–35; and Jay Belsky, "Early Human Experience: A Family Perspective," *Developmental Psychology*, 17 (1981): 3–23.

5. Lead intoxication and minimal brain disorders, among other biomedical factors, were found to predict male delinquency in Deborah W. Denno, *Biology and Violence* (Cambridge: Cambridge University Press, 1990).

6. G. R. Patterson, P. Chamberlain, and J. B. Reid, "A Comparative Evaluation of a Parent-Training Program," *Behavior Therapy*, 13 (1982): 638–50.

7. J. M. Chaiken and M. R. Chaiken, *Varieties of Criminal Behavior* (Santa Monica, Calif.: RAND, 1982).

8. J. C. Ball, L. Rosen, J. A. Flueck, and D. N. Nurco, *The Drugs-Crime Connection* (Beverly Hills, Calif.: Sage, 1981); and Michael Tonry and James Q. Wilson, eds., *Drugs and Crime* (Chicago: University of Chicago Press, 1990).

9. D. S. Elliott and H. L. Voss, *Delinquency and Dropout* (Lexington, Mass.: D. C. Heath, 1974).

10. Charles A. Murray and Louis A. Cox, *Beyond Probation: Juvenile Corrections and the Chronic Delinquent* (Beverly Hills, Calif.: Sage, 1983).

11. David Farrington, "The Effects of Public Labeling," *British Journal of Criminology* 17 (1977): 112–15; and David Farrington, S. G. Osborn, and Donald West, "The Persistence of Labeling Effects," *British Journal of Criminology* 18 (1978): 277–84.

12. L. J. Schweinhart and D. P. Weikart, *Young Children Grown Up: The Effects of the Perry Preschool Program on Youths* (Ypsilanti, Mich.: High/Scope, 1980); and R. A. Feldman, T. E. Caplinger, and J. S. Wodarski, *The St. Louis Conundrum* (Englewood Cliffs, N.J.: Prentice-Hall, 1983).

13. James Q. Wilson and Richard J. Herrnstein, *Crime and Human Nature* (New York: Simon and Schuster, 1985).

Chapter 14: The Moral Sense

1. Emile Durkheim is an important exponent of the first view. See *Suicide*, trans. J. A. Spaulding and George Simpson (Glencoe, Ill.: Free Press, 1951); *The Division of Labor*, trans. George Simpson (Glencoe, Ill.: Free Press, 1960); *The Elementary Forms of the Religious Life*, trans. J. W. Swain (New York: Collier, 1961). Thomas Hobbes is an important exponent of the latter. See *Leviathan*, ed. Michael Oakeshott (Oxford: Basil Blackwell, 1957). For an analysis, see Jon Elster, *The Cement of Society* (Cambridge: Cambridge University Press, 1989).

2. In 1986, three of a hundred thefts reported to the police resulted in prison sentences. Since at the most only one-fourth of all thefts are reported to the

police, the true probability of imprisonment, given a theft, is much less than one chance in a hundred. Patrick Langan, "America's Soaring Prison Population," *Science* (1991): 1572.

3. David Hume, *A Treatise of Human Nature*, 2d ed., ed. L. A. Selby-Bigge and P. H. Nidditch (Oxford: Oxford University Press, 1978), pp. 486, 478.

4. Philippe Aries, *Centuries of Childhood* (New York: Vintage, 1962); Lloyd de Mause, ed., *The History of Childhood* (New York: Psychohistory, 1974); Edward Shorter, *The Making of the Modern Family* (New York: Basic Books, 1975); and Lawrence Stone, *The Family, Sex, and Marriage in England 1500–1800* (New York: Harper & Row, 1977).

5. De Mause, *The History of Childhood*, p. 1.

6. Shorter, *The Making of the Modern Family*, pp. 203–4.

7. Melvin Konner, *The Tangled Wing: Biological Constraints on the Human Spirit* (New York: Holt, Rinehart, and Winston, 1982), pp. 301–4; see also Robert LeVine, "Cross-Cultural Study in Child Psychology," in P. H. Mussen, ed., *Carmichael's Manual of Child Psychology* (New York: John Wiley, 1970).

8. Michael Anderson, *Approaches to the History of the Western Family, 1500–1914* (London: MacMillan, 1980); and A. Macfarlane, "Review," *History and Theory* 18 (1979): 103–26.

9. G. D. Sussman, "The End of the Wet-Nursing Business in France, 1874–1914," *Journal of Family History* 2 (1977); and Keith Wrightson, *English Society, 1580–1680* (New Brunswick: Rutgers University Press, 1982).

10. Steven E. Ozment, *When Fathers Ruled: Family Life in Reformation Europe* (Cambridge: Harvard University Press, 1983), p. 220, n. 83; cf. also pp. 118–19.

11. Linda A. Pollock, *Forgotten Children: Parent-Child Relations from 1500 to 1900* (Cambridge: Cambridge University Press, 1983). Pollock's conclusion is worth quoting, resting, as it does, on the most systematic review of the evidence that we have: "Despite the individual differences in child-rearing techniques, there are limits of variation. These limits are the dependency of the child and the acceptance of responsibility for the protection and socialisation of that child by the parents. From the material gathered here, it is clear that the vast majority of parents from earlier centuries were operating within these constraints" (p. 271). A similar judgment about child care was reached by David Herlihy in *Medieval Households* (Cambridge: Harvard University Press, 1985) for medieval Europe, by Ozment in *When Fathers Ruled* for sixteenth-century Europe, and by Keith Wrightson in *English Society, 1580–1680* (New Brunswick: Rutgers University Press, 1982) and by Michael MacDonald in *Mystical Bedlam: Madness, Anxiety, and Healing in Seventeenth-Century England* (Cambridge: Cambridge University Press, 1982) for seventeenth-century England.

12. William L. Langer, "Infanticide: A Historical Survey," *History of Childhood Quarterly* 1 (1974): 353–66.

13. John T. Noonan, *Contraception* (Cambridge: Harvard University Press, 1965), p. 86.

14. Langer, "Infanticide"; see also Herlihy, *Medieval Households*, pp. 23–27; and Noonan, *Contraception*, pp. 85–87.

15. Langer, "Infanticide," pp. 358–59.
16. Mildred Dickemann, "Concepts and Classification in the Study of Human Infanticide" in Glenn Hausfater and Sarah Blaffer Hrdy, eds., *Infanticide* (New York: De Gruyter, 1984), p. 433; and Susan C. Scrimshaw, "Infanticide in Human Populations: Societal and Individual Concerns," in *Infanticide*, pp. 449–52.
17. W. T. Divale and M. Harris, "Population, Warfare, and the Male Supremacist Complex," *American Anthropologist* 78 (1976): 521–38; see also Scrimshaw, "Infanticide."
18. Martin Daly and Margo Wilson, "A Sociobiological Analysis of Human Infanticide," in *Infanticide*, pp. 488–95; Martin Daly and Margo Wilson, *Homicide* (New York: De Gruyter, 1988), chap. 3; and Scrimshaw, "Infanticide," pp. 444–60.
19. Martin Daly and Margo Wilson, "Children as Homicide Victims," in Richard J. Gelles and Jane B. Lancaster, eds., *Child Abuse and Neglect* (New York: De Gruyter, 1987), p. 207; see also Melvin Konner, *Why the Reckless Survive* (New York: Viking), pp. 173–76.
20. Mildred Dickemann, "Female Infanticide, Reproductive Strategies, and Social Stratification: A Preliminary Model," in N. Chagnon and W. Irons, eds., *Evolutionary Biology and Human Social Behavior* (North Scituate, Mass.: Duxbury Press, 1979), p. 456; and Melvin Konner, *Childhood* (Boston: Little, Brown, 1991), pp. 173–76.
21. Nancy Scheper-Hughes, "Culture, Scarcity, and Maternal Thinking: Mother Love and Child Death in Northeast Brazil," in Nancy Scheper-Hughes, ed., *Child Survival* (Boston: Reidel/Kluwer, 1987), pp. 203–4.
22. Daly and Wilson, "Children as Homicide Victims," pp. 208–9; Daly and Wilson, *Homicide*, pp. 75–76; Irenaus Eibl-Eibesfeldt, *Human Ethology* (New York: De Gruyter, 1989), p. 194; Scrimshaw, "Infanticide," pp. 440, 448–49; and Wenda Trevathan, *Human Birth: An Evolutionary Perspective* (New York: De Gruyter, 1987), pp. 231–32.
23. Eibl-Eibesfeldt, *Human Ethology*, pp. 193–94.
24. Richard A. Shweder, Elliot Turiel, and N. C. Much, "The Moral Intuitions of the Child," in J. H. Flavell and L. Ross, eds., *Social Cognitive Development* (New York: Cambridge University Press, 1981).
25. Eibl-Eibesfeldt, *Human Ethology*, p. 200; Tiffany Field, *Infancy* (Cambridge: Harvard University Press, 1990), pp. 27–39; and Dale F. Hay and Harriet L. Rheingold, "The Early Appearance of Some Valued Social Behaviors," in Diane L. Bridgeman, ed., *The Nature of Prosocial Development* (New York: Academic Press, 1983).
26. Eibl-Eibesfeldt, *Human Ethology*, pp. 30–31.
27. A. N. Meltzoff, "Imitation, Objects, Tools, and the Rudiments of Language in Human Ontogeny," *Human Evolution* 3 (1988): 45–64; and A. N. Meltzoff and M. Keith Moore, "Imitation of Facial and Manual Gestures by Human Neonates," *Science* 198 (1977): 75–78.
28. Field, *Infancy*, p. 61.
29. Eibl-Eibesfeldt, *Human Ethology*, p. 53.

30. Marian Radke-Yarrow, Carolyn Zahn-Waxler, and Michael Chapman, "Children's Prosocial Dispositions and Behavior," *Handbook of Child Psychology*, vol. 4 (New York: John Wiley, 1983), p. 479.

31. Field, *Infancy*, p. 31, and A. Sagi and M. L. Hoffman, "Empathic Distress in the Newborn," *Developmental Psychology* 12 (1976): 175–76.

32. Radke-Yarrow, Zahn-Waxler, and Chapman, "Children's Prosocial Dispositions and Behavior," p. 480.

33. Ibid., p. 481. Mothers, whatever their cultural background, also behave in distinctive ways toward children. For example, whether they are right-handed or left-handed, the vast majority of mothers carry their infants on the left side; it is almost inconceivable that this is a learned behavior. See Trevathan, *Human Birth*.

34. S. J. Rachman, *Fear and Courage*, 2d ed. (New York: W. H. Freeman), pp. 156–58.

35. There is a good deal of research on the limits of conditioning even among animals. Rats can be trained to avoid a taste that is followed by induced nausea or to avoid a light that is followed by an electrical shock; but they cannot be conditioned to avoid a certain taste that is followed by a shock or to avoid a light that is followed by nausea. They are preprogrammed to associate nausea with eating and light with shocks but not the reverse. See John Garcia and Robert A. Koelling, "Relation of Cue to Consequence in Avoidance Learning," *Psychonomic Science* 4 (1966): 123–24; and Martin E. P. Seligman and Joanne L. Hager, eds., *Biological Boundaries of Learning* (New York: Appleton-Century-Crofts, 1972).

36. Eric H. Lenneberg, "On Explaining Language," in *Biological Boundaries of Learning*.

37. Judy Dunn, "The Beginnings of Moral Understanding: Development in the Second Year," in Jerome Kagan and Sharon Lamb, eds., *The Emergence of Morality in Young Children* (Chicago: University of Chicago Press, 1987); Judy Dunn and Penny Munn, "Siblings and the Development of Prosocial Behavior," *International Journal of Behavioral Development* 9 (1986): 265–84; Carolyn Zahn-Waxler and Marian Radke-Yarrow, "The Development of Altruism: Alternative Research Strategies," in Nancy Eisenberg, ed., *The Development of Prosocial Behavior* (New York: Academic Press, 1982).

38. Harriet L. Rheingold and Dale F. Hay, "Prosocial Behavior of the Very Young," in G. S. Stent, ed., *Morality as a Biological Phenomenon* (Berlin: Dahlem Konferenzen, 1978), p. 119.

39. Bibb Latané and J. M. Darley, *The Unresponsive Bystander: Why Doesn't He Help?* (New York: Appleton-Century-Crofts, 1970).

40. Judy Dunn, *The Beginnings of Social Understanding* (Oxford: Basil Blackwell, 1988).

41. Eibl-Eibesfeldt, *Human Ethology*, pp. 340–41.

42. Jean Piaget, *The Moral Judgment of the Child*, trans. Marjorie Gabain (New York: Free Press, 1965), p. 14.

43. William Damon, *The Moral Child* (New York: Free Press, 1988), p. 172.

44. Cited in Konner, *Childhood*, pp. 299–301.

45. Aristotle, *Nichomachean Ethics* 1131b17.
46. J. Stacy Adams, "Toward an Understanding of Inequity," *Journal of Abnormal and Social Psychology* 67 (1963): 422–36; J. Stacy Adams and P. R. Jacobsen, "Effects of Wage Inequities on Work Quality," *Journal of Abnormal and Social Psychology* 69 (1964): 19–25; J. Stacy Adams and W. B. Rosenbaum, "The Relationship of Worker Productivity to Cognitive Dissonance about Wage Inequities," *Journal of Applied Psychology* 46 (1962): 161–64; E. E. Lawler and P. W. O'Gara, "The Effects of Inequity Produced by Underpayment on Work Output, Work Quality, and Attitudes toward Work," *Journal of Applied Psychology* 351 (1967): 403–10; and Elaine Walster, G. William Walster, and Ellen Berschied, *Equity: Theory and Research* (Boston: Allyn & Bacon, 1978).
47. John Stuart Mill, *Utilitarianism*, ed. George Sher (Indianapolis: Hackett, 1979), pp. 30–31, 33.
48. Charles Darwin, *The Descent of Man, and Selection in Relation to Sex* (Princeton: Princeton University Press, 1981), p. 71, n. 5; see also chap. 3.
49. William D. Hamilton, "The Evolution of Social Behavior," *Journal of Theoretical Biology* 7 (1964): 1–52.
50. J. B. S. Haldane, "Population Genetics," *New Biology* 18 (1955): 34–51.
51. Margo Wilson and Martin Daly, "Risk of Maltreatment of Children Living with Stepparents," in *Child Abuse and Neglect*.
52. Dorothy W. Smith and Laurie Nels Sherwen, *Mothers and Their Adopted Children: The Bonding Process* (New York: Tiresias, 1983), p. 95.
53. Janet L. Hoopes, *Prediction in Child Development: A Longitudinal Study of Adoptive and Nonadoptive Families* (New York: Child Welfare League of America, 1982), pp. 97–98.
54. John Triseliotis and Malcolm Hill, "Contrasting Adoption, Foster Care, and Residential Rearing," in David M. Brodzinsky and Marshall D. Schecter, eds., *The Psychology of Adoption* (New York: Oxford University Press, 1990). The fact that adopted children are at greater risk than natural children for psychological problems and conduct disorders does not invalidate the argument that the former are cherished equally with the latter. Adopted children have more personality problems because their biological parents had those problems, which have a large genetic component. See Michael Bohmann and Soren Sigvardsson, "Outcome in Adoption: Lessons from Longitudinal Studies," in *The Psychology of Adoption*; and Remi Cadoret, "Biologic Perspectives of Adoptee Adjustment," in *The Psychology of Adoption*.
55. James Serpell, *In the Company of Animals* (Oxford: Basil Blackwell, 1986), chap. 4.
56. The animals that are most likely to become pets are those that have some of the characteristics of the human infant, such as eyes that are large relative to the face, a soft epidermis, and a prosocial disposition. The most common pets supply an object of affection that returns the affection through obedience, loyalty, purring, or posing. Serpell, *In the Company of Animals*.
57. Richard D. Alexander, *The Biology of Moral System* (New York: De Gruyter, 1987); and Robert Trivers, "The Evolution of Reciprocal Altruism," *Quarterly Review of Biology* 46 (1971): 35–57.

58. Henry Sidgwick, *The Methods of Ethics*, 7th ed. (Indianapolis: Hackett, 1981), pp. 386–87.
59. Latané and Darley, *The Unresponsive Bystander*.
60. Leda Cosmides and John Tooby, "From Evolution to Behavior: Evolutionary Psychology as the Missing Link," in John Dupré, ed., *The Latest on the Best* (Cambridge: MIT Press, 1987).
61. Eibl-Eibesfeldt, *Human Ethology*; Konrad Lorenz, "Die angeborenen Formen möglicher Erfahrung," *Zeitschrift für Tierpsychologie* 5 (1943): 235–409; James J. McKenna, "Parental Supplements and Surrogates among Primates: Cross-Species and Cross-Cultural Comparisons," in Jane B. Lancaster et al., eds., *Parenting across the Life Span* (New York: De Gruyter, 1987); Sarah Hall Sternglanz, James L. Gray, and Melvin Murakami, "Adult Preferences for Infantile Facial Features: An Ethological Approach," *Animal Behavior* 25 (1977): 108–15; Charles M. Super, "Behavioral Development in Infancy," in R. H. Munroe, R. L. Munroe, and B. B. Whiting, eds., *Handbook of Cross-Cultural Human Development* (New York: Garland, 1981).
62. William Golding, *Lord of the Flies* (New York: Coward-McCann, 1962).
63. John Rawls, *A Theory of Justice* (Cambridge: Harvard University Press, 1972).
64. John Locke, *An Essay Concerning Human Understanding*, ed. Peter H. Nidditch (Oxford: Clarendon Press, 1979).
65. Hobbes, *Leviathan*.
66. Jean-Jacques Rousseau, *Emile*, trans. Allan Bloom (New York: Basic Books, 1979); Allan Bloom, "The Education of Democratic Man: *Emile*," *Daedalus* 107 (1978): 135–53.
67. Judith Jarvis Thomson, "The No Reason Thesis," *Social Philosophy and Policy* 7 (1989): 1–21.
68. Richard Rorty, *Contingency, Irony, and Solidarity* (Cambridge: Cambridge University Press, 1989), p. 189.
69. Ian Shapiro, *Political Criticism* (Berkeley: University of California Press, 1990), p. 296.
70. Ibid.
71. Martha Craven Nussbaum, *Aristotle's "De Motu Animalium"* (Princeton: Princeton University Press, 1978), p. 60.
72. Aristotle, *Politics* 1252a30; Aristotle, *Nichomachean Ethics* 1155a17; Aristotle, *Politics* 1252b11.
73. Aristotle, *Eudemian Ethics* 1242b1; Aristotle, *Politics* 1253a29.
74. Larry Arnhart, "A Sociobiological Defense of Aristotle's Sexual Politics," paper presented to the annual meeting of the American Political Science Association, San Francisco, 1990; Stephen G. Salkever, *Finding the Mean: Theory and Practice in Aristotelian Political Philosophy* (Princeton: Princeton University Press, 1990).
75. Robin Fox, *Encounter with Anthropology* (New York: Harcourt Brace Jovanovich, 1973), p. 13.

Index

About the Author

James Q. Wilson has advised four U.S. presidents on crime, drug abuse, education, and other crises of American culture. He was chairman of the White House Task Force on Crime in 1966 and chairman of the National Advisory Commission on Drug Abuse Prevention in 1972 and 1973. In addition to serving on the Attorney General's Task Force on Violent Crime in 1981, Mr. Wilson served on the President's Foreign Intelligence Advisory Board and the Commission on Presidential Scholars from 1985 through 1990. He was chairman of the Police Foundation from 1984 to 1993.

Since 1985 Mr. Wilson has been James Collins Professor of Management and Public Policy at the University of California at Los Angeles. For twenty-six years he was Henry Lee Shattuck Professor of Government at Harvard University.

His extensive publications on urban problems, government regulation of business, and the prevention of delinquency include *Bureaucracy, American Government, Thinking About Crime, Varieties of Police Behavior, Political Organizations, The Investigators, Crime and Human Nature* (with Richard J. Herrnstein), and *City Politics* (with Edward C. Banfield).

In 1990 the American Political Science Association awarded Mr. Wilson the James Madison Award for distinguished scholarship. From 1991 to 1992 he served as the association's president.

The author has been elected a fellow of the American Academy of Arts and Sciences and a member of the American Philosophical Society.

He was educated at the University of Redlands and received his doctorate from the University of Chicago.

Mr. Wilson is chairman of the AEI Council of Academic Advisers and serves on the AEI Board of Trustees.

Acknowledgments

Chapter 2 originally appeared as "The Rediscovery of Character: Private Virtue and Public Policy" in the *Public Interest* (Fall 1985). Reprinted by permission.

Chapter 3 has appeared in several versions, most recently as "Incivility and Crime," in Edward C. Banfield, ed., *Civility and Citizenship* (New York: Paragon House, 1991). Reprinted by permission of the Professors' World Peace Academy. Some of the material in this version was first published as "Crime and American Culture" in the *Public Interest* (Winter 1982).

Chapter 5 originally appeared as "Raising Kids" in the *Atlantic Monthly* (October 1983).

Chapter 6 originally appeared as "A Guide to Reagan Country: The Political Culture of Southern California" in *Commentary* (May 1967). Reprinted by permission.

Chapter 7 originally appeared as "The Young People of North Long Beach" in *Harper's* (December 1969). Reprinted by permission.

Chapter 9 originally appeared as "Liberalism versus a Liberal Education" in *Commentary* (June 1972). Reprinted by permission.

Chapter 10 originally appeared, jointly authored with George Kelling, as "Broken Windows: The Police and Neighborhood Safety" in the *Atlantic Monthly* (March 1982).

Chapter 11 originally appeared as "Adam Smith on Business Ethics" in *California Management Review*, vol. 32, no. 1 (Fall 1989), copyright 1989 by the Regents of the University of California. Reprinted by permission of the regents.

Chapter 12 originally appeared as "Against the Legalization of Drugs" in *Commentary* (February 1990). Reprinted by permission.

Chapter 13 originally appeared as chapter 1 in David Farrington, Lloyd Ohlin, and James Q. Wilson, *Understanding and Controlling Crime* (New York: Springer-Verlag, 1986). Reprinted by permission of the John D. and Catherine T. MacArthur Foundation, the copyright holder.

A Note on the Book

This book was edited by
the staff of the AEI Press.
The index was prepared by Shirley Kessel.
The text was set in Palatino, a typeface designed by
the twentieth-century Swiss designer Hermann Zapf.
Publication Technology Corporation, of Fairfax, Virginia,
set the type, and Edwards Brothers Incorporated,
of Ann Arbor, Michigan, printed and bound the book,
using permanent acid-free paper.

The AEI Press is the publisher for the American Enterprise Institute for Public Policy Research, 1150 17th Street, N.W., Washington, D.C. 20036; *Christopher C. DeMuth,* publisher; *Dana Lane,* director; *Ann Petty,* editor; *Leigh Tripoli,* editor; *Cheryl Weissman,* editor; *Lisa Roman,* editorial assistant (rights and permissions).